Aspects of Colour

Aspects of Colour

Edited by Harald Arnkil
and
Esa Hämäläinen

Published by
the University of Art and Design Helsinki UIAH

Cover: Thirty Vertical Systematic Colour Series with Red
Diagonals 1943/1970, oil on canvas, 165x165cm. Photo by
courtesy of the Richard Paul Lohse-Foundation, Zürich.

Publication series of the University of Art and Design Helsinki
UIAH B 42

Edited by Harald Arnkil
and Esa Hämäläinen

Graphic Design
Riitta Piuva
© UIAH and the authors
Photos by courtesy of Josef Albers Museum, Hamburger
Kunsthalle, Richard Paul Lohse-Foundation, and the authors
Proofreading of the articles by Felicity Kjisik
Printed at the University Printing House
Helsinki 1995
ISBN 951-9384-78-2
ISSN 0782-1778

Distribution
University of Art and Design Helsinki UIAH
UIAH Information and Publishing Unit
Hämeentie 135 C
SF-00560 Helsinki
Finland

Contents

Foreword

The articles contained in this book are a selection of the lectures presented at the International Conference on Colour Education held in Helsinki, Finland, in August 1994. The conference was organised by the Faculty of General Studies of the University of Art and Design Helsinki UIAH. The proceedings of the conference are published here in a form that will hopefully provide information and generate discussion among a wider public on the subject of colour and colour education. The editors are convinced that, although originally intended for a limited audience of professionals, these talks carry an interest for anyone wanting to know more about the function and role of colour in general.

Serious and organised discourse around colour has upto now been maintained chiefly by the scientific community. It seemed the right time to gather in the conference and in this book views, ideas and experiences of the world of visual arts education that will hopefully throw new light on the present state and future possibilities of colour education in art, architecture and design. The articles all deal with crucial and vital issues of the process of creating with colour. Some of them present personal findings in the world of colour as manifested in the intimate creative process of the artist. Some offer well-proven and original methods of teaching that have become refined through many years of classroom experience. The range of topics is wide, reaching from discussions of existing colour systems to presentations of new approaches to colour grouping, from colour in the painting studio to colour as part of town planning. The articles are grouped under six headings: Vision and Logic, Design, Fine Art, Environment, Research, Language.

Colour is at the heart of visual creation. It is the life-blood of paintings, moving images, designed objects, the environment. It is also a phenomenon that is deeply embedded in the fundamental and the most primordial functions of all biological existence, as Ellen Marx points out in her essay *The Three Fundamental Colour Syntheses*. Furthermore, colour is a way of relating to and communicating with the world. It is neither a property of the eye nor of the brain nor of the world outside alone, but of all three together, forming a bridge between the observer and the observed. This is why colour has for centuries fascinated not only artists but also philosophers, psychologists, physicists, physiologists, biologists, chemists, ... One wonders is there any other area of experience touched by so many branches of human knowledge. In science colour can act as an indicator of incidental phenomena (medical diagnosis, physical and chemical analysis, etc.), but it can also be a 'window' that reveals important truths of a more universal kind that would otherwise remain in the dark. Ludwig Wittgenstein, for instance, turned his attention repeatedly to colour in all the phases of his career. He looked at colour in order to solve problems concerning logic, language and meaning. Although colour was never the prime motive of Wittgenstein's investigations, but merely a tool for philosophy, his remarks on the subjects are highly interesting for also artists and educators, as Antero Kare outlines in his paper *Wittgenstein, Colour Concepts, Teaching,*

It would not be fair to say that our age is more aware of the significance and potential of colour than any other age. People who lived a hundred, three hundred or five hundred years ago were, indeed, probably more sensitive to the spiritual and symbolic aspects of colour than we are today. But there is no denying that colours as physical entities, in all forms and combinations, have become more readily and universally available, not only due to the successes of modern chemistry, but also through the printed and electronic media. Consequently the need to understand the potential of colour more deeply has increased rapidly in recent years among people from all walks of life from elementary school teachers to art directors.

8 It may seem surprising that although colour is such a universal experience (excepting the phenomenon of 'colour blindness') there is no 'universal harmony' or theory of colours that would fulfill the same function as, for example, laws of harmony and counterpoint in music. This is not to say that there have not been attempts to create one. Perhaps the most famous examples are contained in Friedrich Wilhelm Ostwald's *Die Harmonie der Farben*, 1918 and Albert Henry Munsell's *The Color Primer*, 1915. Ostwald exerted a major influence on the Bauhaus and its teaching in the 1920s and '30s and Munsell's system of colour organisation is still much in use at art schools in the USA. Neither must one forget Wassily Kandinsky's search for universal principles of composition and harmony in *Über das Geistige in der Kunst*, 1912. He went further, trying to arrive at a kind of 'universal language' of forms and colours that would constitute the basic elements of abstract pictorial composition. But ultimately even Kandinsky shunned the idea of rigid rules for art.

In the publication at hand David Burton's article *Stanton MacDonald-Wright and the Synchromist Theory of Color* also sheds light on the interesting subject of the relationship of colour and musical harmony. Stanton MacDonald-Wright and Morgan Russell are not the only artists who have attempted to reach an analogy between colour and music, but they belong certainly among the most interesting ones to have delved into this area.

There exists a large number of books on colour (mostly in English and German) written from the viewpoint of colour science. Thus, information on recent findings concerning colour vision, physics of light, perception psychology, etc. is readily available to the artist and teacher who reads these languages. What is lacking, though, is literature that combines contemporary scientific findings with artistic vision and pedagogical clarity. This is also affirmed by Jan Janssens's article *The Impact of Colour Research on Design Practice and Education*.

As far as literature goes, colour education still has to rely to a large extent on the leagacy of the Bauhaus. The two most influential pedagogic works on colour available today, Johannes Itten's *Kunst der Farbe* (The Art of Colour), 1960 and Josef Albers's *Interaction of Colour*, 1963, were published over thirty years ago. Nothing of equal pedagogic stature or universal artistic vision has appeared since. While keeping in mind their very different approaches to the subject of teaching colour, it is significant that Albers was a pupil of Itten, who in turn was a pupil of Adolf Hoelzel. Some of the ideas presented by Itten and to some extent also Albers can be traced - through Hoelzel and Goethe - back as far as the nineteenth century and earlier. In the light of today's practical knowledge and colour research some of these concepts, notably Itten's colour circle and its derivate contrasts and colour mixtures, are outdated - and were even in Itten's time. Without underestimating the immense value of the work of Itten and Albers and their role in both carrying forward and modernising the nineteenth century colour tradition, it has become quite evident that new pedagogical books and universally applicable methods of colour teaching based on up-to-date findings are needed.

From another point of view and as both *Juhana Blomstedt* and *Wade Thompson* point out in their articles, teaching painters and teaching designers are tasks that probably call for quite different approaches. In any case the real life world of light, sound, movement and other sensory stimuli confronted in, for example, architecture and interior and stage design, present colour problems that cannot be solved or taught in two dimensions. Neither is the world of art any longer the same as it was in Itten's and Albers's day: its fragmetation and denial of cohesive ideologies is perhaps reflected also in the realm of colour education as a lack of universally accepted authorities.

The eternal question: can one *teach* art is epitomised in the question: can one *teach* colour - and what is the role of theoretical knowledge in the process of training an 'eye for colour'. Ultimately colour will not, of course, be learnt by studying literature or even pictures, but by getting to grips with the physical material, by immersing oneself in the sensory and sensual experience that colour is, an experience whose essence is beyond words. Nevertheless, it would be a mistake to rely entirely on intuition and deny the value of verbal knowledge and analytical thought in trying to make sense of the often contradictory and perplexing situations brought up by colour design tasks. To be understood properly, colour demands a holistic approach, encompassing perception, cognition and instinct, that is best summarised in the following words by Ellen Marx: " ... it is not enough to have eyes to see and a brain to think. The whole human body is necessary and it does not stop at the skin. It forms an organism with the earth, with the sun and with the whole cosmos."

January 1995
Harald Arnkil

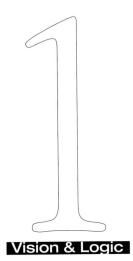

Vision & Logic

The Three Fundamental Colour Syntheses
Additive, Subtractive, Integration - an Experience of Meditating Colour

Today a fragmentary vision opposing the body to the spirit, the subject to the object, the creator to the creation, is replaced by a systemic vision of interrelations and interdependences of all phenomena. Light and matter are not fundamentally different, because all matter is potential energy. I venture to say all matter is potential spirit. Human consciousness is not an epiphenomenon. If we want to understand colour, we must also ask the question: what does consciousness mean and how does our mind function? The two complementary functions of vision, differentiation and integration, permit an analogy with the two principal expressions of being conscious:

First, a symbolic consciousness of the world - related to language, to scientific language as well as to artistic language.

Second, an innermost consciousness of the world - the consciousness of the mystic, where all the dualities transcend in a cosmic fusion.

Quantum mechanics as well as astrophysics today are aware that the world is intimately interconnected and that the nature of light is neither a wave nor a grain of matter, neither a continuous phenomenon, nor a discontinuous phenomenon. These are only images of reality depending on the experimental conditions, but at this level the mind reaches paradoxical thinking behind all language.

How not to feel a great emotion, when we imagine that the material of the human eye was the first trace of life in the primordial sea 3.5 milliard years ago, with archaeobacterium composed of rhodopsin, a precursor of our retina - red-purple the first col-

our of life. A little later, about three milliard years ago the cyanobacteria with their capacity of photosynthesis create also green and blue. It's not life creating colour but colour creating life. When I wrote my first book *The Contrast of Colours* in 1969, the artistic and scientific worlds seemed irreconcilable. The laws of physical optics and the laws of printing inks and artist's pigments seemed very different. At this time I was curious to know why the colour yellow had two different complementaries: blue for light and blue-violet for pigments. But only years later I found the answer to this question in studying colour sensation itself. I recognized that all the laws find their origin at the psycho-physiological level where all the different points of view can find an explanation.

My latest book *Méditer la couleur* shows through concrete examples how the eyes can increase, diminish or integrate the energy of the electromagnetic radiations which touch the retina. It was very fascinating when I realized that the three fundamental systems of colour synthesis, synthesis of light, synthesis of pigments and filters and synthesis of optical integration can be evoked experimentally under certain conditions with successive images. But before we go on, we must discuss the fundamental primaries. The optical phycisist says that there are three principal lights: blue, red and green. The photographer and the printer say that there are three principal inks and filters: blue-cyan, red-magenta and yellow. The colour psychologist says that there are four fundamental colours, which are yellow, blue, red and green. Through experiment we can find that the psychophysiological complementary of the eye reveals to us six chromatic thresholds which are subjective sensations. They correspond approximately on the one hand to the three primaries of the reproduction systems of light - red, green and blue, and on the other hand to the three primaries yellow, magenta and cyan of the reproduction systems of photographic filters and printing inks.

Black and white as well as grey can be generated by the six chromatic thresholds. As will be shown below.

To be successful in the experiments, alertness, steady concentration and above all physical and mental relaxation are required. Preoccupations, contractions and distractions may prevent you from seeing any trace of the successive phenomenon. On the other hand, a state of meditation predisposes in its favour.

With the successive image of this group of colours, we will understand the correlative reciprocity of the six chromatic thresholds. First we begin to stare at the white point in the black centre (figure 1, page 17) while counting mentally up to 30 without moving our head, our neck and our shoulders. The arms as well as the rest of the body are entirely relaxed and the breathing should be quiet and regular. Immediately afterward we project the physiological complementaries on the blank area by focusing on the small cross in the centre with the same concentration and the same relaxation, while counting mentally up to 10.

You have seen this after-image (figure 2, page 17). Now again let us stare at the black point in the white centre (figure 2, page 17) while counting up to 30, and then up to 10 for the projection as before.

Light
Additive Synthesis

Colour in the form of light as electromagnetic radiation of the visible spectrum situated between ultra-violet and infrared can derive from a natural or an artificial source.

Light reveals itself by the laws of additive synthesis. In an additive system, for example, television, three colour beams composed of the short wavelenghts blue, the middle wavelengths green and the long wavelengths red can reproduce the whole spectrum. It's extraordinary that we can simulate with the successive complementaries exactly the same additive synthesis as with superimposed rays on a blank area.

Here let us recall a writer and poet profoundly interested in the visual phenomenon of physiological complementaries, Johann Wolfgang von Goethe, who said:

"Wär nicht das Auge sonnenhaft,
Wie könnten wir das Licht erblicken?"
*"If the eye were not like the sun itself,
How could we see the light?"*

And here another famous quotation from Goethe:

"Denn das ist der Natur Gehalt,
dass Aussen gilt, was Innen galt."
*"But this is the sense of nature,
that what is right outside, was right inside."*

Before we will realize the additive synthesis of yellow, let us focus on the black point in the centre of the yellow form here again while counting up to 30 (see page 18, figures 3 and 4).

Then we focus on the centre of the blank area to see the complementaries while counting up to 10. Now we proceed to do the inversion in exactly the same way (figure 4).

When we superimpose on a blank area a green colour and a red colour we obtain yellow by an additive synthesis. With each additional light, there is an increase of energy. This is the reason why we call this synthesis additive. We will perform this synthesis of yellow inside our eyes exactly as if superimposing a green colour and a red colour on a blank area, exceptly that the projected light will not come from an exterior source but from the complementaries of the eyes themselves.

Optical Additive Creation of Yellow, Cyan, Magenta

The optical additive synthesis in the eyes is only possible with the energy of a white surrounding field during the induction. In staring at the red circle, the background around will take on a red haze. At the same time it will slowly desaturate more and more but at its border simultaneous effects will provoke, on the one hand, an oversaturation of the red and, on the other hand, the complementary green will overflow. The simultaneous effects are caused by the reflex movements called saccades of the small muscles around the eyes. In the beginning they are very difficult to control. In focusing later on the blue-cyan circle don't worry about the successive green circle which is complementary to the first induction. With the complementaries of magenta and cyan, which are green and orange, we will now create yellow by an optical additive synthesis (see page 19, figure 5).

First count mentally up to 45 while gazing at the white point at the right of the magenta circle, and next up to 10 while gazing at the blue-cyan circle at the exact place of the white point of the left, and finally up to 10 for the projection on the blank area.

If your experiment has been successful you have seen an after-image as illustrated in figure 3. The same way that we have created yellow, we could produce also blue-cyan and magenta by optical additive synthesis.

With the successive complementaries of yellow and magenta focused on a white background we could superimpose blue-violet and green in the eyes to get blue-cyan; and also with the complementaries of yellow and cyan focused on a white field we could superimpose blue-violet and red-orange to evoke successively magenta.

Matter
Subtractive Synthesis

We can study the colour in form of matter by the laws of subtractive synthesis with printing dyes which are actually beside colour photographic filters the purest and the brightest. The subtraction is possible by superimposition of different coats of transparent dyes on a white background. This synthesis is called subtractive because each extra coat will diminish the total energy. This culminates in black which absorbs all the chromatic rays. To reproduce the whole richness of coloured matter, what is the minimum number of colours needed and what are their characteristics?

These primaries are yellow without red and without blue, a red called magenta without yellow or blue and a blue called cyan without red and without yellow.

Optical Subtractive Creation of Blue-Violet, Red-Orange, Green

Translucent cyan-coloured ink and magenta coloured ink printed together will give a blue-violet (see page 18, figure 4). The first time I was really very astonished when I realized that the eyes have not only the ability to add colours like light. They can also create colours by subtraction, behaving like the matter of inks and filters under one condition: the colours must be focused on an entirely black surrounding field.

Creation of Blue-Violet

We can create blue-violet by an optical subtractive synthethis. The total absence of light in the surrounding field makes the eyes capable of a successive substraction.

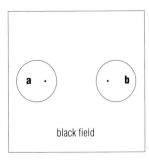 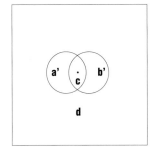

black field

Focused colours in black field:
a left = red-orange
b left = green

Produced complementary
successive colours:
a' left = cyan
b' right = magenta
c centre = blue-violet
(the optical subtractive
synthesis of cyan and
magenta)
d = white surrounding

Just as for blue-violet, our eyes would be able to create red-orange with the successive complementaries magenta and yellow by gazing at green and blue-violet surrounded by a black field; and green with the successive complementaries cyan and yellow by gazing at red-orange and blue-violet likewise on a black surrounding field.

The Complementaries

If we ask now: how many complementaries exist for one colour, we come exactly to the point of my research where I found the answer to the question, why the colour yellow has different complementaries. In exploring the six primaries with the physiological complementaries, we had the opportunity to realize the six chromatic thresholds of vision. We'll now see that all colours, except one pair, have not only one complementary but a whole scale of them: from the additive complementary on one side to the subtractive complementary on the other.

When an orange light is superimposed on a blue-cyan light they will produce white by synthesis. The orange, which is the additive complementary to cyan, has about 50% less magenta than the subtractive complementary.

A translucent blue-cyan dye requires a complementary red-orange with a 100% magenta. In preparing my book *Optical Colour and Simultaneity* I discovered that the successive product was exactly the same red-orange when I removed all the light energies from the surrounding field of blue-cyan during the induction.

Blue and yellow rays superimposed produce white in the additive system but yellow needs a blue-violet ink in the subtractive system.

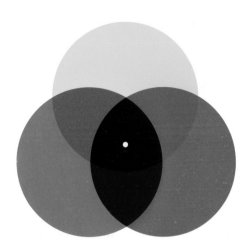

Figure 1

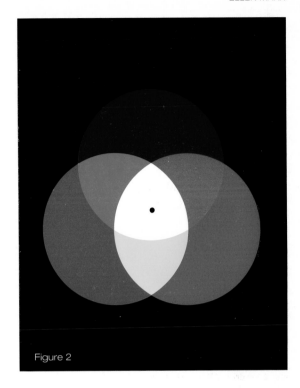

Figure 2

+

Cover the other figure with a piece of paper during the after- image experiment.

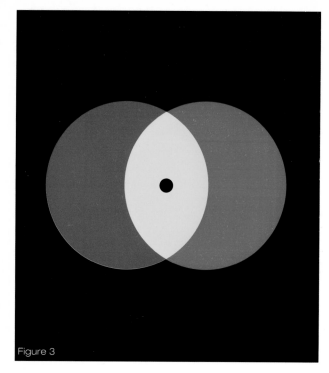

Figure 3

Figure 4

Cover the other figure with a piece of paper during the after-image experiment.

+

Figure 5

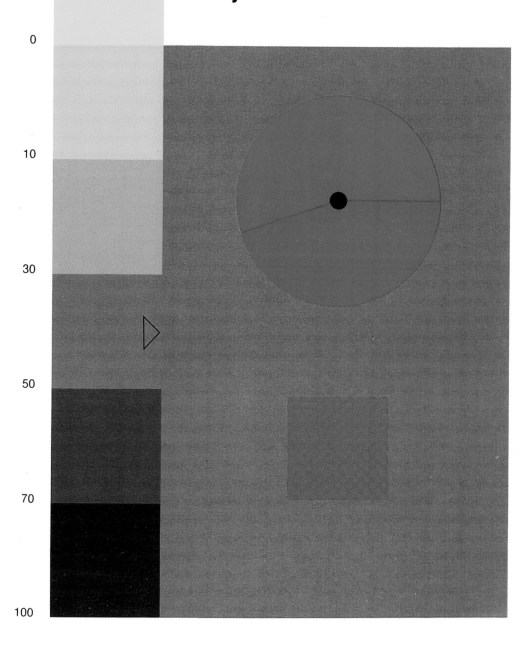

jaune + 50% noir

Figure 6

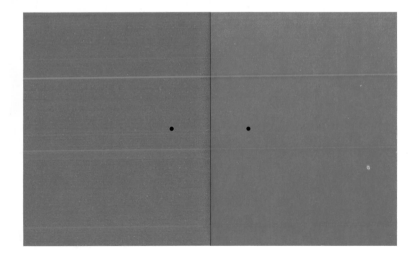

Figure 7

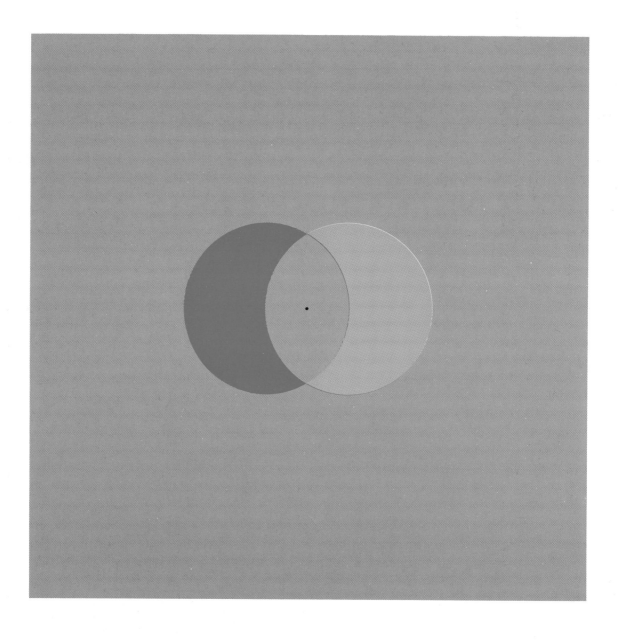

Figure 8

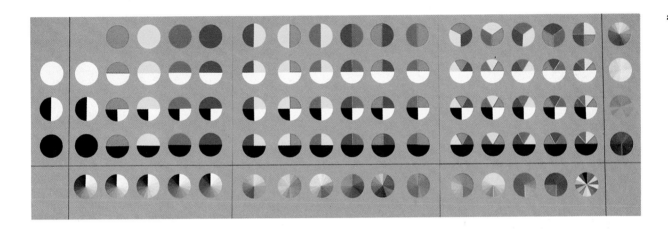

Figure 9
The 64 colour combinations with the resultant colour groups.

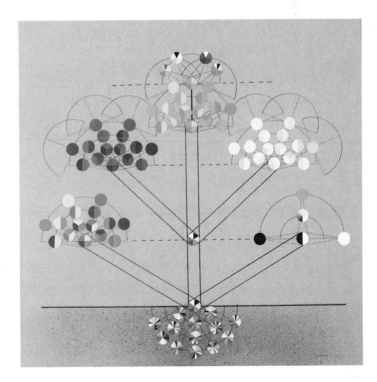

Figure 10
Diagram of the tree for the methodological approach.

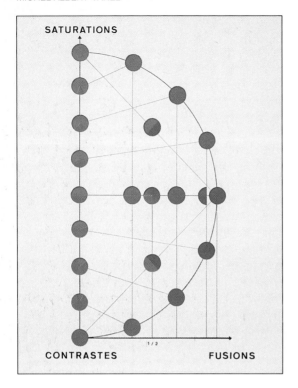

Figure 11

Diagram of saturations

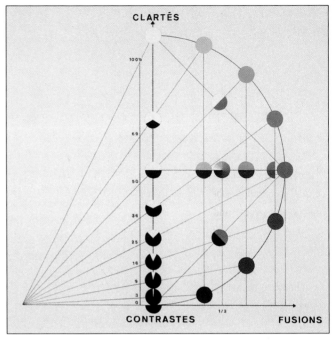

Figure 13

Diagram of lightness contrasts

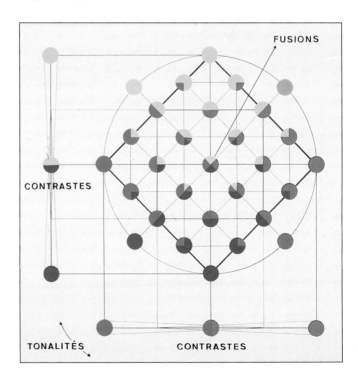

Figure 12

Diagram of lightness dominants and contrasts

The couple yellow and blue induced on the white background remains identical in the successive image - with about 30% to 40% less magenta in the complementary blue. On the other hand the subtractive complementary of yellow induced on a black background is rather a blue-violet (composed of cyan with 100% magenta), and the complementary to blue induced on a black background produces successively orange.

Gazed on a grey background, the successive complementary is located midway between the subtractive and the additive complementary.

Creation of White

The successive creation of white with the pair yellow and blue will confirm that only the energies of a white surrounding field can produce at the psychophysiological level the characteristics

of light on a screen. We already have a certain experience now: first we'll count to 45 in gazing at the yellow circle. Next to 10 in gazing at the blue circle immediately afterward. Finally, minimum of 10 in concentrating your attention on the blank area, where you will see white in the centre.

Creation of Black

On the other hand we could make the synthesis of black by subtraction in the eyes by staring at yellow and blue-violet surrounded by a black field.

Only one pair, namely red and blue-green are an exception. The additive complementary coincides with the subtractive complementary. The additive complementary of magenta has 30% less yellow than the subtractive one. For red-violet the additive com-

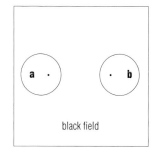

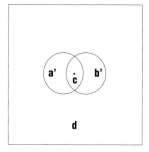

Focused colours on a white field.
a left = yellow
b right = blue

Produced complementary successive colours:
a' left = blue
b' right = yellow
c centre = white (the optical additive synthesis of yellow and blue)
d = black surrounding

Focused colours on a black field:

a left = yellow
b right = blue-violet

Produced complementary successive colours:
a' left = blue-violet
b' right = yellow
c centre = black (the optical subtactive synthesis of yellow and blue-violet)
d = white surrounding

plementary has more blue-cyan. For blue-violet it is subtractively yellow but additively yellow-green.

All these demonstrations prove that black or white surrounding energies which seem neutral, have not only an influence on the brightness of the colours but also on their hue. Likewise we become aware that the six most important colours of the subtractive system need six different complementaries in the additive system. To become neutral, the eye operates a sort of correction concerning the total physiological basic chromatic capacity: overall, the additive complementaries compared to the subtractive complementaries, are composed of more blue-cyan and less red-magenta, as the relative percentages indicate. Yellow remains more or less balanced in the middle - it constitutes about a third of the total.

Here are the proportions to neutralize by integration: only 20% of magenta, but 53% of blue-cyan (and 27% of yellow) are needed to create a neutral grey by rotation.

Only 19% of red-orange against 41% of green and 40% of blue-violet produces by rotation a neutral grey.

You can realize, there are more blue colours and more green colours than red ones. Why is this? The following hypothesis appears the most probable: the eye mirrors not only the physiological interior world but also the exterior world with which the body is jointly interdependent. The analogy of the quantities of the global chromatic perception in the additive system and the neutralizing of the primaries on a turning disc, is not a mere coincidence. In the long history of animal evolution, the adaptation of the eye took place originally in relation to the cycles of light and darkness in the alternation of day and night; and subseqently in relation to a polychromatic environment in which

the division of colours is determined quantitatively: the blue of the ocean, which was the first life environment of human origin, and the blue of the sky predominated. Seen from space, our earth is a blue planet. Afterwards come the greens of the forests which were the second life environment of our ancestors. Rocks, soil, and sand display beiges, ochres, browns, all of them desaturated hues. In nature, blues and greens unfold in all their brilliance; conversely red, orange and yellow are seldom found in saturated form - but only among fruits, flowers, certain fish and insects and the blood within the animal body. The fire and the sun itself, especially at sunset and sunrise are contrasting with the dominant blue-green.

This fundamental need for blue and green explains why we can see every week-end those monstrous migrations of the city dweller to the countryside. Architects, cityplanners and decorators should be very conscious of this.

The location of the cones sensitive to red-orange and green toward the centre of the retina, and those sensitive to blue toward the periphery, mixed with rods, is supposed by Walraven and Vos to be in the following average proportions: red - 32, green - 16, blue -1. These quantities put red in the majority and blue in the minority - in other words the reverse of the proportions found in nature as discussed before. It is logical that the visual apparatus should be more developed for dealing with the colours which are rarer in visible reality, since they have to be distinguished from a background in which blue and green predominate and were therefore of great importance for human survival. These physiological arrangements may explain to some extent why the attention is drawn even on small surfaces of warm saturated hues which become even agressive in large quantities.

The greatest colour contrast of warm and cold, red-orange and blue-green represents also the most important symbolic duality: Fire, hell, blood and the animal instinct and passion is red-orange against the blue-green of the intellectual and spiritual values.

Integration

Exactly midway between light and matter, the additive system and the subtractive system is the third fundamental system, called integration. Integration can be shown experimentally with discs which turn at a sufficiently high rotation speed to cause the colour-sections to fuse into a single impression or with narrow lines or small points extremely close to each other which thus lose their individuality becoming a uniform coloured surface.

Even today there are artists and scientists who mistakenly try to identify integration with additive synthesis. Isaac Newton was probably the first who attempted to reconstitute white by rotation of a disc on which he had arranged his seven colours. Seven was a magic number suggested more by the superstitions of his time than by any physical reality. We have already seen the proportions of the different primaries on a turning disc. We have also seen that the product always being grey rather than white is not due to impurities in the coloured material. It is rather that integration means that the optical chromatic impulses are juxtaposed in the same space-time of the visual field. They are not superimposed like this in the case of addition or subtraction. Integration provokes the phenomena of equalization. The totality of the impulses integrates into a single impression representing an average value of lightness, hue and saturation. The greatest lightness contrast is opposing yellow to blue-violet. The green and red colours are located in the middle, analogous to grey between black and white.

We can imagine six different lightness levels, going from lightness level 1 with white on the top reflecting all the colours to lightness-level 6 at the bottom with black absorbing all the colours.

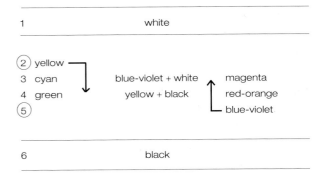

Yellow, which is closest to white, is all alone on level 2, opposed to blue-violet which, closest to black, is all alone on level 5. Cyan and magenta at the third level are lighter than green and red-orange at level 4. This explains why yellow which is the integrated product of green and red-orange, needs 50% of black to fall from the second lightness-level to the fourth lightness-level. This darkening corresponds exactly to the complementary blue-violet which gains about 50% of white in the integration product of cyan and magenta, which allows it to climb up from the fifth level to the third.

Successive images can reveal exactly the same integrated colours as the very dense structures on the one hand and the turning discs on the other. The eyes offer the intimicy of an integrated imprint on only one condition: the colours looked at must be juxtaposed with at least one common border. A little while ago we produced in the eyes an additive synthesis of yellow. We will see presently that integration, on the other hand, produces a dark yellow.

Integration of Green and Red-Orange
Creation of Yellow + 50% Black

To organize this astonishing experience, I have chosen two rectangular surfaces which have a common border and two points for focusing the gaze on the left and on the right side near the common border. Our gaze should persist a little longer on the colour magenta which is situated at the left side of the border because its complementary green prevails in quantity in the mixing on a turning disc - as you can see here (see page 20, figure 6)

Red-orange and green mixed rapidly on a turning disc makes yellow darkened by 50% of black. The structure below composed of very small red-orange and green dots in the same proportions as the sections on this rotating disc integrates to the same darkened yellow as the background.

In the after-image of our experiment there will appear also a dark yellow in the centre which is the integrated synthesis of green at the left side and redorange at the right side (see page 21, figure 7).

Now we look in a swinging movement first a little longer at the left point, then at the right point, again at the left point a bit longer and so on whilst counting mentally up to 30, for example like this: look at the left o-n-e, look at the right two, look at the left t-h-r-e-e, look at the right four, and so on up to 30.

Then at the blank area while counting up to 10.

Integration of Cyan and Magenta
Creation of Blue-Violet + 50% White

If we integrate cyan and magenta with the complementaries of red-orange and green, we become aware, that the successive result is not a saturated blue-violet as with the optical subtractive synthesis - but a hue containing about 50% of white colour.

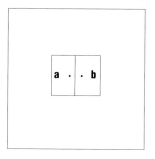 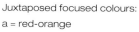 

Juxtaposed focused colours:
a = red-orange
b = green

Produced complementary
successive colours:
a' = cyan
b' = magenta
c = blue-violet + 50% white
(Integration of a' + b')

A similar clear blue-violet is produced by a turning disc or a structure composed of cyan and magenta dots in the same proportions.

We have not enough time here to discuss also the integration of the other primaries and of the complementaries. You can find this in *Méditer la couleur*.

The successive complementaries have been laid open by the experiments which we have achieved together. They are identical with the simultaneous complementaries. They differ only in space-time: the successive complementary appears after having gazed at the image - the simultaneous complementary is seen simultaneously with the image underlining the borders of the colours. The contrasts due to these simultaneous effects reveal our power to objectify the world, which means to discriminate the insight in separate objects. Only this separation permits us to give a name, to articulate a language. At the quantum level its matter in the dimension of the particle. It is the world of Newton. We know today that his theories are right only in part. They are incapable of translating the whole reality. The discrete representations characterize essentially the left hemisphere of the brain which still exercises a sort of dictatorship in our technical and scientific society.

Whereas the wave-quantum level corresponds more to the chromatic integration, the space-time activities of the right hemisphere of the brain is largely determined by a holistic and global process of analogy and continuous representations. Nevertheless we have seen that integration or differentiation have a common origin: the complementary of the eye which can unite or, inversely, separate visual objects. It can adapt or, on the other hand, accentuate the difference. For example, in photography you need filters to rectify the spectral composition of the light but with the phenomenon of constancy the visual system produces with its complementaries an automatic and uninterrupted rectification in such a way that even under different lights, the objects seem identical.

In every day life the complementary is able, first: to accentuate the individuality of colours. The gaze then is in constant movement exploring and analytical; second: to equalize the light energies, when smaller parts are fusing into greater systems.

We can observe these two trends of visual perception in every healthy ecological system where you can find the individual and the common spirit in a steady balance.

The reality of the infinite is not elsewhere and eternity is not tomorrow or yesterday. Infinity and eternity can be lived in the present of here and now. This enlighted present needs the whole human being with his muscles and his breath, with his intelligence and his feelings. An immense mental and emotional experience which must nevertheless remain quiet and simultaneously alert to plunge into the multidimensional unique reality which is impossible to reach with concepts.

The experiment which we will discuss now with this pair of complementaries on a grey background requires long minutes of complete relaxation, a very regular and nearly imperceptible breathing, the nerves and all thoughts at rest. The attention is directed on the very instant of here and now and simultaneously the infinite. Here and now is the focused space-time of a determined very small point in the centre. The infinite is motionlessness, the mental and emotional emptiness, the non-intention. Just before the integration in a uniform grey, where the background and the form fuse together, the borders of the two complementary colours brighten up to an intense flash of lightning.

This phenomenon of the chromatic perception finds an analogy in the social sphere: before the integration of the mentalities into a world-wide universal consciousness, each person, each community, each entity requires and proclaims its autonomy, its specificity.

At the crucial moment of the zero-point, there is a total adaptation. The complementaries disappear in the background - the complementary orange of the eye integrates with the cyan, the complementary cyan of the eye integrates with the orange. All is grey. The exterior Universe and the interior Universe are looped.

This experiment can give us a notion of a paradoxical space-time of a full emptiness, of an empty fullness, of silence containing all the noises. A neutrality composed of the duality and a profound comprehension that the duality is in fact a complementarity necessary to all manifestations... (see page 22, figure 8).

The eye as a receiver as well as a projector can give us an idea of the close identity of sight with what has been seen. I think we've made it clear that it is not enough to have eyes to see and a brain to think. The whole human body is necessary and it doesn't stop at the surface of the skin. It forms one organism with the earth, with the sun and with the whole Cosmos. But it is the consciousness which determines its limits: It can be a small prison confronted to a world of hard matter - or it can be a manifestation of a living and indivisible Universe.

Michel Albert-Vanel

The Planetary Colour System
Methodology and Applications

1. Approach to Colour Groups

My teaching in colour began in 1968, the year of the mini cultural revolution in France. In the image of this period, my teaching has continued to be experimental for the last 26 years. At the beginning I based my approach on a special colour space, intermediary between Munsell and N.C.S., giving us a classification of the colours by equal lightness, equal saturation, equal hue... But I had some difficulty understanding the restiveness of some of my students. For them colours could not be reduced into only these few categorisations. And finally I had to become aware of the fact that it is very damaging that colour spaces, as in the theories of Munsell, Ostwald or N.C.S...., do not take into account the differences of material and the effect of colour combinations.

The Role of the Material

All of this is evident concerning the role of the material. I could notice that students have a great sensitivity toward material aspects: the effects of material and the use of pastel, gouache, water-colour, ink, pencil and so on... And they do not want to reduce the colours to very poor uniform samples, simply because it is possible to classify them in a cartesian colour space.

In contrast, they are capable of building very original spaces incorporating transparency, reflection, etc... if we leave them a certain freedom. But a colour space incorporating transparency is not representable in three dimensions, it would be at the least a four-dimensional space or more with reflection, etc., depending on the number of parameters.

Finally we arrive at the conclusion that colour science needs only three physical parameters to represent a colour in three-dimensional cartesian space, just as everything in the universe could be only in three dimensions according to the conception of the 19th century! For example in the C.I.E. triangle 1931, light and pigment, transparent and opaque colours are confused in the same point. But it is very easy to demonstrate that white and transparency are not the same thing: one can make a progression from a glass of milk to a glass of water.

If this multi-dimensional representation is more difficult to conceive, it has the enormous advantage of opening into a new colour space where all the fancies, all the sensibilities can find their place. In doing that, we simply imitate Nature which combines excessively different materials and textures in endless combinations.

In these classical spaces a painting can be represented only by a constellation of dots of which we know nothing concerning their relative importance. In fact they display only the similarity between colours or progressions from one colour to another, but they ignore the differences between contrasts, e.g. black and white, yellow and blue, etc...

So it was necessary to create another pedagogical method to introduce a relationship between theory and practice.

Basic Principles

Considering the above, we can assert that colours are relative, they are never fixed, but susceptible to modification in time and space. So, why should the colour universe stay fixed and immutable, when the theory of relativity gives us a glimpse of a universe in perpetual mutation, variable according to different points of view?

In fact, a colour can be completely transformed by its surrounding, because of contrasts and optical fusions. When we look at a painting or a landscape, we do not see isolated colours, but a relationship between these different colours. We perceive that the painting is very colourful or more greyish, or with a dominant blue, bright or dark... Different colours play a secondary role inside this global impression.

Thus our perception of this image is a global perception and not a fragmentation into small units. That is why an isolated colour is a complete abstraction. This is also precisely why this notion of colour groups is so fundamental.

Definition

A colour group is a colour combination inside which the different components lose their own characteristics to the profit of a global perception. Thus colour groups are families of colours which reflect this global impression and comply with the laws of gestalt theory. The consequence is that all the colour groups which do not possess a strong dominance will be confused as identical although they are different.

But this determination of different colour groups was taking too much time and was very empirical. We started by printing images in silkscreen to see if the modifications of colour could modify the images' sense.

Working some time later in the photography department, I had the idea of building a special tri-chromatic machine to permutate colours in an image. That was better, because the students really enjoyed experimenting with this machine. But it was still taking too much time and it was necessary to use computers. So I created some programmes of colour permutation, which enormously accelerated the research. In some ways this made more evident the reducing aspect of visual perception.

Entropy

It is very commonly believed that colour groups are infinite in number. In fact it is nothing like this and only a small number of characteristic colour groups can be identified and memorised. All the colour groups that do not have a strong dominance will be confused as identical even if they are in fact different. They give an impression of randomness, of aleatory choice. Entropy characterises a state of disorder opposite to negentropy which brings a strong structure and an elevated level of communication. Aleatoriness is the ideal point of entropy of the colour groups, and all the colour groups which are perceived are negentropic. But this notion is also relative: a colour group may be entropic for one and negentropic for another one. So the question is, how can colour groups be identified as being really different?

Research based on images could proceed directly to colour associations. I began by determining the opposites in only 6 colour groups, and I progressively increased this number, arriving finally at 22, this number being an optimisation.

When we try to determine what are the most different colour groups, we soon see that this research is extremely difficult. In fact it is easier to develop similarity in a personal palette than differentiation.

Therefore we can note that students generally work with very limited colour groups and do not recognise others. This situation is very unfortunate and can be compared to a pianist who plays only on a small part of the keyboard.

Indeed it takes a great personal effort to become conscious of one's own limitations, to stand back in order to understand the other preferences of people in a group and extend the grasp to all the possibilities of the colour spectrum. In this way we increase the student's capacity to realise and communicate.

Thus we can conclude that the famous question of harmony in colour is not a real problem. Harmony is a subjective and limited choice in the greater possibilities of the colour groups. And finally harmony or disharmony is only a question of communication and application in colour following the goal of the practice.

The Planetary Colour System is not in conflict with other representations of colour, but incorporates them and permits the understanding of their differences and provides something more.

2. Description of the Colour Groups

For the sake of pedagogical clarity, we will try to investigate further this notion of colour groups. Far from the material problems concerning colour reproduction in terms of additive, subtractive, or proportional primaries, it is necessary to consider the 'psychological primaries' as the domain of chromatic perception.

Following Hering's theory, the different colours are perceived according to three antagonistic pairs resulting in six fundamental colours which are responsible for the whole of our colour perception. Hering's theory was for a long time in conflict with the tri-chromatic theory of Young. But now we recognise that these two theories are in fact complementary, the Hering theory describing simply a more elevated level of perception.

But it is necessary to add to this model ABSENCE (absence of colour) which characterises transparency and reflection. Absence is at the origin of the different colours and colour groups.

These fundamental colours opposed in antagonistic pairs are:

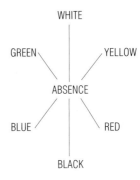

The visual field of the observer can be compared to a 'window' through which these fundamental colours enter in combinations of variable proportions to constitute the 'colour groups'.

Now we can develop this new conception: from the combination of the four hues YELLOW, RED, GREEN and BLUE result 15 configurations, and a 16th case with absence of colour.

COMBINATIONS OF HUES

	1 HUE	2 HUES	3 HUES	4 HUES
A -	R G Y B	Y R G Y B G	Y B G R	R
		B Y B G R R	R G Y B	G
			B Y R G	Y
				B

Symbols: A = absence of colour, R = red, G = green, Y = yellow, B = blue

34 But it is also necessary to take into consideration the neutrals BLACK, WHITE, BLACK AND WHITE, which are combined with the 16 preceding typical combinations of hues. These new combinations generate 64 possibilities.

COMBINATIONS WITH VALUES (See page 23, fig. 9)

	1 HUE	2 HUES	3 HUES	4 HUES
P →	R G Y B	Y R G Y B G	Y B G R	R
		B Y B G R R	R G Y B	G
			B Y R G	Y
				B
W + →	" " " "	" " " " " "	" " " "	"
N + →	" " " "	" " " " " "	" " " "	"
N+W+ →	" " " "	" " " " " "	" " " "	"
GS+ →	" " " "	" " " " " "	" " " "	"

Symbols: P = pure colours, W = white , N = black, GS = grey scale

These 64 configurations permit a classification of the colour groups, because all the situations in everyday life are necessarily included in one of these combinations or intermediate between any two of them. But it is necessary to imagine a third dimension giving us a progressive fusion in each of these contrasted colour groups through integration of little dots of colours or by optical fusion with rotating disks.

These 64 possibilities and their fusions can be reduced into 22 typical cases which constitute the sequence of fundamental colour groups. The sequence of 22 fundamental colour groups is necessary and sufficient to represent the main colour perceptions in everyday life.

THE SEQUENCE OF 22 FUNDAMENTAL COLOUR GROUPS

ACHROMATICS:	White
	Black
	Black and White
	Scaled Greys
1 HUE:	Red
	Yellow
	Green
	Blue
2 HUES:	Yellow + Blue
	Red + Yellow
	Yellow + Green
	Green + Blue
	Blue + Red
	Red + Green
3 HUES:	Yellow + Red + Blue
	Red + Blue + Green
	Blue + Green + Yellow
	Green + Yellow + Red
4 HUES:	Red + Yellow + Green + Blue
	" " " + White
	" " " + Black
	" " " + Black and White

We can add two non-significant colour groups: Absence (Transparency and Reflection) and Aleatory. Absence is similar to zero in mathematics because it signifies absence of colour. Aleatory is similar to infinite, because we can multiply endlessly the number of aleatoric groups to obtain the same unique perception. The two-hue colour groups such as Yellow and Red, Yellow and Green, etc., give the nuances such as orange, lemon yellow, turquoise, purple... The four-hue colour groups are 'polychromatic' by balance between the principal hues, so the addition of other hues inside these colour groups modifies nothing.

The result of this is a conception of 22 main stars around which revolve planets representing the 64 colour groups described above. But as it is possible to endlessly vary a colour group, with partial contrasts or fusions, so we add to these planets some more satellites, the constellations becoming denser and denser, presenting more and more subtle variations. When these variations become too subtle they are no longer perceived and we are back in a situation of losing sense, near the aleatory situation of the beginning.

3. Methodology of Application

Colour scenography is the result of judicious choice in a colour group or a sequence of colour groups present in the system. The steps will follow a tree diagram showing the successive choices to be accomplished. That is to say that we will have to follow a certain pathway in the planetary colour space. (See the Scheme on the right)

Semantics

Semantics is very useful in practice, because we can state that all the applications in colour finally depend on communication: the impression you want to communicate with your painting, or with your architecture... Each colour group has a particular signification and semantics give very simple rules for making your choices in these colour groups. You can be sure of the semantics when you have a good correlation between public surveys,

SCHEME OF THE TREE (See page 23, fig. 10)

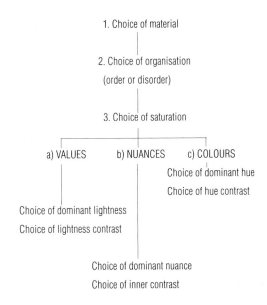

the use of colour in publicity, studies in colour sociology, and so on.

We give here the result of many years of research on this subject. But it is also really important to declare that semantics is only correct in a limited area which changes with time and geography. The semantics developed here is only valid for Europe and America at the end of the 20th century! It is also very important to make clear that colour significations are not only positive. We have three terms to characterise a colour: one positive, one neutral and one negative. Now we have to examine these different choices in more detail:

1. Choice of Material

Possibilities: LIGHT - MATTER
TRANSPARENT - OPAQUE
REFLECTIVE - MATT

These materials constitute colour groups, too. So a transparent or translucent material can have also a red or blue dominance. This choice of material is predominant in architecture and permits a special relationship with light. This choice in light or material also affects the choice of the primaries: RED - GREEN - BLUE in additive for light, YELLOW - MAGENTA - CYAN in subtractive for matter, RED - YELLOW - GREEN - CYAN - BLUE - MAGENTA for proportional or visual integration. This last criterion is the most important in everyday life.

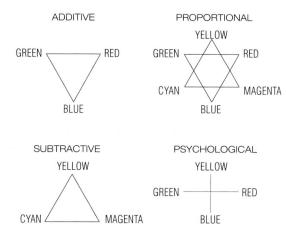

But we can reduce these primaries in our approach to RED - YELLOW - GREEN - BLUE, which are generally sufficient, because these psychological primaries are in fact a simplification of the proportional primaries.

However we can say that this is the most usual case, and that colour reproductions and mixtures simply have a tendency to be either more additive or substractive, given that we use more light or more matter.

2. Choice of Organisation

Possibilities: ORDER - DISORDER

At first it is necessary to be reminded of the fact that all the colour groups not characterised by a strong dominant will seem identical, aleatory and non-significant. But it is equally possible to use disorder as a principle of organisation. Remember also the non-significant colour groups that belong to the category of disorder: non-significance results equally from lack or excess of colours.

3. Choice of Saturation

Three possibilities: - COLOURS
- VALUES
- NUANCES

This choice is essential, because it corresponds to three fundamental esthetic categories. Generally, all colour problems come from the fact that we do not clearly choose between these three categories and we are in an intermediary position of compromise.

SEMANTIC SCHEME OF SATURATIONS (See page 24, fig. 11)

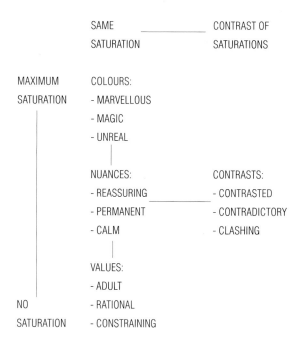

	SAME SATURATION	CONTRAST OF SATURATIONS
MAXIMUM SATURATION	COLOURS: - MARVELLOUS - MAGIC - UNREAL	
	NUANCES: - REASSURING - PERMANENT - CALM	CONTRASTS: - CONTRASTED - CONTRADICTORY - CLASHING
	VALUES: - ADULT	
NO SATURATION	- RATIONAL - CONSTRAINING	

This criterion of saturation is also the most important concerning the integration of architecture with landscape. Generally it is the half-tone, or nuance which permits the best integration and eventual camouflage. We can state that inside buildings the saturation of a space should be in inverse proportion to the time spent in the space.

Thus circulation spaces, such as passages can be in very saturated colours, because we are only passing through them and different bright colours permit a good memorisation and identification of the main directions in the building. But public spaces such as a refectory or library suppose a longer frequenting and require less saturated colours. And finally spaces such as classrooms should be neutral, because of the long period of frequenting and the liveliness brought by different documents stuck on the walls. This question of time is very essential in architecture.

a) Colours

Here neutrals will play only a secondary role of compensation, allowing a chord between pure colours, lightening a Blue, if necessary, or darkening a Yellow, etc. This effect is more accentuated in three or four hue compositions, with the possibility of obtaining Pastels or Shades. This was expressed by colouristic painters such as Fusch, Van Gogh, Matisse...

Choice of the Dominant Hue

Possibilities:	YELLOW DOMINANT
	RED "
	BLUE "
	GREEN "

The dominant hue can also be an intermediary between two hues, for example Orange between Yellow and Red. This choice of dominant hue can be made in compensation for or in accentuation of the natural light. So the light coming from the north is, for examle, dominant blue and the light coming from the south is dominant orange. The role of the curtains and blinds is also essential here.

The choice of the dominant hue can be made also according to psychological and semantic criteria. Thus yellow gives an impression of sun and is especially interesting for underground spaces which never receive natural light. Blue is more celestial, like sky and water and gives a correspondence with these elements. Green evokes nature, and so on...

Choice of Hue Contrast

Possibilities: MONOCHROMATIC
                  DICHROMATIC
                  TRICHROMATIC
                  POLYCHROMATIC

Polychromatic colour groups animate space, making it more cheerful, more dynamic. But in excess they can result in a 'cacophony'. At the opposite end of the scale, monochromatic colour groups give a greater unity to space and make it sober.

SEMANTIC SCHEME OF HUES (See page 24, picture 12)

PASSIVE		ACTIVE
LIGHT		
YELLOW-GREEN:	YELLOW:	ORANGE:
- SPRING	- ENERGETIC	- VIVIFYING
- HUMID	- SUNNY	- HOT
- PUTRID	- DESSICATED	- DISTURBING
GREEN:	POLYCHROMATIC:	RED:
- NATURAL	- JOYFUL	- WARMING
- VEGETABLE	- FREE	- LIVING
- SICKLY	- BARBARIAN	- VIOLENT
TURQUISE	BLUE:	PURPLE:
- COOL	- QUIET	- SPIRITUAL
- COSMIC	- NOCTURNAL	- ETHEREAL
DARK - ICY	- NOSTALGIC	- VAPOROUS

b) Values

Naturally we find here White, Black, Black and White, and Scaled Greys, but equally monochromes: Red, or Green, Yellow, Blue, where different Greys can bring important variations between dark and light. In this category you can find everything which is employed to reconstitute the effect of light, the hue playing here a secondary role to accompany the values. This was expressed by painters such as Latour, Rembrandt, Turner...

Choice of Dominant Lightness

Possibilities: WHITE OR PALE
                  GREY OR MEDIUM/NEUTRAL
                  BLACK OR DARK

Here also we can act by compensation or accentuation: a very bright room seems brighter if it is painted white. But too much light can be softened by a dark colour on the wall. Semantics also guide the choice for the mysterious aspect of black, the immaculate aspect of white, or the discretion and refinement of grey.

Choice of the Lightness Contrast

Possibilities: BLACK AND WHITE CONTRAST
                  SCALED GREYS
                  FUSION IN A LIGHTNESS VALUE

The lightness contrasts essentially affect the legibility of a space or the legibility of a message. This legibility is maximum with strong contrasts between light and dark. On the other hand a form becomes illegible when the lightnesses are equal, but that could give more comfort in a space such as an office. Halfway, scaled grays give an effect of light, of succession in the different planes of the space, or an effect of mist.

SEMANTIC SCHEME OF VALUES (See page 24, fig. 13)

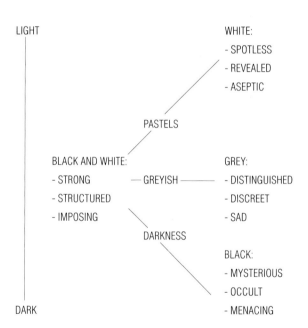

CONTRAST OF ———————————— FUSION OF
LIGHTNESSES   LIGHTNESSES

LIGHT

WHITE:
- SPOTLESS
- REVEALED
- ASEPTIC

PASTELS

BLACK AND WHITE: GREY:
- STRONG   — GREYISH — - DISTINGUISHED
- STRUCTURED   - DISCREET
- IMPOSING   - SAD

DARKNESS

BLACK:
- MYSTERIOUS
- OCCULT
DARK   - MENACING

c) Nuances

These different hues and values combine to create nuances. We find here the preceding categorisations, but with more complexity. In nuances, there is a very short distance between the different components of the colour group. But in compensation it is necessary to have a very great number of nuances to enrich this colour group.

The subtle variations around a central point of colour are the most important here. It is more often a secondary colour, like Orange, Turquoise, Yellow-Green, or Purple, that is to say, an intermediary between two basic colours. We find in this category all that would constitute an effect of physical matter. The extremely nuanced colours of nature enter in this categorisation. This was expressed by painters such as Chardin, Braque, Morandi...

Choice of the Dominant Nuance

Possibilities: MORE RED OR GREEN
                   MORE BLUE OR YELLOW
                   MORE WHITE OR BLACK
                   MORE SATURATED OR DESATURATED

In certain cases of tolerance, it could be interesting to take into consideration the possible variations around a colour group. We can measure the deviations permitted around a colour group and all the colours comprising this colour group. This notion is especially useful in industry.

Choice of the Inner Contrast

Possibilities: FUSION OF HUES and CONTRAST OF VALUES WITH:
                   BLACK
                   WHITE
                   BLACK AND WHITE

                   FUSION OF VALUES and HUE CONTRAST WITH:
                   YELLOW
                   RED
                   GREEN
                   BLUE

40 In fact, fusions or contrasts between hues and values can be more or less complete, so there could be some partial fusions and partial contrasts. These partial contrasts animate space. And the colours can be so saturated that they are used in reduced areas. Like time, space is a very essential notion in architecture. But if we extend in surface a specific colour in a colour group, this colour group changes in dominance and becomes another colour group.

When a colour group loses its identity by time or space, by ageing or taking distance, it returns to entropy. A painting by Rembrandt, for example, is a struggle against disorder, but entropy threatens it in time by attenuation of the colours, yellowing of varnish, and also with space: from a distance this painting is only a small surface of brown. Thus a colour group in which the internal contrasts of hue, lightness and saturation have disappeared is none other than a uniform colour. Like aleatoriness, uniform colours are endless in number but they are not perceived as colour groups.

Conclusion

The consideration of these different parameters, in relationship with semantics, permits us to foresee with accuracy what will be the spectator's appreciation of a colour group or a colour group sequence. This notion of colour groups permits the building of a bridge between art and science, which was impossible before, because there existed no relationship between the isolated colours in science and colour combinations in art. This pedagogy also completely revises colour teaching and permits focus of attention on the personal development of the student. And finally, this method gives a very efficient scheme of working in various colour applications, such as textile, design and architecture.

Bibliography

ALBERT-VANEL, Michel
- (1976) Harmonie et sémiologie de la couleur. In: Colour Dynamics 76. A.I.C. Budapest.

- (1981) Rôle des permutations colorées dans l'image numérique et analogique. In: A.I.C. Color 81. Berlin.

- (1981) Les ensembles colorés, une nouvelle approche de la couleur. In: Information Couleur 15 - C.F.C. Paris.

- (1982) The Planets-Colour-System. In: Dynamic Colour Symposium A.I.C. Budapest.

- (1982) Le Planètes-Couleur-Système. In: Catalogue exposition E.N.S.A.D. Paris.

- (1983) Jouez la Couleur. In: Information Couleur 20 - C.F.C. Paris.

- (1983) Das Planeten-Farb-System. In : Farbe und Raum 5/1983. Berlin Ost.

- (1983) Colour Chart Mesures in Planets-Colour-System. In: Färg rapport A.I.C. Kungälv Sweden.

- (1984) A frog's eye view. In: Color Education A.I.C. Salamanca.

- (1985) Typologie des Ensembles Colorés. In: Mondial Couleur A.I.C. Monte-Carlo.

- (1985) Cosmologie de la Couleur. In: Mondial Couleur A.I.C. Monte-Carlo

- (1986) Application des Ensembles Colorés à la pédagogie. In: Colloque "La couleur à l'Ecole, la couleur et l'Ecole". Paris: C.F.C. et Ministère de l'Education C.E.S.T.A.

- (1987) Des couleurs pour nos Ecoles. Paris: Ministère de l'Education.

- (1987) Color Approximation by relative groups. In: Symposium "Colour Appearence" Volume 15. Annapolis U.S.A.

- (1988) Colour approximation by relative groups. In: Colour Dynamics Budapest 88.

- (1988) Les mécanismes de la nature par les ensembles colorés. In: La couleur et la nature dans la ville. Académie Nationale des Arts de la rue, Editions du Moniteur Paris

- (1989) Planetary System. In: The Color Compendium by Hope and Walch. New York: Van Nostrand Reinhold Book.

- (1993) Basic colour groups sequence. In: Colour 93 A.I.C. Technical University of Budapest.

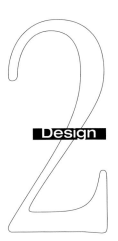

Design

Development of the Colour Sense
Basic Colour Education at the Basel Design School

Basic Design Course

At the Basel Design School the education begins with a basic design course, which lasts one to two years. To be admitted further into the professional classes one must first take the basic course. Here the student becomes acquainted with principal design problems on an elementary level. The following subjects are part of the curriculum:
– Drawing
– Methods of design in two and three dimensions
– Basics of photography
– Lettering
– Studies of materials
– Colour studies

The general idea of the basic course is, to develop separately the students' specific sensitivity and talent relative to the different subjects. Afterward in the professional classes these subjects are integrated into more extensive projects. Colour is a separate subject taught only in the basic course. We do not have a fixed school curriculum. Each teacher presents his course in the way he sees fit. In spite of this freedom, there is a consensus among the teachers concerning the general goals of design education: The main goal is that students should be able to make independently professional decisions when they leave the school.

The following points are characteristic of the teaching method / philosophy in the basic course:
– First hand experience is of the upmost importance,
– This experience comes through comparison,
– Comparison requires differing possibilities,
– The more variable the possibilities are, the richer the experiences are, and
– To make comparisons the student needs a set of criteria. We

do not take such criteria from known theories. The student must develop his own criteria by observing his possibilities.

Colour Education

Colour is known to be a highly subjective matter. Therefore colour theories are attractive to a teacher. When colour appears more objective through the rules of a theory, it seems to be more manageable. But theoretical studies are not helpful in developing the students' colour sense. Studying colour theories makes more sense later on, when the student is able to compare his/her own colour experiences with the meaning of such theories. At this point theoretical studies help to reflect the personal approach to the colour and to open new perspectives.

For an introduction to colour design many colour theories are too *general*. They speak about primary colours and principal contrasts. But the students have to learn to work with all colour gradations and with a lot of reciprocal influences between them. Other colour theories are too *individual*. Some of the theories of famous painters are very interesting in context with their personal work, but not directly applicable to a beginner's problem with colour.

For such reasons we do not apply known colour theories or colour systems in basic colour courses. Theories cannot replace the personal experience of a designer. We try to generate conditions for the students to acquire personal experiences with colour. Therefore in the beginning we do not tell students
– what physics says
– what psychology says
– what the history of art says
– what this or that artist says
  about colours,

but we ask each student
– what *he* sees
– what *he* feels
– what *he* remembers
– what *he* thinks
when *he* is looking at his colours.

In the first year of the basic course the program encompasses a 40 hour week. Colour studies take up 5 hours of that time and consists of two different subjects which are complementary: *Colour as material* and *Pure colour studies*.

Colour as Material

In the first year colour course the student must research:
– Visual characteristics of different painting materials such as dyes, paints, and pencils,
– Different tools for processing colours, and
– Different ways to apply colours on a surface, including the student's movement for directing tools.

The student doesn't learn to apply the paint techniques in a classical way, but the subject is to experiment and to play with the painting material, for exploring new and individual visual structures. The character of a picture *results* from this play. The student doesn't pre-imagine a picture *before* painting, but rather he becomes surprised by the result of his action. For many students it is hard work to learn to play again, but this attitude is an indispensable presupposition for real creative activity.

In the second year colour course the student integrates the aspects "Colour" and "Material" in a more extensive way. Not only are traditional painting materials used but non–traditional materials that can result in coloured surfaces. Such three dimen-

sional materials include for example sand, wax and coffee and can be combined with even further materials that result in diverse self-made coloured surfaces.

The student learns to control many different visual aspects of a work in the same moment:
– colour contrasts (hue, value, saturation)
– even and uneven
– glossy and matt
– coarse and fine materials
– ordered and disordered materials
– personal associations
– emotional values.

Pure Colour Studies

This course consists of investigations on
– the different qualities of colour,
– the influence of one colour on another, and
– the relation between quality and quantity.

In the basic colour courses normally we use the gouache technique, but sometimes we also work with cut coloured papers. (For some advanced projects we use silk screen).

To mix colours by hand may appear outdated because the current student generation will do their professional work on the computer and not with pencil and brush. But there are good reasons for maintaining this elementary technique in basic colour education. Mixing colours on the palette, to follow the subtle change of one colour on another and to be surprised by a new, unexpected colour is a very sensual and instructive way to explore the personal world of colours.

If colour is the subject of the investigation, the form has to be as simple as possible. Form and colour must always be controllable for the student. Limitations activate students' creativity.

In the beginning exercises are very elementary, they can become more complex later. Here are some exercises from simple to more complex:

– To order small pieces of coloured paper cut from magazines. Ordering the samples according to hue (horizontal) and value (vertical). This is an excellent eye training exercise. In each sample the student must judge twice. The student learns to distinguish clearly the different dimensions of colour.

– To paint some colours and to describe afterwards the personal associations, feelings and ideas associated with each colour. Comparing the descriptions of all students in the class. The students learn to appreciate each colour. They observe how feeling can change a lot, while colour changes only a little.

– The combination of two or three colours in an elementary form (squares, stripes). Many different variations occur. Comparing his own propositions the student learns to differentiate more and more. Finally he groups his attempts according to his personal criteria.

– To choose one or two colours and to confront them again and again with two or three new colours. Added to this exercise is the possibility of changing positions and proportions. Again many different attempts occur. Observation of the interdependency between quality and quantity of a colour becomes more finite. To group and to order the attempts finally.

– To paint colour compositions on a grid. Such composition consists in shapes with similar forms but different sizes. The student tries to balance the composition in a long process, painting one layer over another, changing colours and shapes. Every change influences the whole composition. The student has to run a risk when he decides the next change, because there is no way backwards, but only forwards.

The teacher's function in such education processes is:
– to ask the student's a question, to propose him a simple problem to develop,
– to stimulate the students' curiosity,
– to animate him to search wider and deeper,
– to show him unexplored fields in his investigation, and
– to help him develop criteria for grouping and ordering his variations.

The criteria aren't *good* or *bad*, *nice* or *ugly*, but: how *large* and *rich* is a student's investigation, what is the level of *differentiation* in his work, is it *boring* or *interesting*. Such criteria are evident for every student. Teaching respectively learning methods must be evident for students. (See figures 14 and 15, page 57).

Andrew M. Tomcik

Design and Color
Expanding the Scope

The stimuli for restructuring design and art programs in North America are various and powerful; from economic emergencies to information technologies; from the reconsideration of the formalism of much of modernist design and art to the contextual theories of much newer work. Though the pressures for change are often external to the teaching experience, they have provided an opportunity to reconsider the content and presentation of the material.

Having said this as a general context, I would like to explain our particular situation at York University in Toronto. Though having the largest and most varied fine arts (and design) faculty in Canada, we are primarily a university offering a 'liberal' education somewhere between the strict academic form of English universities and a more varied structure of American universities. As well, how design education fits within a university and how university design programs are different from the specialized training and professional programs of other institutions are questions being asked by long term planners. For the first time in many institutions, design is now being accepted as a distinct activity of cultural and economic importance rather than as a sub-function of the fine arts.

York undergraduate students in design and art spend at least half of their education in academic courses outside the studio, including the natural and social sciences, humanities, languages, other arts, and more. Rather than a handicap, we who teach in design feel this broad educational foundation is especially important as preparation for a profession undergoing constant and rapid change.

As at many educational institutions, difficult times financially create a substantial pressure to either shrink programs or to enlarge classes to keep cost-per-student low. To the administra-tors directing the restructuring, the small size, personal contact and unique activity-based format of the studio classes are puzzling. Lecture courses are deemed efficient because they reach large numbers of students at one time, studio courses are seen as financially inefficient because they must of necessity be small. Faced with this paradox, rather than shrink, we at York have tried to take advantage of both teaching formats by devising a number of foundation design courses that include a single large lecture portion taught by experienced faculty members, and a number of smaller tutorial studios, directed by younger professional designers.

By integrating the intellectual and manual activity within a single course using two teaching methods, it is hoped the students will see their work in design and the arts not as a mysterious hybrid talent isolated within the university, but as an activity that is both intellectual and instinctual, and integrated in the university.

More practically, this is how we have taught the Design and Color course for the last several years. It is a semester-long course of 13 weeks, which includes 13 one-hour-long lectures, and 13 three-hour-long studio sessions, all designed, coordinated and supervised by the senior lecture professor. The student work is evaluated as the semester progresses and portfolios of term work are reviewed by the professor and the tutorial instructors at the end of the term.

The Lecture Content

As much as possible, the lecture portion of the course parallels but is not limited to the problems being considered in the studio. Meant to introduce the student to the broad and varied study of color in many fields, the lecture content includes the scientific aspects of color and vision; psychological and social considerations; pragmatic information on materials including the new electronic media; color theories used by designers and artists; the use of color in commerce and marketing; and large selection of current work in art and design.

The lecture schedule begins with an introduction to the physics of light and color, along with discussion of some of the historical scientific theories from Aristotle and Newton through Goethe and Helmholtz to Land. Aristotle, Goethe and Land are interesting in this section because of their renown in fields other than science; Aristotle the philosopher, Goethe as a creative writer and Land, the inventor of the Polaroid camera. The discussion of physics and vision has been greatly aided by some recent books, including Moritz Zwimpfer's *Color, Optics and Perception.* These lectures are accompanied by explanatory slides, and demonstrations using projections of colored cells onto objects of various colors and values.

If students wish for more complete scientific explanation of color, they can study the physics of light in the Faculty of Applied and Natural Sciences of our University in courses such as *Light, Sound and Motion* a course for non-science majors, or in advanced physics courses as part of their university, non-fine art/ design requirements. Our students often have secondary interests, or 'minors' as we call them, in other areas of the university.

Discussion of physics is followed by biology, particularly the optics of humans, and the vision/brain relationship. The lecture would discuss among other things, the lens and iris (and the parallels to cameras), eye coloration, and particularly the function of the rods and cones. The rods and cones relate to such things as color reception, the evolution of vision in animals, night vision and the value studies which the students would be working on in the studio. Comments like Sir Francis Bacon's

"All colors will agree in the dark" become understood as not just an ancient witticism, but an observation of some scientific merit. Again, more complete study of optics could be had in courses in the biology department.

Natural science is followed by the social sciences and psychology, particularly color distinctions in various societies, the perception of color at various ages, and color constancy, all reinforcing the eye/brain, brain/eye connection. At this time, color symbolism and the similarities and differences between cultures, religions and periods can be mentioned. Color nomenclature is discussed including the varying need for color names in different societies; 11 basic terms in English, only 5 for the Kung bushmen of Africa. Discussion continues from basic language to associative terms, to materials, to marketing and ultimately to color naming and organization systems such as Munsell and Ostwald. This discussion parallels the value, hue and chroma studies in the studio.

This lecture naturally leads to the pragmatic issues of colored pigments, paints and dyes, natural and man-made materials, transparency and opacity, permanence and so on. In addition to the conventional artists' materials, photographic materials both positive and negative are discussed including dye layers, light temperature, as well as the issues of reflective and refractive sources.

The new electronic media of television and computer follows; how color is generated on screen, and the difficulties of relating refractive on-screen RGB (red,green blue) images to reflective printed results in the CMYK (cyan, magenta, yellow, black) system of printing. These difficulties become more evident in the advanced years of the design program when students are spending more time on computers. For your information, most of the hands-on use of computers happens in years three and four on our Macintosh based system, using Quark Express, Adobe Illustrator, Photoshop and Interactive multi-media programs plus a variety of output devices.

Creative Theories and Examples Used in Lectures

Up until this point, all the lectures may seem to have been technical or academic, but in each lecture I attempt to ground the issue in creative art and design examples. The materials discussion that includes paintings, plastics, computers, film and more, can also include the sand paintings of the Hopi Indians and Buddhist sand mandalas in which lack of permanence is as much part of the work as permanence is to most other work. The color theories of Chevreul, a chemist by trade, can be illustrated by threads in tapestries, the original impetus for Chevreul's study, or the more common example of Monet's paintings of haystacks, despite Monet's denial of influence. But one can also include the posters of Monet's contemporary Jules Cheret, Roy Lichtenstein's pop art versions of Monet's haystacks done in the Benday dots of mechanical reproduction, or the pixeling and 'morphing' on computer screens.

To make the link between the technical issues and creative processes, we discuss theories and creative formulations used by designers and artists to 'make sense' of the world of color and experience. Kandinsky has left a rather explicit account of his ideas in his *On the Spiritual in Art*, and Klee did as well. Again, some recent publishing, such as Manlio Brusatin's *A History of Colors* and *Primary Sources, selected writings on color from Aristotle to Albers* edited by Patricia Sloane, has presented us the ideas of artists of many earlier periods. By extending to earlier periods references of creative work linked to the color ideas prevalent in their time, we can address a common misconception of beginning students that the history of art and design is divided into an earlier 'realistic' period of unselfconscious craft, and the art of the twentieth century burdened with ideas and ideologies.

Rather than presenting the student with mute examples of design and art, names and dates, this discussion of history, theory and the intellectual context enables the student to link designer/artist with the ideas and processes that informed the work. The context of the Bauhaus where Kandinsky worked, his reference to music, his specific vocabulary of color and shape relationship, and his 'orchestration' of paintings using these vocabularies are a case in point.

The Broader Intellectual Context

To cite Wittgenstein, "We cannot think what we cannot say, (Tractatus Logico-Philosophicus, 1921), and language forms an important part of how we think about color. The classic humors of the fifth century BC still infiltrate our language relating mood to color: sanguine, choleric, melancholic and phlegmatic.

Attempts to link color with physical, psychic and spiritual spheres are common in history and continue to arise regularly. Both Mondrian and Rudolf Steiner espoused theosophical views, Steiner translating them into the color rooms at the Goetheaneum. More recently there is a growing interest in chromotherapy .

Though some color/mood associations can be traced back to the humors and other early sources, the origin of these associations is often lost. Yellow as cowardice, blue as sad, black as mourning, white as celebration are meanings common in North America, their source not always certain and their associations not universal. Some use is very local in origin. "He was fired on gray paper" is a Danish saying suggesting humiliation, owing its origins to the manner of dismissing disgraced public officials 200 years ago. If linguists are correct in describing language as a system of arbitrary symbols, color nomenclature and color association languages would be as various and arbitrary as other symbol languages.

The intellectual context need not be confined to visual material. Significant examples from literature, such as Melville's extended consideration of the color white in *Moby Dick* or Diane Ackerman's book *A Natural History of the Senses*, underscore the importance of color in experience and expression beyond the visual arts. Such study also reveals that in some periods, the importance of color and description is less important than other issues. Though Homer spoke of "the wine-dark sea", more important in his literature are the elements of physique, stance, and events.

Reference to other visual forms, particularly theatre and film, make a natural connection with students who are avid movie goers. The stunning black and whiteness of early Bergman films, the artificial comic book color of *Dick Tracy*, Peter Greenaway's color changes as people move through rooms in *The Cook, The Thief, His Wife and Her Lover*, and the very selective use of color in Spielberg's *Schindler's List* are common examples in the students' experience.

Commercial and Popular Contexts

The symbolism of color has both its elite and popular proponents. The study of color symbolism in paintings is well developed, while a host of books and consultants advises anyone who wishes popularity, beauty or power on the secrets of color. For example, consultant David Ushewitz in his *The Color of Success* states that "no doubt dark colors mean power and authority, that's why Hell's Angels and IBM executives wear dark outfits." Though I question the absoluteness of these statements, I feel students should be aware of these common assumptions about color and be willing to question their authority.

Our world is rife with color usages outside the arts. For some time, commercial enterprises have used corporate colors for identification, just as sports teams do; note the '*Big Blue*' of IBM and the '*Azurri*' of Italian soccer. These uses have continued to evolve. After a series of controversial advertisements, Benetton now considers its trademark to be, not one color, but 'The Colors of Benetton' allowing all that name might encompass from characteristics of race to the color of sweaters.

Though the use of poetic, associative names for colors of garments or products by merchandisers is often a ploy in establishing a mood or 'niche' in the market, these associative names are not always what they seem. Some product colors have been selected not for their mood association alone, but also their usefulness as for computer inventory control codes. For example, the names Tahini, Tangerine, Tearose and Thunder (e.g. navy blue) are coded as TAH, TAN, TEA, and THU.

Design and Art, Similarities and Differences

As this course is *Design and Color*, the lectures and projects tend to be more analytical and controlled than in most art courses, hopefully contributing to an understanding of color in use, rather considering color as intuitive only, a mystical inborn 'sense'. Not denying the importance of intuitive expression, I do believe there is much that can be learned about color by anybody willing to apply both aspects of their creativity.

Because this course is offered in the foundation years, students are usually not aware of much recent art, and are less aware of new design. Within the lecture format, they are introduced to advanced work in architecture, industrial and interior design, graphic design, photography and fashion, with the particular emphasis on the issues of color in the work, as well as color in the significant movements of the visual arts of painting and sculpture. This is an opportunity to link the scientific and technical issues with the creative issues, and bridge the gap between their studio projects and work being done today.

Design examples range from the colors of 'natural' materials in much modernist and Scandinavian furniture, to the bright plastics in Sottsass's Valentine typewriter and the 'artifical' colored laminates in Memphis furniture, the vibrating colors in 60's rock posters and the op art of the same period, and the sense of volume via color in Michael Graves' architecture. The crisp primary distinctions of De Stijl, Alfred Jensen, and the Pompidou Center in Paris can be contrasted with the veiled atmospheres of color field paintings of Jules Olitski and selected interiors. As an interesting parallel contemporary with color field paintings, when speaking of atomic and quantum physics in his later life, Albert Einstein would not refer to them in terms of 'space and time' but only as 'the field'.

By linking current work to the scientific, technical and theoretical discussions held earlier, we are attempting to avoid the oversimplification of color to only scientific data, a set of formulae or a basic instinct, none of which completely explain color's importance.

The Studio Projects

The studio activity is the prime interest of most of our students who are majors in the Department of Visual Arts, and in the expanded courses, the studio is definitely not subsidiary to the lecture portion. Having taught this course for years before and after restructuring, I have come to seek a few useful basic insights for the students from the studio activity. First, I would like them to see and understand the basic distinctions of color including the terms hue, value and intensity (chroma), an ability which is still rare in young students. Next I would like them to discover in a disciplined fashion, particular qualities or interactions of color. Third, I would like to see them begin expressing ideas by using color primarily.

Course Materials and Sources

I use projects from Albers' *Interaction of Color*, not just because that is how I was first introduced to color, but because it stresses the particularities of experiencing color. In a lecture, Albers described himself as a romantic, and was very skeptical of formulaic systems. He included them in the back of his book, reserving a grudging praise for Goethe's color triangle because of its relating of colors to mood. The Albers' projects also relate well to the issues in the lecture portion of the class, such as; Albers' color quantity and mixture relates to the Impressionists and Chevreul; Albers' additive and subtractive project is akin with paint and light discussions; color change is linked with ideas of context, etc.

The studio portion of the course then moves regularly week by week with variations of problems from Albers. These are paralleled with longer term projects that are painted; such as the hue, value, intensity studies; a project in three dimensions; some experiments with materials, techniques and textures; and a final project that uses color to express a feeling or state of mind. The mix of exercises and expressive projects keep the students' creative interests active while focusing more than they realize on a fairly narrow range of devices available to a designer or artist.

The methods and materials are basic and support the analytic nature of the course. Though old technology, the use of gouache demands control and forethought, and is flexible, being useful for value or hue studies as well as later expressive projects. The fact that gouache is not easily changed is infuriating at first, but it slows down the making-process enough to encourage analysis and technical care.

Drawing on the Local Environment

Canada is a land of abundant nature, many trees, big skies and many painters who have attempted to capture its natural glory, and the Albers' leaf project ties history, place, art and personal experience with a special poignancy. To gather leaves for color and shape in an autumnal atmosphere that screams with the reds and yellows of our maples seems at first too easy, and then, as students begin to place them into areas of color, more difficult and more subtle. What seems intense in mind is much more varied, subdued, and flexible in use.

As we do this project, we look at some recent work of the English artist Andy Goldsworthy and his surprising use of natural objects *in situ*. Another tutorial instructor in this course has directed her students outside the classroom into our natural landscape to create works in place, photographing them as a record.

The Tutorial Leaders' Role

In our reorganized format, the tutorial leader is the person in direct contact with smaller groups of students (about 20). It is the tutorial leader's job to distribute the studio problems, assist the students in their work as they work, and critique the students' finished projects and grade them. In this arrangement, it is the Professor's job to create the studio assignments and oversee the studio leader's activity, making sure there is equity in workload and assessment between sections of the course and that helpful criticism is consistent with the aims of the projects. As the tutorial leaders are professional designers and artists outside the university and not full-time teachers, they are freed from most of the administrative demands of teaching, providing their professional insight directly to the students.

The Professor's Role

The reorganization of our basic foundation program has put a substantial burden on the senior faculty. First, as experienced teachers we usually have an incidental knowledge of much of the material mentioned here, but to teach that material as a series of formal lectures to classes of 50 to 100 students (and some basic classes are as large as 250) requires a major change in method and preparation. One cannot casually command an audience of this size, the relationship is no longer the personal one we know from the studio.

Second, the amassing of sufficient research material to support the broad, interlinked curricular aim of the course requires the professor to delve into unfamiliar areas. Science explains itself differently than design or art does. I don't claim to be equally versed in science, social sciences, design, art, history and so on, and I let the students know this, but I believe the effort to relate the issues outside the particular disciplines of design or art is appropriate and appreciated. The increasing complexity of the context in which all design is used and needed today suggests that an outward vision is essential. There is no safety in preparing for a narrow craft.

Third, the experienced studio teacher becomes a director of others who are the ones involved in the person-to-person activity of leading the individual students through the studio projects. This new distance between student and course director is often discomforting, course appraisals and other formal means of assessment are not quite the same as personal contact and feedback.

Students are having a period of adjustment as well. Being more familiar with a clear division between studio and lecture, which suggests an artificial division of intelligence and creativity, they are asked in this course to integrate material from two methods of teaching and two people, into one course.

These issues notwithstanding, the structural change in the course has encouraged us to reinvestigate the foundations of color in design and our experience with it, and how color can be introduced to the student of today. Change is always unsettling at first but, in the long run, I believe it has improved the course.

Though 13 weeks is a short time to introduce the breadth of material mentioned, it is my hope that the student will begin to realize the complexity of color. Color is not only an aspect of creative work, color is a phenomena experienced and used by all, seen through a myriad of physical, cultural, social, and educational filters.

I hope to introduce students to how color is *produced*; how it is *received* physically and psychologically; how it is *explained* by science, the social sciences, language and other fields; how it is *interpreted* by various cultures and eras; how it is *utilized* by society in many ways from maps to religious symbolism to fashion and commerce.

On a more personal level, I hope to encourage the students to *experience* color directly putting aside the pre-determinations that come with art and other education; to *discover* how designers and artists have formulated and directed their use of color through conscious consideration of color's many aspects; and finally with confidence and humility, to begin to *create* new work using color.

Garth Lewis

Colour Theory for Textile Design Students

I received my serious introduction to colour as a teaching assistant to Herb Aach at Queens College, C.U.N.Y., in 1970. The course that Aach taught was initiated by John Ferrin, who was also Aach's teacher. It covers some of the same ground as Albers *Interaction of Color*, but significantly included colour mixing with pigments, something Albers' purposefully avoided.

I have subsequently taught versions of this course to a broad range of art and design students, editing and re-presenting ideas in a number of educational formats. My work with textile students has been my most intensive and thorough colour teaching. I have found art and design education still retains residues of that old prejudice that drawing can be taught but not colour. This coupled with widespread misunderstanding or vagueness about basic colour ideas and terminology has meant my contribution in this field retains a measure of novelty and freshness. Colour ideas, like simultaneous contrast, reveal magical colour changes that go beyond most students initial expectations of colour.

The colour programme I teach at Central St. Martins happens in the first term of the B.A. Textile Design course. Students then relate the experience and knowledge to their work in Woven, Knitted and Printed textiles.

The colour programme is in two parts: the first consists of colour problems, done in colour-aid paper and found materials, that are based on Chevreul's ideas of successive and simultaneous contrast. Here students make hue and value changes, explore extension, and create transparency effects with opaque colour swatches. In all cases there is a transformation of basic coloured materials, illusionary colour mixtures are created without physically mixing pigments.

The second part of the course involves mixing two colour charts: a Value chart consisting of a grey scale and between 10 and 15 different hues, stepped from light to dark; followed by a Chroma chart, which again uses 10 to 15 hues, but here the values are kept constant and the mixed scale is from the pure hue to the neutral, which has been mixed with the appropriate complement. The colour circle and colour solid are implied by the two charts, but are not actually represented.

The charts are followed by a painting study of a colour master, where the aim is to maintain the values of the original but reverse the colours. This requires identifying and mixing complements, and matching the original values and degrees of saturation. The study promotes the colour thinking of the chosen artist; in some cases the results can appear arbitrary, but often there are interesting insights gained by reversing the colour logic of a particular painting.

The colour programme presents the idea of a language of colour with its specific terms, ideas and methods that enable clearer and more determined colour expression; but colour use is also a visual process, it is practised and is practical.

Initially I describe three basic qualities: Hue, Value and Chroma. These are fundamental but can prove difficult, value being the easiest to identify. To locate a hue which may have a fugitive identity, to recognise value differences between different colours of variable saturation and to use chroma which is often confused with value, is an essential part of the process. Each colour problem involves and tests these qualities, while introducing new and distinct colour ideas. The mixing of colour charts enables students to get whatever colour they want, rather than be stuck with what they've got. Simultaneous contrast helps students make more of what they already have.

56 The control of colour and paint which is desirable for any artist or designer becomes critical when matching pigments for textile printing or dyes and yarns for weaving. Colour can often be the sole aesthetic issue with textiles. Successful handling of concept and craft is vital. That colour relations can be effective in specific ways, can be developed and refined; that elegant solutions can be achieved for particular colour problems is an important outcome.

Working within a broad and expanding design syllabus, recent additions are C.A.D. and new technology in each textile area means the benefits of studying colour are varied and far reaching; it can indicate new areas of research or provide the means to pursue and assess existing practice.

The colour problems I teach are common to both Aach and Albers and are those that derive from Chevreul, plus the transparency problem, which also involves value and colour change. Chevreuls other ideas of colour harmonies derived from the colour circle were taught by Aach as split complements, analogous harmony, primary and secondary triads, etc., but not by Albers. I discuss these ideas but do not use them as, I am not convinced of their relevance for the student-designer at this stage. A seemingly useful guide to colour harmonies can become a dull and predictable formula, when applied to creative work.

In practice, the grasping of the concepts of hue, value, chroma, saturation, transparency, colour mixing of various kinds and simultaneous contrast is sufficiently complex and demanding to occupy most of my structured colour teaching. The application of ideas of colour harmony, of whatever order, are beyond my immediate remit and would usually concern the specialist, textile tutor.

The textile design industry has its ideas of colour harmony: brights, naturals, pastels, seasonal colours correspond roughly to primaries, complements, analogous harmony, warm and cool colours in technical colour language. Students' colour choices can derive from the colour circle or spectrum but most often their approaches are pragmatic and eclectic, they are influenced by diverse materials and colour sources, or by the specific design requirements they set, or are asked to address.

That simultaneous contrast can help create new colours from a fixed range, can increase or subdue brilliance, or help change opaque material to transparent is all the encouragement students need to realise the potential and relevance for their own ideas, and the textile experience. In professional textile practice there are conventions, ways of doing things, that can be addressed directly by this colour knowledge; they include colourways, which present alternative colour schemes for a fixed design, co-ordinated colour ranges or colour storyboards which use coloured yarns, fibres and fabric, but mainly the student-designer is interested in new and independent colour formulations.

Textiles is a natural medium for colour. The varied materials that are dyed, painted, printed, woven, variously treated and mixed means the process is steeped in colour. Even natural and untreated yarns, fibres and materials, when woven or printed, are raised to a level where we can respond to colour as distinct from form.

The history of textiles has offered many significant colour developments and innovations which have then been extended to other fine and applied arts. There are examples of contemporary colour names, that derive from types of fabric: The Spanish term *purpura* referred in the 10th century to a silk fabric

Figures 14 and 15

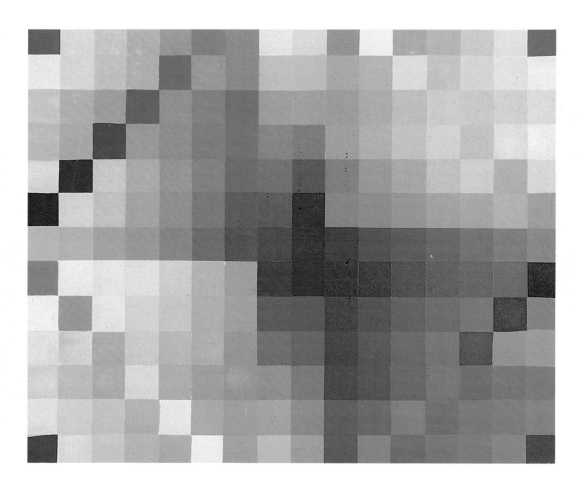

Figure 16
Limited Palette -Transparency Effect.
Ohnmar Han, University of Kentucky, 1993

Figure 17
Design Gestalt Variations – Palette Constant.
Alyssa Bibart, University of Wisconsin, 1994

Figure 18
Reflective Color: 3-D Modular Design.
Wendy Schaeffer, University of Wisconsin, 1993

Figure 19
William B. Warfel: A daytime scene from a production of
Shakespeare's Much Ado About Nothing at The Yale Repertory
Theater, New Haven, Connecticut, USA. Setting: Joel Fontaine,
Lighting: Peter Maradudin.

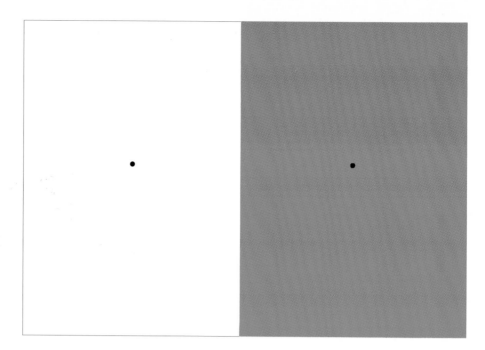

Figure 20

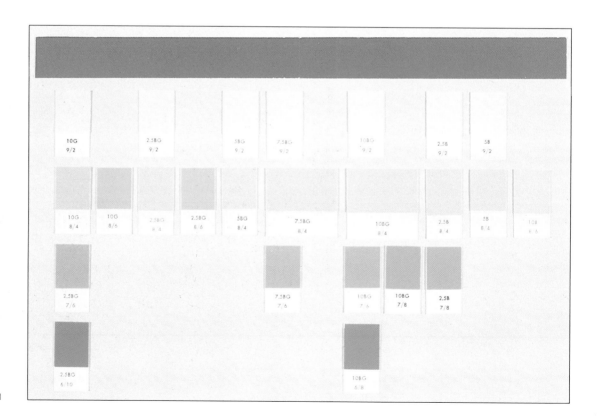

Figure 21

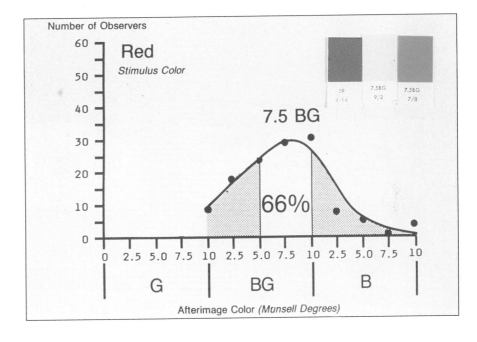

Figure 22

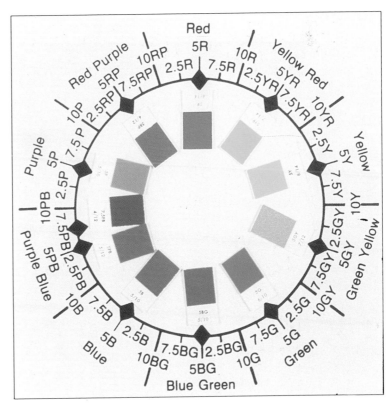

Figure 23

64

Figure 24

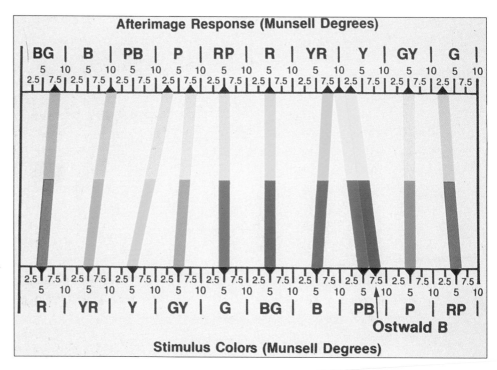

Figure 25

which could have been of any colour. By the Renaissance 'purple' became the established colour name. 'Scarlet', a German 11th century term for a fine shorn wool of great value, progressed to the abstract colour name.

Painting styles of Modernism, from Impressionism, to Abstraction have been influenced by the experimental language of the colour laboratory, that was often located in a textile context. Chevreul made his discoveries while experimenting with colour dyes for the Gobelin manufactory. His *Principles of Harmony and Contrast of Colours* were intended for a broad range of art, design and craft practice. The formal means used to experiment with colour are familiar in Textiles: colour swatches, yarn winding, stripes, dye samples, colour scales are part of the practical work of the Textile artist and designer. For painters, these colour elements were novel and needed radical adjustment to be absorbed into their pictorial language. Chevreul was able to relate his colour ideas to the formal and practical aspects of textiles because with tapestry, carpets and decorative painting he could see the use of flat or broken colour to create spacial and formal illusions. Broken tones of contrasting coloured dots or hatchings had long been used in decorative work, that needed to be seen at a distance. Chevreul recommended painting in flat colours for textiles and decorative painting, however he did not realise its significance for fine art, and what became modernism.

In recent times, translucence and iridescence are among textile designers new concerns, metallic pigments, light sensitive pigments, new techniques of bonding metals and synthetics onto yarn and cloth enable the designers' experiments to move beyond our usual systems of colour description, creating new relationships between pigment and light.

Judged by appearances, the colour problems and charts suggest a degree of order and calculation, an ideal world of colour geometry that promotes specific aesthetic and ideological values. To broaden its context, and relate the laboratory ideas to students' own painting and designing, I refer back to Chevreul and the Impressionists to recover some of the complexity, variety and meaning of these discoveries.

A comparison of the Neo-classical paintings of Gerome and Cabanal, based on chiarascuro with an almost contemporary Monet, that is more direct, flat and painterly, best illustrates the Impressionists' radical alternative of style and technique. Part of Monet's invention was to create pictorial signs that can describe observed reality and also function as colour shapes. A range of colour ideas representing the collective of Impressionists and Neo-Impressionists can be related back to some aspect of Chevreul's researches. To discuss these paintings through colour is to remind students of the radical nature of a style of art that has become so acceptable and popular today.

Neo-Impressionist paintings are direct and largely explicit in their colour relations and physicality, they accommodate coloured dots, stripes, patches, a mosaic of shapes, to the needs of representation. That such practical and mundane elements can contribute to complex and expressive figurative and later abstract works is something at once familiar and surprising. The Modernist dictum that a painting is an arrangement of coloured shapes before it is a representation has particular significance for the textile designer. To progress from initial design to finished fabric requires a reconstruction of the image, that turns this truism into a practical methodology.

Extending this colour analysis, it is possible with Monet's career to trace a move from representation to a more abstract expressive and autonomous style. With his late works, in the 20th century, we have a Cubist multiplicity of levels and viewpoints coupled, unlike Cubism, with a full-blooded, almost abstract and expressionist use of colour. To begin with Monet is to confront a fuller, more complex colour reality than is available in the subsequent, reductive direction of late 20th century colour painting.

This offers the textile student an introduction to art that is a rich and broad arena of colour knowledge and experiment. At the same time it is a practical help to their own painting where use of colour and structure can bring results that are often more advanced than their drawing skills may permit. Drawing tends to progress here, once the need and use of colour 'engineering' becomes clearer.

That pictorial space can be represented and articulated largely by colour, whether as broad, flat areas, or in broken sequences of more or less saturated colour or by chiaroscuro effects created by value changes across a flat colour is an enrichment of the painting process for most students and helps shift the emphasis away from literal recording and arbitrary, abstract colour relationships. Colour here, can function as description but also

as an autonomy that is more readily adapted to decorative and expressive ends.

Colour is one means to establish a practical as well as aesthetic relationship between Fine Art and Textiles. The development of the student-designer who can embrace both traditions is part of the aim. To understand the role of colour and to apply that understanding to the shaping of the environment is the challenge for the artist and designer, the vitality of the subject is that students feel the possibility is there for the individual to make a fresh and significant contribution.

Bibliography

ALBERS, J. (1963) Interaction of Color. Yale University Press.

BIRREN, F. (1980) The Textile Colorist. Van Nostrand Reinhold.

CHEVREUL, M.E. (1967) The Principles of Harmony and Contrast of Colours. Van Nostrand Reinhold.

COLCHESTER, C. (1991) The New Textiles. Thames and Hudson.

FINKELSTEIN, L. (1986) Painting of Herb Aach. Queens College Magazine.

GAGE, J. (1993) Colour and Culture. Thames and Hudson.

J.H. Dohr & M.B. Portillo

Color in Design Education
New Approaches beyond the Bauhaus

Background

Color theory crystallized and advanced by the Bauhaus movement has exerted longstanding influence in design education (Wingler, 1978; Whitford, 1984). Namely, the legacy of Johannes Itten (1970) and Joseph Albers (1974) through color contrast theory and methods of exploring color phenomenon in two dimensional design, provides the basis for color education in most programs today. However, what is not as readily apparent or emphasized in Itten and Alber's work is the *developmental* structure inherent in color and color use.

That is, it becomes critical in color instruction to consider the sequencing of thought, production, and evaluation that occur as students progress from a mastery of direct concepts to more complex color relationships. This developmental perspective is an important factor in our approach to studying and teaching color as discussed in this paper.

Analysis of additive color theory and subtractive color systems of Munsell, of Ostwald and of the red-yellow-blue theory describe the positioning, mixing, and integration of hue, value and saturation (Hope & Walch, 1990). Learning these basic systems provides the groundwork for further color testing and experimentation. Likewise, perceptual responses to harmonies, contrasts, and illusions — presented by Itten and Albers — contribute yet another level of understanding color relationships. Students gain abilities to predict and control color through exercises of design where one color is made to look like two different colors, when they adjust multiple hues to constant value or when they generate color film transparencies (see figure 16, page 58).

Add to these examples, exercises that entail manipulating the design gestalt across like patterns with different placements of

the same palette (see figure 17, page 59) and one sees students interest and confidence in color usage increase. But how do we move beyond this foundation to teach color in the context of environmental design education?

When teaching design from an environmental perspective — the design of lighting and theater sets, product design, interior design, architecture, and landscape architecture — students and instructors must supersede two dimensional color phenomena to explore color in a light-space-object relationship (Hope & Walch, 1990; Linton, 1991). For example, learning that color on horizontal planes (under overhead lighting) generally will be lighter in value than the same color on a vertical plane enables students to manipulate this more normal effect by changes in lighting, position, and/or value of the color.

Color in environmental design consciously entails light, material surface, time, environmental surrounds, and human context. With these relationships realized, color may be experienced as bound to the surface, as filling a volume, or as a film in space (Swirnoff, 1976; 1988). Acquiring skills for systematically visualizing color in three dimensions and anticipating its complex effects enable students to better use color in design. The reality of color in a three dimensional context needs inquiry that is inclusive of, and sympathetic to, two dimensional color theory, yet demands new ways of explaining and learning color.

One asks, "How might we develop new approaches that (1) are consistent with basic color theory teachings, (2) respond to the environmental context, and (3) acknowledge stages of the design process and students' developmental needs? How might we account for these objectives enabling students to gain a greater understanding and mastery of color theory?"

Design Phases, Creative Process and Color Theory

In responding to the previous questions and exploring new approaches, we revisited our earlier studies on creativity, the design process, the pedagogy of design and students' development of problem-solving (Portillo & Dohr, 1989; Dohr & Portillo, 1991; Portillo & Dohr, 1992/93). This work supports a time and place construct of creative design with phases of preparation, production and presentation where thinking, making and evaluating cycle through design problem-solving.

The earlier findings demonstrated that students perform at different maturity levels or stages in their design thinking and ideation, production and technical skills, and assessment abilities (Portillo & Dohr, 1989). Whereas students may vary from each other in level of overall development, an individual student also may profile different developmental levels in problem-solving. For example a student may have more advanced assessment abilities, yet lower maturity levels in the generation of innovative and elaborated ideas or in the production of designs. Given that design educators seek to facilitate students' growth in design, where students demonstrate creative thinking abilities, sound, skilled production, and effective evaluative judgment, we maintain that color education in design fields must also consider and be consistent with the development of the learner and the phases of the design process.

Generating design ideas for color requires perceptual and imaginative abilities that relate in some way to the manual and structuring abilities required to execute color designs. The combination of these abilities guide students' judgments, but again differ from the articulation of why a project is successful, meaningful, or expressive. The challenge for the design instructor is to teach to these capabilities in creative problem-solving.

Students should be actively engaged to see creatively and to generate fresh insightful ideas. They must develop discipline and exercise their technical skills that enable a clear communication of ideas. They need to test their ability in evaluating work on sound criteria. The instructor facilitates this while recognizing that his or her students may be at different levels of maturity in these design phases.

Using the previous reasoning within the context of design where the light-space-object relationship is dominant, questions emerged for teaching and studying color.

To Enhance Creative Design Ideation
(1) How might creative thinking about color relationships in three dimensions be initiated?
(2) What role do color dimensions play?
(3) How might creative elaboration with color be improved, since elaboration is critical to optimizing an innovative design idea?

For Disciplined Production and Skill Development
(1) How does media or surface application techniques in three dimensions influence color use?
(2) How might color contrast theory be used to explain color use in interior environments?

For Sound Color and Design Evaluation in Presentation Stage
(1) What criteria and meanings of color need to be understood by students from multiple perspectives?
(2) How might different criteria be incorporated in color projects to acquaint students better with the roles of color in the built environment?

From these questions, we present design projects that have been completed by beginning undergraduate students in color courses, or examined and written about by graduate students. We will also present some of our own research on color use of noted designers. The following sections address each question and provide examples of studies and results that have been discovered.

Creative Seeing and Ideation of Environmental Color

Traditionally, color is described in terms of hue, value, and saturation. Each of these dimensions can be manipulated and controlled, yet value is the only dimension that can be separated from color. As such, value provides a good entry point to begin designing with color. Once value relationships are established, it becomes a question of developing the hue and intensity. It has been our experience, however, that students initially come to the study of color expecting to focus on hue. Their initial concerns surround hue preferences. It remains an objective of the design instructor to shift the emphasis from hue to value. Hue becomes a secondary concern in a student exercise demonstrating the Bezold Effect. The purpose of this assignment is to create a pattern that raises the key in one section of the design by introducing white elements while lowering the key in another section by adding black elements.

Value assumes added importance in the built environment where even an achromatic form is defined by its highlights and shadows. This underlying patterning of values can be reinforced or contradicted through selective color use (Swirnoff, 1988). Yet work on color-form interaction remains relatively uncharted with many opportunities to test phenomena. Further study could systematically examine the Bezold illusion in the context of form. For example, how would the scale of the pattern be adjusted to create the strongest shift in value?

It is difficult to underestimate the importance of placing value at the center foundation of color planning; however, there are myriad possibilities for developing greater sensitivity to hue. The composition of a single hue can be described as flat and mundane or complex and unique. One of America's foremost colorists, Donald Kaufman (1992), creates colors for major museums, art galleries, public spaces and residential designs that appear luminous in appearance. The subtlety and nuance of his hues shift with changes in lighting and angle of viewing. In contrast to standard manufacturers' paint formulas that contain three or four hues toned with black and white, Kaufman's mixtures often contain at least ten hues where the dominant color is toned with its complement. His principle method involves representing all areas of the spectrum to create emphasis and counterbalance. His precise color mixing is tested and refined on site. These methods can be presented to design students as they become more adept at seeing "color within color" (e.g. seeing a red as either yellow/orange-based or blue-based). It further becomes a foundation for controlling neutrals and introducing subtle shifts observed in environmental settings. Mixing with complements and within one's palette develops "new" seeing on the part of students.

After establishing the value, creating precise, complex hues, and adjusting the intensity, the next phase of the process involves creating color relationships that enhance form. This developmental progression is not in any way intended to imply a rigid, linear sequence. Instead, the iterating cycle allows refining and elaborating and interplay among phases of thinking, making, and evaluating while moving toward a color solution for a design problem.

In examining color planning in the realm of environmental design, two major projects — an undergraduate class assignment

70 and a graduate thesis — further illustrate this initial phase of creative seeing and thinking. Since the classic research of Guilford (1950) and Torrance (1966) on creative thinking identified fluency of idea (numbers of ideas), flexibility of idea (direction of ideas), innovation (novel or different ideas), and elaboration as key components, we sought first to address fluency, flexibility, and innovation in color studies. In an intermediate level, color theory class, a reflective color project — focusing on the integration of light-space-form — adapted the ideas of Lois Swirnoff (1988) to encourage fluency and flexibility of idea (see figure 18, page 60). Principles of modular design were central to this assignment. Modular design has an organic nature, where the unit shape — as an individual three dimensional module — plays the same part as the motif in two-dimensional patterns. The gestalt of the designs varied with systematic changes as students manipulated spacing and multiplicity of the module. Further, the proximity of one module to the next provided a fascinating mechanism with which to study the interplay of color and light.

Finally, creating a reflective color palette resulted in a memorable experience in which the students obtained knowledge that could be applied to other design problems. A discovery-type experience consistently resulted.

When Patricia Raney (1992), a graduate student, sought to understand the relationship of color use and creative elaboration of design ideas, she first tested beginning design students' creative elaboration abilities using the Torrance Test of Creative Thinking (1966). She then asked students to complete a color mixing study within a controlled framework and using one pair of complementary hues and neutrals of black and white. From the work of students in high and in low ability groupings, she compared and tested the color result. Students with high elaboration scores significantly mixed a greater number of colors from the two parent hues and neutrals, and they had greater ability in using tones than students with lower elaborative abilities. However, both groups of students were similar in displaying good control over value changes (Raney, 1992).

Several conclusions are drawn from this study. Value appears less complex for students to manipulate than other dimensions of color. Students readily understand value and achieve competency more quickly which further supports having students begin work with this dimension. Tones and saturation variations, on the other hand, are developmentally more complex. Yet, a competency in their use allows students an advantage in elaborating and enriching their color designs and ideas.

These findings provided a rationale for student exercises addressing elaboration of color ideas. These exercises entail completing many mixes to create tonal hues within a limited palette that stem from environmental study. One source employs the traditional approach of analyzing natural forms and materials, while another source focused on creating complementary neutrals displaying temperature variation. Neutral scales are developed by mixing complements that represent neutrals changing in different lighting conditions to portray temperature variations with a cool or warm hue dominance. The scales then are changed to a woven design and later become the basis for three dimensional color projects employing complex neutrals in form or in space.

Equally, this type of learning experience supports the philosophy of Albers, who advocated the discovery of color theory through experiencing color followed by analysis of the color phenomenon and color theory.

Studio Production Techniques and Studies of Light-Space-Object Relations

What becomes evident from the previously discussed exercises is the fact that exploration of ideas cannot be separated from media use and production. Through wide exposure to color experiences, students gain an understanding of which materials and techniques are more appropriate to the design problem. For example, a greater elaboration of ideas occurred through the mixing of pigments for the environmental color exercise, while colored papers offered more flexibility for testing ideas in the reflective color project. Furthermore, the three dimensional modules created subtle washes of reflected color that changed in intensity and resulted in a complex and interesting surface quality. In this case, paper also often proved to be a more economical medium than pigment.

In expanding on this realization, we introduce other studies and student projects that further compare two dimensional and three dimensional media and production skills. Advantages and limitations separating the studio techniques relate to the intent or purpose of each phase in design development. It also becomes apparent that effective teaching of light-space-object interaction requires three dimensional models, vignettes or environments.

An empirical study of Itten's seven contrasts in built environments by Madeline Sattler, a graduate student, raises new questions on the use of this theory in environmental design. Sattler (1992) measured and analyzed color contrast in full scale design vignettes. These vignettes were created by noted designers who operated under similar parameters of size and project type. Temperature was found to be the most significantly manipulated contrast, with value contrast next although low (23%). The

other contrasts — hue, saturation, complements and extension — had even lower degrees of use in these interior settings. Given that temperature conveys associative meaning and value relays formal compositional meaning, the results of the study indicate that designers emphasize warm/cool contrasts, and less spatial-planar definition. It appears that the three-dimensional volume was first neutralized — almost as if a canvas was being prepared — and then color was introduced to compose that environment.

Value ranges and complements existed in a designer's palette, but the colors were not juxtaposed in space to take advantage of the contrast effects. While literature clearly suggests that lightness and saturation contrasts be used to define space and manipulate form (Swirnoff, 1988), Sattler did not find designers exploiting contrast to do so. Perhaps, we as educators need to teach this better. Also, contrasts such as saturation, hue and complements might to a greater extent contribute to color layering or detailing that occurs after establishing the space and form. (Note: Sattler only considered finishes/color of the architectural envelope features and major interior fixtures, not accessories.)

The findings do raise questions, however, about using Itten's contrast theory to explain environmental color phenomenon. Itten's contrast theory may explain three dimensional spatial and perceptual effects on two-dimensional planes, but does not fully explain color in three-dimensional spaces. The harmonizing and unification of colors have greater dominance in color usage three-dimensionally. Further, additional research is needed to test the intriguing possibility that certain contrasts may be more fundamental than others and may even need to be considered sequentially when developing interior color. For example, why is temperature contrast manipulated to such an extent especially related to environmental color balance and human need? Does contrast of saturation or of complements serve surface, layering or time interest?

Drawing from Sattler's study, we ask students to consciously observe compositional meanings of color demonstrated in light-space-form relationships and the counterparts of associative meanings. The power of value contrast used to create dimensionality or control spatial response may be reinforced when students are asked to simulate color of light and surface interaction of material.

Similarly, symbolic meanings and associations not only bring into consideration the environmental temperature surrounds, but are an introduction to the topic of cultural meanings and associations of color (Spillman, 1985; Boeschenstein, 1986).

Evaluation of Color in Presentation Stages of Design

The emergence of associative/symbolic and compositional meanings of color from investigations of models and built environments sets the stage for asking students to return to an initial purpose or their design concept when using color, and to apply criteria to guide their environmental color decisions. Equally, while students evaluate ideas and techniques as they are completing color studies, it is often in the final presentation stage that questions arise on the totality of color-form interaction. Multiple levels of color meaning (Hietzman, 1989) address the reality that color is a language serving designers' and users' needs, and affecting different aspects of human existence. Neither color nor design have a singular nature. Intermediate and advanced students in many design areas understand that design is multidisciplinary (Hillier, Musgrove, & O'Sullivan, 1984). Students consider economic, social, psychological, aesthetic and

technological issues when designing products, interiors, theater sets, architecture, or landscapes. In examining the multi-disciplinary nature of design processes and structure, and color criteria that expert colorists and designers used, Portillo & Dohr (1992/93) identified five criteria that these acclaimed designers normally apply to their decisions about color. The criteria consistently related to the larger purpose for color application in a project. Compositional, symbolic associational, behavioral, preferential, and pragmatic criteria comprise the five.

Yet, compositional, symbolic, and behavioral criteria were significantly used more often by the expert colorist-designers, while preference and pragmatic criteria were seen as givens or client considerations. The findings speak to a hierarchical sequencing of criteria where the ability of color to define space, convey symbolic meaning, and influence human behavior appear to be key considerations in color usage. One concludes that color preferences and current market hues enjoy the popular view of color, but the more complex compositional, associative and behavioral meanings engage and comprise color needs of designers. In using this study to guide color education, we encourage students to examine the layers of meaning that color contributes to a design and again return to these criteria in evaluating its success. For example, projects that address the impact of color on identity, emotionality and cognition of users or clients may be explored. Students are challenged to explain forms and spaces where humans have expectations of color, and where color is associated to the identity of form. These projects illustrate how criteria guide the design process and they further give students vocabulary and understanding of color that gets them beyond the preferential, "I like it" stage.

Studies using five criteria for evaluating and selecting color are also helpful when teaching students the larger history and evolution of environmental color knowledge. Whereas the Bauhaus theories and subsequent studies of value, hue and intensity undergirds objective, compositional knowledge, more recent work from environment and behavior studies provide understanding of functional, behavioral response. Further cultural, associative meanings of color, originally discussed in the earlier 1900s by Jung, is receiving current renewed interest.

As environmental designers do more international and regional design projects, teaching a depth of cultural meaning associated to color is critical to having students move beyond stereotypical applications. Amy Milani, a graduate student, looked at cultural metaphors interpreted from interiors of the American Southwest (1994). People from within and outside the region responded to slides of numerous interior environments, and rated them from most to least Southwest in appearance. From the most and least categories, she analyzed responses to the design characteristics and the environmental meanings derived. Color, as would be expected, was a frequently identified attribute. Color quality, placement and pattern were primary cues consistently associated to *place-based* meanings of regional light and sky, indigenous soil, animals and vegetation. Cultural artifacts of Native American Indians and Spanish settlers and their grammar of color represent *people-based* meanings associated to historical events, life experience, ritual, emotions and values. The study's respondents sought authenticity in the gestalt of design and color that conveyed metaphorical interpretation of ruggedness, perseverance, and ties to the natural environment and mystical qualities of the region.

Milani concludes a layered complexity of design color engages the imagination of people and offers meaning far beyond the simple interpretation of style.

Summary

The totality of these color experiences reinforces several competencies in using and explaining color phenomena in three-dimensional space. Color as a language with individual elements, the pattern and grammar of structure, and multi-leveled meanings provide a rich grounding where students may shift from making a superficial statement, to imaging a new color concept and then to creating complex, poetic environments. Discussion of the intent of color, association of color and ultimately composition provide students the experience to see and test their understanding of color complexity and development. With an education in the nuances of color in the environment, students gain a depth and breadth of color theory from multiple perspectives. The new explanations remain developmentally grounded in the Bauhaus teachings, but provide expanded avenues for new expression, additional explanations and new discoveries.

74 ## References

ALBERS, J. (1974) Interaction of color (2nd Edition). New Haven, CT: Yale University Press.

BOESCHENSTEIN, W. (1986) Expressive urban color. In: Journal of Architectural Planning Research 3, 275-285.

BONTA, J. P. (1979) Architecture and its interpretation: A study of expressive systems in architecture. London: Lund Humphries Publishers Ltd.

DOHR, J. H. &FORBESS, L. (1986) Creativity, arts and profiles in aging: A reexamination. In: Educational Gerontology, 12:123-138.

DOHR, J. H. & PORTILLO, M. (1991) Developments in design education. In: J. Perioct (Ed). Design pedagogy: Themes of design (tri-lingual edition). Barcelona, Spain: Elisava Publishers. 173-190.

DOHR, J. H., SARMADI, M., & PORTILLO, M. (1990) Volume Color: Environment & Behavior Systems Approach. Paper presented at Environmental Design Research Association, Urbana, Illinois.

HEITZMAN, F. (April, 1989). Color in recent Chicago architecture. Paper presented at the Inter-society Color Conference, Chicago, IL.

HILLIER, B., MUSGROVE, J. & O'SULLIVAN, P. (1984) Knowledge and design. In: N. Cross (Ed.) Developments in design methodology London: Wiley & Sons. 245-264.

HOPE, A. & WALCH, M. (Eds.) (1990) The color compendium. New York: Van Nostrand Reinhold.

GUILFORD, J. P. (1950) Creativity. In: American Psychologist, 5, 444-454.

ITTEN, J. (1970) The elements of color. New York: Van Nostrand Reinhold.

KAUFMAN, D. & DAHL, T. (1992) Color: Natural palettes for painted room. New York: Clarkson/Potter Publications.

LAWSON, B. (1990) How designers think (2nd ed.). Cambridge, Great Britain: Butterworth Architecture.

LINTON, H. (1991) Color consulting: A survey of international color design. New York: Van Nostrand Reinhold.

MAHNKE, F. & MAHNKE, R. (1987) Color and light in man-made environments. New York: Van Nostrand Reinhold.

MILANI, A. (1994) Visual metaphors in interior design: Regional perceptions of the American Southwest. Masters thesis, Interior Environments, University of Wisconsin-Madison.

PORTER, T. & MIKELLIDES, B. (Eds.) (1976) Colour for architecture. London: Studio Vista.

PORTILLO, M. & DOHR, J. H. (1992/93) A study of color criteria used by noted designers. In: Journal of Interior Design Education and Research. 18 (1-2), 17-24.

PORTILLO, M. & DOHR, J. H. (1989) Design education: On the road toward thought development. In: Design Studies. 10 (2), 96-102.

RANEY, P. (1992) Color development: Dimensional variation & creative elaboration. Unpublished Masters Thesis, Interior Environments, University of Wisconsin-Madison.

SATTLER, M. (1992) A method for analyzing three-dimensional color interaction and color contrast and placement patterns with interiors. Masters Thesis, Interior Environments, University of Wisconsin-Madison.

SPILLMAN, W. (1985) Color order systems and architectural color design. In: Color Research and Application, 10:(1), 5-11.

SWIRNOFF, L. (1976) Experiments on the interaction of color and form. In: Leonardo, 9, 191-195.

SWIRNOFF, L. (1982) The visual environment: Consider the surface. In: The environmentalist, 2, (3), 217-222.

SWIRNOFF, L. (1988) Dimensional Color. Boston, MA: Birkhauser Boston.

TORRANCE, E. P. (1966) Torrance tests of creative thinking. Princeton, NJ: Prentice Hall.

WINGLER, H. M. (1978) Bauhaus. Boston, MA: MIT Press.

WHITFORD, F. (1984) Bauhaus. London: Thames & Hudson Ltd.

William B. Warfel

Colorimetry in the Teaching of Stage Lighting Design

The applied techniques of Colorimetry are not complex and are in common use. It is true that understanding the process by which the commonly used diagrams were derived through the Tristimulus Values and Trichromatic Coefficients requires some understanding of physics and mathematics, but the resulting diagram, the Chromaticity Plot, is something almost anyone can understand after a few minutes of explanation. For example, a leading lamp manufacturer uses it in sales literature as a guide to the color of fluorescent lamps.

In the late 1960's we at Yale set about finding ways that students and others engaged in the art of stage lighting design could organize their knowledge about the various groups of color filters which were then in use. There were about 350 different filters available in the United States in those days, both gelatin and acetate based, and we thought it might be helpful if there was a way to make informed comparisons between, for example, two similar blue filters from two different manufacturer's products.

The early efforts amounted to holding up samples in front of some light source, and making a visual evaluation. Attempts were made to organize samples into groups by hue and saturation, all by the "hold it up and look" technique. Inevitably, a filter would be found which would not fit in any color family which the researcher had established, and so another family had to be created. Color families began to proliferate. Moreover, the resulting listing would not quantify the hue or saturation of the filter, nor, in fact, would it help the user to do anything except file the samples in some predetermined order. Clearly, some new approach was needed.

At the same time that we were trying to organize the filters in a descriptive arrangement, I was searching for a method by which beginning students might make sound choices of color filters for use in their productions without aimlessly flipping through samples until some color struck them as possibly useful. One answer which we found for both of these concerns is described herein.

The technique which we adopted was hardly new, but rather has a history which extends back to the work of James Clerk Maxwell, the great Scottish physicist, in the latter half of the nineteenth century. Maxwell would seat people in front of his colorimeter and have them mix red, green and blue light on one small area in order to match a sample he placed in an adjacent area. Colorimetry, in the form finally standardized and published by the International Commission on Illumination (CIE) in 1931, provides a technique, based upon many tests with human subjects, for quantifying the observable qualities of a color: the *Hue*, which is expressed in terms of the *Dominant Wavelength* (DWL) of a color; the *Saturation*, which is defined in terms of *Purity* (PUR); and the *Value*, which is called *Brightness* (Y). If one understands these three qualities, it is an easy matter to make a precise definition of a color, either in pigment or, in our case, in a transparent filter.

Perhaps some definitions and explanations are in order here to help those readers who are not familiar with Colorimetry. Setting aside for now the way in which the shape of it was derived, the Chromaticity Plot lies in the positive quadrant of a Cartesian graph (Fig.1). The curve, which is often referred to as the *Spectrum Curve*, represents the visible spectrum from 380 nanometers (nm.) to 780 nm. The straight line which joins the ends of the curve, which we call the *Purple Line*, does not represent spectrum colors, but rather additive mixtures of light from both ends of the curve.

Standard source colors have been defined by various agencies,

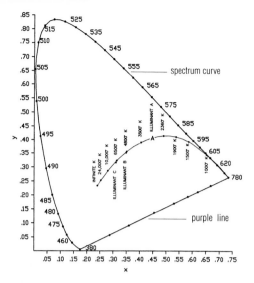

Figure 1: The Chromaticity Plot in relationship to its Cartesian coordinates. The numbers around the Spectrum Curve are the wavelengths of the various colors of light expressed in nanometers (10⁻⁹ meters). Various standard illuminants and certain color temperatures of light are located in the Chromaticity Plot. The Black Body Locus shows the location of the theoretical perfect radiator at various temperatures on the Kelvin scale. Below 3500°, the temperatures are a rough approximation of the temperature of a tungsten filament, and thus provide a scale which describes the color of an incandescent lamp at various intensities.

in particular the CIE, and their locations can be identified on the Chromaticity Plot as Illuminant A.B and C (Fig. 1). To understand the measurable properties of a color, it is necessary to know both the location of the source and that of the sample. For the work we have done with stage lighting color filters, we used CIE Illuminant A (1931) which has the coordinates x = .4476 and y = .4075. This is equivalent to a tungsten lamp burning with a color temperature of 2848° Kelvin (K) which is roughly equivalent to a 3200° K lamp operated on a dimmer set at approximately 65% of maximum output. Thus, the work is related to a recognized standard and a device commonly used in theatrical practice.

As applied to transparent color filters, the *Dominant Wavelength* for a color on the Chromaticity Plot is determined by

drawing a line from the location of the light source, in this case Illuminant A, through the location of the filter, and on to the spectrum curve (Fig. 2). The wavelength at which this line touches the spectrum curve is the dominant wavelength of the filter, and is a good indication of the hue which the combined filter and source will produce. In the cases where the line does not reach the spectrum curve, but rather, the purple line, the dominant wavelength is expressed as that of the compliment of the sample filter by extending the line in the direction opposite until it reaches the spectrum curve.

Using the same line from the source through the filter location and the spectrum curve which helped define the dominant wavelength, we can now understand *Purity*. It is useful to think of each color represented by a location on the Chromaticity Plot as a mixture of light of the source color and light of the pure spectrum color at the dominant wavelength. *Purity* is defined as the percentage of the pure spectrum color in the mixture as opposed to that of the source. A very pure color is only slightly "diluted" by the "white" light of the source. Purity is expressed as the percentage of the distance from the source to the spectrum curve that is represented by the distance from the source to the filter location (Fig. 2).

Finally, *Brightness* is that quality which equates to value in pigment-based systems. In the case of color filter studies, it represents roughly the percentage of transmission of a sample as related to the sensitivity of the eye of a "standard observer".

Colorimetry is, in my opinion, a far more useful technique for a lighting design practitioner to use in order to understand the qualities of a color filter than other common techniques such as a spectral distribution curve or the Munsell Color System. The former, while probably the most accurate way to describe a cer-

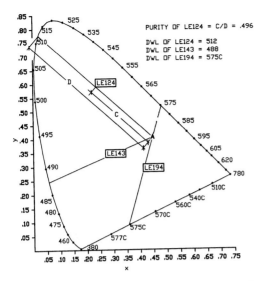

Figure 2: The Dominant Wavelength (DWL) of three colors found by extending a line from the source (A) to the color's location and thence to the Spectrum Curve. Note that the DWL of LE194 is defined in terms of that of its compliment since the Purple Line does not represent natural spectrum colors. The expression of the Purity of LE124 is also shown.

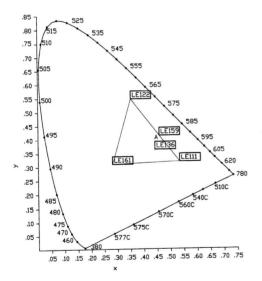

Figure 3: The ability of Colorimetry to predict the results of additive color mixture is shown. Since LE159 lies on a direct line between LE122 and LE111, those two colors will mix to produce a match. Both A and LE136 can be mixed by balancing the three colors at the corners of the triangle formed when LE161 is added.

tain colored light, is not immediately translatable into an impression of the observed color; while the latter relies on pigmentation techniques which are awkward to apply to color in light.

At the outset, as I said earlier, we had turned to Colorimetry simply to find a good way to classify and compare color filters. As we became more familiar with Colorimetry, it became clear that we had a much more powerful tool at our disposal than we had previously thought. We had assumed that it would help designers to select substitutes for color filters which were not available, and to select, say, a filter of roughly the same DWL and PUR of one in use if more light of the same color was needed on the stage. However, one of the most interesting properties of Colorimetry is its ability to predict the results of additive color mixture. This property is very useful, and makes it possible to provide student designers with a method of selecting and using color filters.

If a spotlight with a Lee #122 filter and another with a Lee #111 filter are focused at the same surface, and both are connected to dimmers, one can mix any color which lies along the line between them, for example, Lee #159 (Fig. 3). Moreover, if a third color is added, any color which lies in the area inside the triangle can also be mixed. When a Lee #161 filter is added to the picture, many new possibilities arise, such as mixing Illuminant A, or Lee #136.

Some limitations become obvious once one starts to experiment with color mixture. For one thing, colors which one wants to mix on the stage should be fairly consistent in the direction in which they are aimed at the stage. A light from the front of an actor will not mix well with a side light, though there will be some mixture on irregular surfaces and curves. Two lights

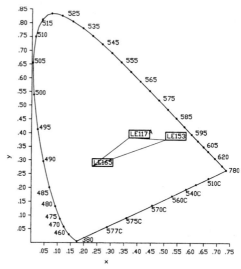

Figure 4: White Light for Madame Bergeret. The colors of light required to reproduce those in the painting all lie within the triangle.

which are 45° apart, however, will mix on a non-specular surface.

Also, in mixtures of two colors which differ widely in either purity or brightness, the less pure or the brighter color will dominate, and this will limit the range of the mixture except when the brighter or less pure color is at very low dimmer settings. (Then it will, in fact, be another color, as we will see shortly.) The widest range is available if the two colors are within 30% purity of each other, or are of similar brightness.

Colorimetry also makes it easy to understand the change in a color when the source lamp is dimmed or brightened. The so-called *Black Body Locus* is a curve which traces the path of the theoretical black body radiator as its temperature in Degrees Kelvin changes (Fig. 1). The tungsten filament of a lamp, sometimes called a "gray body radiator" approximates the behavior of the black body, and so can be understood as moving up and down that curve when the dimmer setting is changed. As the filament cools, it's location changes, it "drifts" toward amber and then red. It ceases to be a practical source of light at about 1000° K. The change in the location of the filter on the Chromaticity Plot varies according to how far from the red end of the spectrum a color's DWL lies. The lavenders and blues drop away much more quickly, while dark ambers and reds persist well into the fade. If one source is operated at a dimmer intensity much lower than the other in a two color mixture, the line between them will move, the range of colors which can be mixed will change, and the brighter color will dominate.

In 1981, in collaboration with Walter Klappert, a graduate student at Yale, I published *Color Science for Lighting the Stage*. By that time, there were about 660 different filters on the market. The appearance of polycarbonate and polyester bases had greatly expanded the market, and the need for a system to keep track of them was urgent. The book listed all of the color filters we could find at the time with their DWL, PUR, Y and x and y coordinates. For each filter, the book listed a group of similar filters one could use as a near match for the initial color. We also printed all of the information on chromaticity plots. The text of the book described Colorimetry, and presented information on amber drift and its effect on the shifting of a filter's location and on mixing colors.

With the information available in print, I turned my attention to ways in which Colorimetry might help lighting designers to make color choices for production. To do this, I began to apply the techniques of Colorimetry to a way of thinking about color for stage lighting which I call "Working with White Light". At that time the late Thomas Skelton, a well known American designer, was teaching with me at Yale, and we spent a good deal of time discussing the White Light theory, which had originated with him. White Light is simply light which is of the correct color for a scene, an act, a whole production. We call it "white" because it is so much a part of the scene - the setting, the costumes, the action - that even though it might be quite colored, it is not obvi-

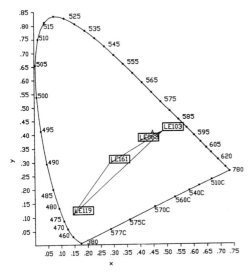

Figure 5: The white light diagram for Much Ado About Nothing. A daytime palette can consist of LE103 and LE063 which will mix an approximation of A. However, the basic light for all scenes can be realized within the triangle LE103, LE161, and LE119.

ous. The audience accepts the entire picture, and does not ask "What is *that* color doing there?"

This is not to say that there is only one color on the stage, or even that we are not aware of different colors, but rather that all colors used work together to produce a range of tonalities which are appropriate, natural and in harmony with the scene.

My favorite example of this is not from a play, because I have trouble getting good pictures of my productions, but from a painting: François Boucher's "Madame Bergeret" (1746). For this "scene" Madame Bergeret appears as a very aristocratic figure in a cool, shaded garden. In the light, there is a warm, nearly colorless, tone accenting the gentle pinks in the flowers and the lady's face, and then there is a blue tone to the light throughout rest of the scene, becoming deeper and somewhat greenish to the background. The color of the light is in complete harmony with the seemingly serene, aristocratic lady, with the silken rustle of her gown, and with the cool garden foliage around her.

To select color filters which would enable me to design this moment, I would probably choose three colors which form a triangle near the source anchored in a pink, crossing to the greenish blue area, and including a true blue (Fig. 4). This will enable me to control, with dimmers, a foreground clear color, a middle ground tone, and the deeper colors of the background. All of these colors are within the triangle.

Obviously, white light will change from scene to scene in a play. A scene from a production of Shakespeare's *Much Ado About Nothing* (see figure 19, page 61) offers a further illustration. The daytime scenes can be lighted with a two color mixture which provides a range that is centered at Illuminant A (Fig. 5), and which can make the stage substantially cooler or warmer than A depending upon dimmer settings. In the daytime scene, the shift is toward the warmer side, with the cooler tones visible at the edges. Night is a mixture of a darker blue and pale blues with patterns. Note that the cooler color (LE063) in the daylight pair could be replaced by one of the colors in the night time system (LE161) with little penalty. Also, one area in a night time mode can strongly be accented by adding the warmer daylight color to it.

For the student Colorimetry is a method to translate his or her vision for the production into reality with confidence. Once the white light zone on the Chromaticity Plot is established, the designer is assured of a coherent color system which is consistent with his or her vision. The point is to start with a choice of the area on the Chromaticity Plot which will best suit the design, and then to search for filters. Aimless, uninformed leafing through filter sample books hoping to find a pretty color is eliminated. Experienced professional designers may not use this system, but students do, at least until they become comfortable with their own technique and build up a file of their preferred colors.

80 A long time goal of mine, to use Colorimetry to discover the percentage of purity at which an observer becomes aware of the color of light, remains unrealized. To date, I have devised no way to set up the test environment so that an even, calibrated progression from the source color toward a pure spectrum color can be achieved. I also suspect that too many subjective, personal factors will be involved in the subject's responses to make the test valid. This part of the research will have to wait.

In Beijing in 1992, I had an opportunity to work with a mixed group of students and professionals who were all attending a two week lecture series I was delivering. I had introduced the concept of Colorimetry and the mechanics of it to mild interest. Then I began to illustrate it with *Much Ado ...* and other productions. Suddenly, the excitement began to build as the people realized that there could be a systematic approach to color selection. They could predict what will happen when two or more colors are mixed.

They have their own color filter manufacturers in China, one of which is called "Weikang". One afternoon, the class was given over to a workshop in which we tested all of the colors in the Weikang sample book. In typical Chinese fashion, the project was divided up so as to employ as many people as possible. One held the color over the meter, one pushed the button, one read the numbers, another wrote them down, and so forth. By late afternoon, all samples had been tested.

A drawing board was brought into the theater where the classes were being held, and some of the people took turns entering the data on the map and copying it into lists. The acid test came the day after the map was finished when two colors were chosen and put in spotlights and, as predicted, light matching that produced by a particular third filter was produced. My satisfaction came from seeing a group of lighting designers suddenly move from making instinctive guesses about what colors might do on the stage to having a method of predicting it, and thus gaining control over a vital portion of their art.

There is new research under way which will probably produce useful results in the next few years. There are now almost 1000 different filters available in the United States and Europe. A new edition of *Color Science for Lighting The Stage* is long overdue, and is now being produced, this time accompanied by a computer disk which will make the data more accessible.

Also, a student at Purdue University conducted a series of tests of the commonly used filters with a certain high intensity discharge (HID) lamp often used in followspots. With Colorimetry, he was able to show what filter one should use in the followspot to match the color on the stage produced using other filters with incandescent sources. That particular student has dropped the project, but I am hopeful that someone will carry it forward and make such information available, since HID sources are becoming so wide spread in modern stage lighting.

Knowledge of Colorimetry will not make a person a lighting designer. But it is a useful tool to explore the world of color filters while making those vital decisions that all designers face. It is also a fascinating topic to explore.

Marian-Ortolf Bagley

Color in Design Education
Perceptual Studies and Studio Practice

Afterimage (AI) is a familiar experience that has interested many color-minded artists and teachers and researchers (Bickley-Green 1990). Much has been written on the subject, but little of it has been accessible to designers or to design students. Scientific jargon impedes understanding: neat definitions often serve rhetorical purposes but lack directive power for practitioners. Albers (1971), for example, defined complementary pairs as colors accompanied by their afterimages. His definition is at least partially true, but of little practical value.

Another feature of the literature on afterimage is particularly striking. Most writers have assumed that afterimages are uniform across populations. Albers is exceptional in suggesting that the afterimage of red may be green *or* blue-green. The assumption that afterimages are uniform is false, as studies at the University of Minnesota have shown (Bagley, Maxfield,1986).

Given the confusing state of the literature, designers are, so to speak, left in a twilight zone — a condition less than ideal for colorists. To illuminate the subject, answers to basic questions are required: first, what do we really know about color variation in the afterimage experience? Second, how can such knowledge assist designers? Can color information be accessed through use of universally accepted color standards? Answering these two basic questions is the purpose of this discussion.

The discussion here divides into three parts. Part One is introductory. Here we will review the experience of negative afterimage. We will also take a brief, preliminary look at how this experience has been treated in the Minnesota studies of color afterimages. Part Two presents studio applications of the procedures and findings in the Minnesota studies. Part Three returns attention to the Minnesota studies, summarizing the research basis which may guide uses of color afterimages in the studio. Illustrative charts, shown here for the first time in color, express patterns of interrelations of source color and afterimage color derived from aggregated reports of color-matching.

Part One
The Afterimage Experience

To prepare for the experience of negative AI, turn to figure 20 on page 62. Cover one eye. Fixate on the center of the red field for some 30 seconds, then switch to the adjacent plain field. Blink the fatigued eye to bring back the afterimage. Then cover the fatigued eye, and look with the rested eye. Go back and forth between the fatigued and the rested eye to compare.

You may be able to find your afterimage on the following chart for red (figure 21, page 62). The chart shows the range of the most frequently reported afterimages matched to Munsell color by the 125 respondents in the Minnesota study. The next chart shows that 66% of the afterimages for red fall into the continuum of the blue-green hue family (figure 22, page 63).

The third chart (figure 23, page 63) summarizes the most frequently reported afterimages for the ten Munsell hues and for one Ostwald blue (Bagley and Maxfield, 1986). The afterimage is usually paler than the stimulus color; for example, red calls for a *pale* blue-green. Compared to two complements in a traditional 12 hue color circle spaced 180 degrees apart (Itten 1966), an afterimage color pair has a narrower hue contrast, perhaps 160 degrees. We looked for color pairs rather than for the ultimate hue circle, since hue circles come and go.

Part Two
The Color Curriculum

Experience shows that students' individual afterimage colors can serve as color references for creative projects. Many graduate students who had completed the basic and advanced color courses later taught the basic color course as teaching assistants. Practical application of afterimage colors is evident in their work from the advanced color course and from their independent masters' degree projects. If frequency of use is an indication of success (Mager, 1962), then the courses were successful, as these graduate students often chose afterimage colors for their creative projects.

Two key points emerged over time in the successive projects created by students in various media, including fiber arts, book illustration, letterform art, and package design. Successful use of afterimage colors is more likely 1) when color proportions are carefully considered and 2) when color proportion is tempered through gradation of colors. Because of this, all levels of the color courses stress design strategies that give careful attention to color proportion and gradation along with reliance on perceptual color (i.e., personal afterimage colors.) Students in the color courses are encouraged to work in a closely related series so that color can be viewed as the dominant variable.

Inspiration for projects in the intermediate and advanced classes projects come from three main sources. Transformations of historic works by color innovators, observation of nature forms, and practical problems. Within these frames, students have wide latitude of choice.

Examples of designs shown here (figure 24, page 64) suggest guidelines for studio practice. It can be seen that perceptual complements may be used together, or they may be combined with traditional complements — for example red with perceptual opposite blue-green and traditional complement green — to create a lively color balance. Gray may be consciously used as a chameleon field that takes on the tinge of afterimage color. Clues for background colors for any object can be found through the afterimage process. Afterimage color backgrounds *sharpen* the given colors (Hurwich 1981). Afterimage or successive contrast is a temporal effect. (For more on the question of successive contrast and simultaneous contrast see note 2)[2]

Curriculum Details

The first ten-week course in the undergraduate color curriculum serves university students preparing for careers in interior, graphic, and clothing design. The first course explores alternative approaches to experiencing and understanding color, ranging from color interaction discovery exercises modeled after Albers to the measured analyses of Munsell. Students learn to compose color purposefully with an understanding of color interaction in problems that introduce the design strategies of proportion, gradation, and working in a series. Study of partitive, additive, subtractive, and subjective color goes beyond traditional studies in color theory based on a red-yellow-blue color wheel. After observing demonstrations and completing assignments, students prepare study sheets and design their own "varying viewpoints" summaries to explain the concepts to themselves.

In subtractive color exercises, students create two triangles, each with nine steps, to compare color mixtures from painter's and from printer's primaries. Visually equal color intervals are at issue here. When they discover that red and blue can be mixed from printer's process colors, they disprove traditional paint dogma for themselves. Students follow the measured approach of Munsell in painted achromatic and chromatic scales which must vanish side-ways. They employ the same colors in modular designs for their portfolios.

Students subsequently work through an independent study unit which introduces negative afterimages (Bagley 1988). The unit is part of a course taught in multiple sections and conducted by various instructors. Students read Brindley's *Scientific American* article "Afterimages," partly for its explanation of the psycho-physical basis of afterimage, and partly to practice using his four hues to generate afterimages (Brindley, 1963). Following the directions in the independent study unit, students view surface colors on white backgrounds, as on the printed page and the *Munsell Book of Color* (Munsell 1976). Using Pantone® colors matched to ten Munsell hues, plus an Ostwald purple-blue, students find their afterimage colors through repeated practice. The colors are viewed in alternate order, first red, then blue-green, and so on, to reduce visual fatigue. Instructional objectives are stated to students: generate, identify, match, record afterimages; then arrange them around the rim of a rectangle. Although it was originally thought that simply matching the *hue* family would do, students were found to be intensely self-motivated to continue matching until they were truly satisfied with the afterimage tint.

An afterimage reference chart presented in a common format that allows comparison reveals surprising differences, especially among yellows and purples. For a design experiment, students select a pair of their perceptual opposites from the chart. They paint a chroma-bridge that gradually blends the color with its afterimage in steps. Students have reported that afterimage chroma-bridge colors are pleasant to view. They voluntarily chose them for subsequent projects.

Students often refer to their personal afterimage charts in the studio. They learn to compose color purposefully with a heightened understanding of color interaction. They also become more conscious of how adjacent colors may influence each other, or how a color background *adds* its afterimage to a small area of color placed upon it. They may find clues in their afterimage charts for simultaneous contrast exercises. Many students choose their afterimage pairs for free-choice projects.

Readings

Instead of a single text, readings selected from Chevreul, Brindley, Munsell, Itten, Albers, Harlan, and others, are assigned. The aim is to integrate studio experience with concepts from the color literature. They see many examples, such as the Goethe triangle. A laboratory guide (Bagley, 1988) with questions on readings and directions for the afterimage unit is available to all students.

In the intermediate color class for design communication students, there is a continuing emphasis on making conscious color proportion decisions and working in a series. Students may compare chroma-bridge paint mixtures for perceptual opposites that mix to gray with mixtures of traditional paint complements that mix to brown. Afterimage pairs offer a new option for students who, until now, have known only the traditional paint complements. Students next begin to experiment with color variants, inspired, for example, by electronic imaging of historic or contemporary sources; or by free-choice studies. Projects, such as shopping bag designs, begin the transition to practical application.

The research findings charted in color are, in a sense, sociologically useful when working with groups — whether clients or students — because the findings predict individual differences as well as regularities. While the red and blue-green range suggest commonalities, the yellows and blues may evoke friendly disagreements among students.

Part Three
The Research

The Minnesota research project on color afterimage centered on the question of uniformity versus variability in perception. "Uniformity" was the ruling assumption in the literature. The assumption that afterimages are uniform is not surprising, since prior reports seem to have been based on the response of the single viewer, from Goethe to Chevreul, and down to Brindley and Marx. The literature offered no report of a broad sampling of viewers. The treatment of afterimage in popular color texts was usually brief and undocumented.[3] The situation called for improvement, which led to the Minnesota project.

Color Deficiency Tests

Our participants were 125 volunteers from introductory design lecture and studio classes. Of these, seven volunteers were male. Nine males had volunteered, but the Ishihara and Farnsworth color deficiency tests administered to all volunteers eliminated two.

Controlled Conditions

A written script used by a research assistant guided the color matching process. This was done in a darkened room with the Spectralight set at the daylight setting, creating a low level of illumination. (Goldstein [1977] reminds us that the rods and cones decrease in sensitivity as illumination rises.) Participants

in the study viewed the ten Munsell principal and intermediate colors at the central 5.0 position, plus an extra Ostwald 7.5 purple blue, on a white field. The order of viewing alternated: first red, then blue-green, red-yellow, and so on. Participants could repeat matching to color standards from the Munsell Book of Color (1976) until satisfied.

Findings

Instead of the predicted uniformity, a range of afterimages were reported. However, the afterimage reponses for nine stimulus colors all fell within a single hue family. The majority of the afterimages for the remaining two stimulus colors, purple-blue and yellow- red (a golden yellow), spanned two adjacent hue families.

We also wanted to know if the perceived colors were uniformly reciprocal, as is commonly assumed, even by Brindley (1963). That is, do the colors reverse? If red generates blue-green, does blue-green generate red? When we compared the reciprocity for all eleven stimulus colors and their most frequently reported afterimage, as diagrammed on Munsell degree circles, we did indeed see a neat reciprocity for red and blue-green. For the rest of the colors, however, the reversibility relationships turned out to be close to, but certainly not identical with, the original stimulus colors.

In another interpretation of reciprocity in color, a bar-chart presents stimulus colors along the bottom and afterimage colors along the top (figure 25, page 64). When viewed *together*, the afterimages appear to lean toward a pinkish central point, a relationship that is not evident in the black and white chart in the published report (Bagley and Maxfield, 1989).

Findings for reciprocity presented another surprise. While for reciprocity the most controversial relationships involved blues and yellows, the greatest agreement on afterimage colors for any stimulus color was yellow: 81 % of the reported afterimages were in the purple hue family.

In this connection, afterimage pioneer Goethe pursued color reciprocity for the six hues in his chromatic circle with "demanded"colors opposite each other "contrariwise, " (Matthaei, R. , 1971). Goethe's "plum blossom red" or red-purple, shown correctly by Agoston (1971) "calls for" green across the circle, colors with good afterimage reciprocity. Goethe's nine hue triangle can represent how cyan-yellow-magenta printers process primaries (at the outer points) can be used to mix the additive light primaries within.

The trail from Goethe leads to Helmholtz (1924) and Rood (1879/1973), whose work influenced Munsell. Munsell further refined complementary relationships through a color-by-averaging disk mixture method (Munsell, 1926). Munsell's five principal hues can be viewed with their afterimages from the Minnesota study. The basic Ostwald complements of blue and yellow, red and blue-green, based on additive color, can be compared to their afterimages. Students found that Ostwald's beautiful purple-blue generate his golden-yellow in our afterimage studies.

For technical reasons and photographic limitations, it has been necessary to add a darker version of the afterimage color to the original pair in figure 22, page 63. This observation once again underlines differences which color designers must take into account when shifting from uses of afterimage in projected color and surface color.

Notes

1. I wish to express my thanks to my colleagues Dr. Barbara Martinson, instructor Carol Waldron, and teaching assistants Lori Gilbertson and Linda Krueger for providing slides of student work from their classes. I wish to thank present and former graduate students for allowing me to present their work shown in this order: Lydia Kulesov, Julia Reitan, Margaret Sathre Maxfield, Kristin Peterson, Frances Trice, Alison Wanner, Anne Runyon, Jan Myers, Jean Nordlund, Susan Graves, Kanti Blaz, Barbara Caron. Work shown by undergraduate students includes Waldron students Donald Haney, Julie Parker, Pamela Mayer; Martinson students Hazel Lutz, Ahmed Kashif Asdi; and Bagley students Sharon Edstrom-Gandara, Jim Norkosky, Laura Carlson, Michael Schoenberger, Denyse Madden, and Tim Ricci.

2. Afterimages are sometimes called successive contrast. A parallel term, simultaneous contrast, refers to the way colors mutually influence each other as we view them simultaneously. Successive and simultaneous contrast are sometimes used as interchangeable terms by art writers Sidelinger (1985), and by Sidelinger's probable source Albers, (1971). Marx (1983) also links the two terms when she states that "along with the additive, optical, and subtractive complementaries, the existence of a fourth, the simultaneous or successive complementary, must also be acknowledged."

Lee (1981) points out that simultaneous contrast is "immediately apparent and is equally apparent to a roving gaze as it is to a fixed stare." Fixating on a color for a period of time is required to generate successive contrast. Psychologist Bruce Goldstein states that simultaneous contrast "can be obtained in the absence of afterimages." (1977)

3. Color references that describe afterimages include DeGrandis (1984) who states that the afterimage of red is green, and that staring at green will evoke red, yellow evokes violet, blue evokes orange. Zelanski and Fisher rely entirely on an Albers' diagram that depicts nine yellow disks as they skirt the afterimage domain. Brief directions for generating afterimages for surface colors viewed against white surrounds appear in Albers (1971), Kueppers (1982), and Sidelinger (1985). Marx (1983) and Lambert (1991) direct the reader to project the afterimage on a white screen.

86 **References**

ALBERS J. (1971) Interaction of Color. New Haven, CT: Yale University Press.

AGOSTON, J. (1971) Color theory and its application in art and design. Berlin: Springer Verlag.

BAGLEY, M.-O. (1988) Color in design: process, concepts and resources. St. Paul, MN. Available from Copies on Campus Store, University of Minnesota St. Paul, or from the author. Incorporates directions from 1974 independent study booklet.

BAGLEY, M.-O. and M. S. MAXFIELD (1986). Afterimage color perception for designers. Perceptual and Motor Skills. v. 63 (October), 995-1007.

BICKLEY-GREEN, C. (1990) Afterimage in painting. Dissertation. Athens, Georgia: University of Georgia. Complete literature review to date.

DE GRANDIS, L. (1984) Theory and Use of Color. New York: Abrams.

GOLDSTEIN, E. B. (1977) Review of Color perception in art by Faber Birren. Leonardo, v. 10, nr. 3, 245.

HELMHOLTZ, W. (1962) (J. P. C. Southhall, Ed. & Trans.) Helmholtz's 'Treatise on Physiological Optics.' Vol. 2 New York: Dover. (Originally translated and published by the Optical Society of America, 19214)

HURVICH, L. (1981) Color vision. Sunderland, MA: Sinauer.

KUEPPERS, H. (1982) The basic law of color theory. Woodbury NY: Barrons.

LAMBERT, P. (1991) Controlling Color. New York: Design Press.

LEE, A. (1981) A critical account of some of Josef Albers' concepts of color. Leonardo, v. 14, 99-105.

MAGER, R. F. (1962) Preparing instructional objectives. Palo Alto, CA:Fearon.

MARX, E. (1983) (G. O'Brien Trans.) Optical color & simultaneity. New York: Van Nostrand Reinhold,

MATTHAEI, R. (1971) (H. Aach Trans.) Goethe's color theory. New York: Van Nostrand Reinhold.

MUNSELL, A. H. (1926) A color notation. Baltimore, MD: Munsell.

The Munsell book of color glossy finish collection. (1976) Baltimore, MD: Munsell Color.

ROOD, O. N. (1973) Modern chromatics. (F. Birren, editor) New York: Van Nostrand Reinhold. (Originally published in 1879 in New York: Appleton)

SIDELINGER, S. (1985) Color manual. Englewood Cliffs, N.J.: Prentice-Hall.

ZELANSKI, P. and FISHER, M. (1989) Color. Engiewood Cliffs, N. J: Prentice Hall.

3 Fine Art

Hans Joachim Albrecht

Structuring Colour
Expression and Meaning in Contemporary Painting

It is not the eyes that should be occupied by a painting, the intention of all visual activation is rather the "post-retinal effect". This claim, often articulated by Josef Albers, is the starting point in my concentrated sketch concerning the correlation between colour structure and the character and expressiveness of colour in contemporary painting. Albers literally says: "Only when the painter makes the spectator see more than the painter (physically) has presented will he produce *perceptual* (psychological) effects".

And he continues: "For all art leads sensitive eyes to see, to realize, or to read more than meets the retina. Art adds psychological effects to physical facts".[1] Are these not strange yet obvious demands and observations that Albers cited in 1965 in order to dissociate his art from *Op-art*?

I believe his reaction is understandable considering the excessive attention that several artists paid to optical phenomena. This preference for optical aspects became possible following the recent split awareness between instinctive experience and knowing comprehension. While perceiving, our position interchanges and usually we do not even notice it.

This discrepancy between knowledge and experience has been recognised much earlier. For example, in the last century Ozenfant spoke of "optical syntax" and "psychological syntax" and Walter Hess concludes from this dualistic approach in the beginning of modern painting: "The growing tendency in analytical thought helps the painter not only to liberate the servile use of colour but also divides up the complex effects of autonomous colour".[2]

Now Albers has just demonstrated the optical aspect with his studies on the *Interaction of Color*, and with such baffling re-

sults that many observers are often satisfied with the initial optical experience. Consequently he felt compelled to demand "more" from art. My lecture tries to approach the psychological content.

"It is in the nature of a picture that it says more than it appears to be".[3] This statement precedes Albers's general opinion. It originates from Philipp Otto Runge, a German painter of the romantic era who died in the year 1810 at the early age of 33. Due to the mental clarification of his position Runge stimulated important developments in the art world which now serve as the "undercoat" for my explanatory sketch. The influence of his philosophy reaches as far as the Bauhaus era, to Wassily Kandinsky, Johannes Itten and, as I mentioned, Josef Albers.

It is worthwhile hearing what Runge has to say on the subject: "Colour rests in the air like sound in metal. As the tightening of a string changes the pitch of an instrument so, equally amazingly, the sharpness or obtuness of an angle alters a colour. And the phenomenon where first red, then yellow and then blue flare up in the immediate proximity of the sun is a property that belongs also to painting and we must know it and use it. To make pure and tuneful music only with the air in a picture, that is the figured bass that makes everything sound in harmony ..."[4]

With these few words Runge demonstrates that the *landscape* has to become the central theme for painting. Elementary apparitions of light in the air suffice as a subject for a painting. However, these must be recognised and employed consciously. Red, yellow and blue are the colour elements that originate from light. Their tone must be experienced simultaneously with their acoustic sounds so that a picture can develop by following strict rules and attain musical qualities.

With this statement Runge introduces himself as a clear-sighted and conceptually thinking artist. However, in contrast, his meta-physical ideas remain concealed.

The new appreciation and understanding of the landscape in itself requires a particular note: The painter leaves his immediate surroundings in order to discover symbols of a comprehensive "life on earth" (Carl Gustav Carus said: "Erdenleben"). He strives to grasp the elemental aspects of all structures and appearances in an instinctive, perceptive and knowing manner in order to create symbolic forms. Furthermore, as he believes that "natural life" and "emotional life" correspond (according to Carus in four main stages!), the search for universal rules represents for him a fathoming of the mental state.

The periodical return of day and year, in which all life is included, is obviously suited to the realisation of such ideas. Runge writes that "the year in its four changing stages: *flowering, generating, bearing and destroying ...* sweeps so constantly through the mind" that his longing for this eternal miracle regenerates itself again and again.[5] The great cycle of the *seasons* offers an example of universal events and, contained within them, the lesser cycle of the *times of day*. Runge dedicates his creative energy to this cycle.

The significance of colour for a picture becomes increasingly essential. As we heard in the quotation, the observation of elementary processes in nature secures the programmatic assignment of the colour "trinity" in the times of day. The colour red accentuates the close connection of earth and light. For this reason red is the characteristic colour of morning and evening. However, while in the morning the light expels colour, in the evening it is devoured by it. Blue belongs to the day and, finally, yellow to the night.[6]

Runge was able to execute a colour version of *Morning* only (see figure 26, page 97). But within it, the colour red is in no way dominant. Besides red, other colours appear, diametrically placed in opposite-colour contrast as well as in continuous transition. Light and dark or rather white and black are integrated. Apart from this rare picture we have few examples of Runge's artistic ideas. On the whole, he became well known through his achievements in the field of colour theory.

Around 1800 radical abstraction had released all colours from their real, concrete or material origin. For this reason it is necessary to reconsider and redefine the traditional artistic experience of the totality of colours having a unifying effect on a picture. Goethe worked hard on this challenge. In his neighbourhood an amazingly simple model was being developed. With red, yellow and blue Runge constructs his own comprehensible world following a strict geometrical plan: it is his *Colour Sphere*. A new globe is created which is to provide the orientation and overall view for further artistic work. Johannes Itten included it in his book *The Art of Colour*.

From Runge we will draw a connecting line to Itten and to the Bauhaus. Further we want to deal with Kandinsky, Albers, Rothko and then via Badur and Delaunay we proceed to Lohse and Kelly. However, before we enter our century, we must draw a contrasting line over the 'undercoat' of our sketch.

The self-potraits, *Philipp Otto Runge in a Brown Jacket, 1809/10* and *Vincent van Gogh, September 1889*, are both painted just before the death of each artist.

The concept of recurrence in the way of world bridges the gap between Philipp Otto Runge and Vincent van Gogh, as the latter also considers symbolising the *seasons* with colours and depicting them in a cycle made up of four parts. On this subject he writes:

"The spring is tender, green, unripe corn and apple-blossom (pink). The autumn is the contrast between yellow leaves and shades of purple. The winter is snow with soft shadows. But if the summer were a counteraction of different blues and an element of orange in the golden colour of corn, then one could in this way paint a picture using each contrast of the complementary colours red and green, blue and orange, yellow and purple, white and black, that would accurately express the mood of the seasons."[7]

Van Gogh's programme for a picture series of the *seasons* is based on the principle of opposite colours. He was confident that he would find a binding symbolism within this order. In this respect, he is more determined than Runge, whose picture *Morning* connects symbolic significance in such a way that his friend the poet Ludwig Tieck described the picture as a "guide to beautiful dreams".

Equally foreign to van Gogh is Runge's idea of penetrating the various creations and formations of nature from the inner mental state. The motives and subjects of his painting lie in the visible outside world. The objects appear to him figuratively. He seizes them. Every shape that his eye registers is torn into an artistic stroke. Only after the composition of the material subject is elaborated, can the "high-handed colourist" (van Gogh) intervene. Intense colours remove the drawing from the visible actuality and transform it with their particular colour expression. Van Gogh himself made an exemplary comment on the origin of a portrait that depicts a blond friend in front of a shabby wall. The colours transform the scene and create that particular "mysterious effect of a star in the depth of an azure-blue sky",

caused by the colour of the hair, intensified by orange, chrome-yellow and pale lemon-yellow, on a rich blue background.[8]

All the same, van Gogh's description gives us some impression what enormous importance he ascribes to colour and how he might have processed his strict plan of the *seasons* in his painting. The "suggestion" emanating from his painting hinted at here, has above all influenced "expressive" painters after him.

The "expressive" use of colour was also a challenge to Johannes Itten. In his colour theory he concerns himself with a picture-analysis of van Gogh's *Night Café* from 1888. The text betrays the fact that Itten felt uneasy about the displacement in the areas of violet-blue and yellow-orange. They appear to disturb his sense of harmony due to the flickering simultaneous effects and the unbalanced quantities.

It is clarifying for my sketch to mention that after van Gogh, Itten also concerned himself with the task of symbolising the *four seasons* with colour. Let us hear his interpretation of the great cycle of the world: "Nature could be a perfect example for our lives with its rhythm of the seasons that alternately swing outward and inward. In the spring and summer the strength of the earth surges outwards and brings about the growth of the plants, in the autumn and winter this strength turns inward and prepares for new germination."[9]

Late in his life, in 1963, Itten painted the four pictures. Through the location and compilation of the colour groups which, from his point of view, "belong unequivocally to the expression of the season in question", he refers explicitly to the balanced colours of Runge's colour sphere. For *Spring* and *Autumn* he discovers the following colour-profile:

"The youthful, pale, radiant unfolding of nature in the spring is expressed by bright colours. Yellow is the colour which is nearest to white light and yellow-green is the progression of yellow. Pale pink and pale blue shades intensify and broaden the sound. Yellow, pink and lilac are often to be found in the buds of plants.

The colours of autumn contrast intensely with the colours of spring. In autumn green vegetation dies off, it rots and disintegrates in dull shades of brown and purple."[10]

Itten continues to rely on the constant observation of visible nature. He expects significant insight into the matter. He knows that deep inside he is a "naturalistic symbolist". But how much further than Runge will he go? And which colour definitions do his Seasons have in comparison with van Gogh's concept? Here we ask for a subtotal concerning the picture-function and the colour-symbol.

Itten finds his origin in modern art. Therefore he is acquainted with the method of step-by-step abstraction and uses it to transfer his primarily impressive and later expressive landscape painting to a constructive level. The final version is based solely on a geometrical surface plan. The picture is constructed from precisely proportioned and colour-matched rectangles, without any support or contribution of specific forms or traditional symbols (i.e. flowers). This pattern should contain the feelings or mood of the painter as a complete experience. Finally, it is solely the colours that evoke this specific experience in the observer.

We observe a change in the comprehension of pictures. A traditional composition is concerned with the conclusiveness of all elements in the picture, in appropriate proportions to its size, whereas the modern picture becomes more and more a mirror for the observer. It foregoes representation in order to specifically arouse emotions and encourage insight through the structure of its colours. The type, amount, position and order of the colours are arranged respectively.

But how can a colour juxtaposition accurately reflect and convey a mood? Is its expressive value generally acceptable? In comparison, the last examples demonstrate how varied the seasonal atmosphere and the symbolic evaluation of colour can be.

Van Gogh writes about one of his harvest pictures from 1889: "It is a picture of death, as proclaimed by the great book of nature. But what I have sought is a nearly smiling character. It is completely yellow apart from a line of violet hills, a pale, fair yellow."[11] He transfers the yellow of the harvest landscape to the symbolic meaning of the harvest, finally to death. Itten, on the other hand, speaks of the purple and brown colours as an expression of death. The signs of death are in any case evident to him. Itten comes from the Bern highlands and is familiar with the colour-transformations of his mountain homeland.

The peculiarities of different environments, personal situations and opinions have a long-term influence on the individual assessment of colours. Colours underlie comprehensive connotations. How can observed phenomena lead to binding expressive colour-values? If we pursue the deeper meaning of single colours, we attain at most only an indication of the root of polarity. The might of death could be represented by a *complementary* pair of colours. To van Gogh it is yellow, Itten sees it as purple. Traditionally, black or white are used to express death as darkness or light.

It is hardly surprising that Wassily Kandinsky also derived the themes of *seasons* and *times of day* from landscape paintings (from the beginning of the century until about 1914). But he goes further. True conceptual elements were intended to put his art on a level that could compete with the scientific knowledge of his time. Consequently, he feels compelled to fathom the deeper psychological basis of the colour-world and other fundamental topics, in order to guarantee his epoch-making position.

Kandinsky certainly found it difficult to see colours outside of any object-relationship. He knows exactly how different the colour red can appear, depending upon whether it is seen in a horse, in a dress or in a plain geometric surface.[12] However, he takes the decisive step to abstraction and liberates the colours from all reference to the material world. Now the painter is responsible for all the colours in his picture. This is the beginning of non-representative painting.

Within the bounds of his expression-theory, Kandinsky deals with the characteristics of the most important colours. In his much-quoted descriptions, phrases referring to "acoustic" sensations are most striking. At this point we recall Runge's wish "to make pure and tuneful music in a picture". The idea of "musical" painting proves to be long-lived and in this respect Kandinsky is very typical of many artists of his generation. Particularly non-figurative or concrete painters seek correspondence and analogy to acoustic art. The abstractness of sound and the rules of musical composition appear ideal for their artistic train of thought. Their aim is an art of colour that directly influences the observer in a most complex manner. But that is a subject of a separate lecture.[13]

Kandinsky's urge to research can hardly have impeded his work of art between 1909 and 1914. Being himself at the beginning of the road, he wanted to make the right artistic decisions, guided by his feelings. That obviously occured. The easel has his undivided attention and he spontaneously sets his sign or form ab-breviations onto freely arranged splashes of colour. Both parts of the painting result from the same regressive behaviour and they achieve parallel effects.

We can find a certain explanation for the correspondence of colour and sound in *synaesthesia:* In the field of perception, connections really exist crosswise between different sense-spheres. When stimuli are psychologically processed, e.g. visual stimuli, it is possible that other senses are aroused at the same time. These signal connections which are probably individually formed and mostly of an associative type, were especially extreme in Kandinsky's case. For this reason his personality strongly influences certain opinions concerning colour-characters.

The expressive values that he applies to colours correspond in most points with recent results of psychological research. Naturally he is familiar with Goethe's vision of a *'thorough bass'* in painting. His colour-theory contains the chapter about the "Sinnlich-sittliche Wirkung der Farben" (Sensuous-pure Effect of Colours), that transformed the poet's knowledgeable perception into the first modern character-theory of colour. This theory prepares for colour the way from the symbolic representation of spirituality to the presence of specific colours.

Objections to Kandinsky's theoretical position come from a different direction. Theodor W. Adorno considers the triumph of spiritualisation in art to be a dearly bought Pyrrhic victory, because it neglects the urgent mission of the avant-garde to discover new territory. Adorno's argument is weighty: *convention* determines the symbolic value of colours and convention is the category "against which the complete new-art movement had most fiercely revolted." The critic confirms the obvious connections between radical art and arts and crafts at the beginning of our century (in the tendency towards folklore and ornamental style), and doubts the spiritual pureness. He concludes: "Supposedly significant colours, sounds and whatever continue to play their dull part." [14]

After the second world war, as Josef Albers fully developed his painting at Black Mountain College, his method proved to be rather economic and pragmatic. He did not demand from art a spiritual aspect. However, his picture titles demonstrate a surprising proximity to Kandinsky's artistic sentiments. Who can ascertain to whose work the following titles belong: *Dense-Soft* (1969), *Loose-Fast* (1926), *Decided* (1951), *Definite* (1930), *Tempered Ardor* (1950), *In the Warm-Cool* (1921), *Diverse but United* (1963) and *Division-Unity* (1934). But whereas Kandinsky's pictures are mostly characterised by signs, shapes and figures and these frequently of a droll character, Albers confines himself to the use of colours in simple surface planes. He prefers small, emotionally effective groups of colours, in the sense of colour polarity, (that he demonstrates with Goethe's colour-triangle). Albers is particularly interested in the confrontation of cold and warm, or wet and dry. The direction in which he strives becomes obvious: the *relativity* of colours, formulated in gentle or strong but always moderate and controlled contrasts, creates "climates" and "atmospheres" that are intended to hold the observer in a state of active tension. In this way it is not difficult to understand the picture series of *Biconjugate* (later also called *Variant*) as a further transformation of the landscape theme (*Adobe, Leaf Studies*).

Again we have a picture-title to thank for a reference. A painting of the Square-series is called *Pompeian* and directs the gaze far back to one of the sources that Albers drew from. He studied Pompeian wall-paintings because they showed him parallels to his own colour-art: Just as in an economically run theatre, clear colour-groups appear in "role-play exercises" on simple stages. Each colour alternates as "actor" or "character" between a leading role and a supporting role. The programme runs without a break. In the sense of this metaphor, there is no finished theme, no final version for this painter. Albers patiently works on an endless series of variants.

An observer takes up a conversation with a variant as with a partner. At first, the interaction captures each observer. Like a mirror, the picture can reveal his unknown ego, never having so consciously reacted to colours before. However, Albers calculates this effect far enough in advance to prevent this experience from melting away. In the *Homage to the Square* the separate colours combined in groups of three or four are so defined that they are not absorbed in a floating entirety, but keep returning in intervals. In this way an attentive observer experiences a change of function in every colour in the painting. Each colour first appears as an individual and then as a member of a group. It is this dual-function of colours that Albers discovered in Pompeian painting and acknowledged as its particular acheivement. (Here I give the example of a *Caldarium*, i.e. a hot bathroom with a cool water basin, next to the painting *Tempered Ardor* by Albers, figure 27, page 98).

Albers's square-structure provides the basis to enter the picture and finally to escape from its concentric order. Mark Rothko's paintings centre our view in another way. Two, sometimes three colour areas lie in layers on a uniform background and so this arrangement retains the scheme of a landscape.

The dimensions of Rothko's paintings are nearly always so expansive that he can "climb into" the painting during the work process. This format is comparable to a door in its true size and even more so in an abstract sense. The observer also needs these dimensions in order to accept the painter's invitation. The complete visual field is activated by colour stimuli and is seized by the surface of the painting. If the observer continually looks at the painting, he will slowly be drawn into a flowing, floating colour space. Finally, the clarity that increases through the unhindered occupation with colour, occurs without the influence of memory, history or geometry. Rothko cannot tolerate what he calls these "swamps of generalisation".[15]

It seems to me that Rothko's untitled painting from the year 1963 (*Untitled*, 175 x 127cm) blocks the entrance to its inner depths. The gaze lands on an intensive orange-red in the centre. This resists further progress of the eye and lets it drift away. Two colour zones of extremely different size and intensity take control of the eye. In the upper area a narrow barrier holds it there whereas the lower area gently receives it in a darkened shade. Both surfaces have a somewhat transparent quality that is highly unusual in orange and brown colours. They let themselves be inundated by the central orange-red and combine temporarily with it and subsequently they counteract the appearing blue-green after-images. The orange-red remains almost constant before our eyes.

The picture-space in Rothko's paintings is often governed by a dominant colour whose high intensity is transferred in a weaker form into the accompanying zones. There is a tradition in this kind of chromatic modification, but it definitely needs subtle treatment to gain pictorial significance. Light could have interfered and caused this gradated light and dark of the colours. Rothko himself describes his "Painting as Drama" whereby the free action of the "actors", namely the colour areas, abandon the preconceived plans and ideas and spontaeously achieve the desired completion of the artistic experience.[16]

Now the line in our sketch swivels at right angles. A vertical picture order supercedes the horizontal. The central structures that allowed a meditative, contemplative relationship with the picture, now fade. This puts an end to the forward inclination of the observer and his sinking into the depths of the painting. The vertical structure demands a new attitude from the viewer, a sideways skimming over the surface of the painting or even a broad passing-by. This vertical order characterizes significant groups of work by Barnett Newman, Richard Lohse or Ellsworth Kelly.

A younger German painter, Frank Badur, processes in his vertical structure several aspects that we have already discussed. The observation of natural phenomena is a part of his motivation (possibly due to the light in Finland). The direct colour-experience is still the painting concept. Badur's colour sequences make use of relations that activate simultaneous processes and assimilation; yet the back and forth, the reciprocal tension increases.

It is not only a question of simultaneous effects setting off the visual dialogue, or uniting the painting with the observer. New additional stimuli result from the complex treatment of the colour medium. Badur combines two qualities of colour in the act of painting: their material substance and their light appearance. He can set a shiny surface next to a matt surface or a transparent one next to an opaque one. If one covers or overlaps the other, does it extinguish or transform the colour hue of the other or does one colour make its particular volume apparent? Or do neighbouring surfaces just lie simply next to each other?

The use of different colour media in painting evokes a more comprehensive experience of reality. At the same time this qualitative increase complicates all its relationships. The smooth, rough, opaque, glassy, shiny, matt surface causes a tense or perhaps even contradictory attitude towards the painting. Our attention is easily divided by visual and tactile impressions caused by the different colour materials in the picture field. But we remain attentive, and this is important.

Badur works with this dual attitude towards the painting whereby the vertical order is proved. If approached from the side or regarded from an oblique angle, the vertical fields are particularly interesting for the searching eye. Perspective changes of proportion, the slant of the light and reflections of the surrounding area change the effect of the painting with every movement. The initial involuntary displacement can provoke conscious experiments with viewing distance or viewing angle and controlled movement or position. The observer realises how active his part in the dialogue with the painting really is and how temporally unlimited it begins to be. This dialogue develops the content of an artistic experience that cannot be fixed by any length of time.

It is still possible to establish common ground among such differing works of art. They are "dedicated" to the eye by their colour structures. Their activity is an appeal: gentle, strong or sometimes even "aggressive", as Albers says. It is out of chronological order, but now Robert Delaunay sets an extreme accent in our sketch. He refers to his *Simultaneous Disc* from 1912 as a "punch". The eye is hit by colour stimuli that overtax the senses. Then only in this overstimulated state, can the eye elicit a remarkable part of the light which is contained in the colours. Naturally, Delaunay paints with very pure colours and reduces their material presence. However, the structuring of his painting succeeds in attaining the desired light-effects with colour alone. Delaunay developed the principle of *simultaneity*. He sets this principle above all else.

The attack on the eye demands a rigorous organisation of the colours. There is no escape from the surface of the painting. Polar and complementary pairs (better: opposite-colours) and groups are displaced in ring-segments so that they stimulate the eye in permanent rhythm. In this endless stimulation, the simultaneous effects blend each other out; the after-image -series neutralise each other similarly to a dazzling of the eye. Delaunay's vision of participating in the abundance of light, results from these perceived dynamics of the energetic processes.

Delaunay tries out his elemental model on the contrasting lights of sun and moon. He differentiates further and mitigates it. In several paintings both celestial bodies are even unified so that an alternating rhythm exudes from two different centres. This painter has no consideration for any traditional expressive colour-values. The eye should participate in the extreme strength of colour. For Delaunay it would be a relapse to extract single psychologically defined colour characters out of the powerful totality. But still the painting as a whole becomes an expression because the perceived light-filled glow often is accompanied by an "optimistic" feeling. Perhaps one has to share Delaunay's belief in human progress in order to expose oneself voluntarily to such a strong light. For the first decades of the century, the optimism may be combined with a noticable degree of aggressiveness.

Here we recall Johannes Itten's friendly colours (even in a *Circle Study* from 1916) and how their structure fulfills a dual function. On the one hand they divide up the surface of the painting into clear proportions. On the other hand they have to display a certain atmosphere that an observer can comprehend while he stands in front of the painting and observes.

Figure 26
Philipp Otto Runge, The Small 'Morning', 1808. Oil on canvas,
109 x 88,5. Hamburger Kunsthalle, Germany.

Figure 27
Josef Albers: Homage to the Square, Tempered Ardor.
Oil on masonite, 1950.
Josef Albers Museum, Bottrop, Germany.

Figure 28
Color Design Class.
Student work, acrylic on illustration board, 9" x 12".

Figure 29
Color Design Class.
Student work, acrylic on illustration board,
9" x 12" each panel.

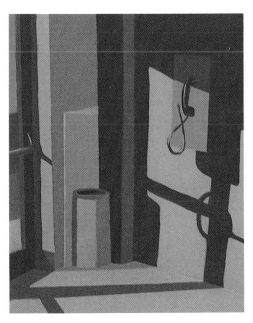

Figure 30
Foundation Painting Class.
Student work, oil on canvas, 30" x 40".

Figure 31
Michael Graves, Portland Building 1979-82

Figure 32
New highrise for downtown
Seattle, design by Sara Bragdon

Figure 33
King County Jail, form
manipulation by color contrast,
design by Reese Kaufman

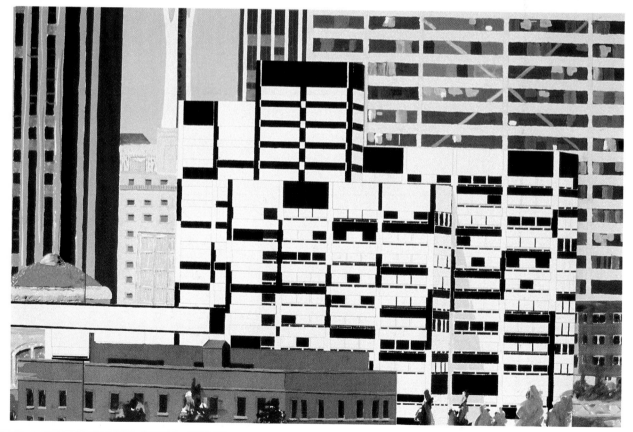

Figure 34

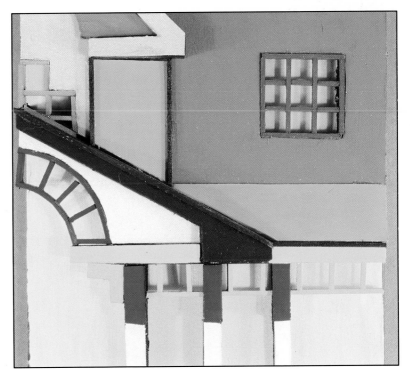

Figure 35

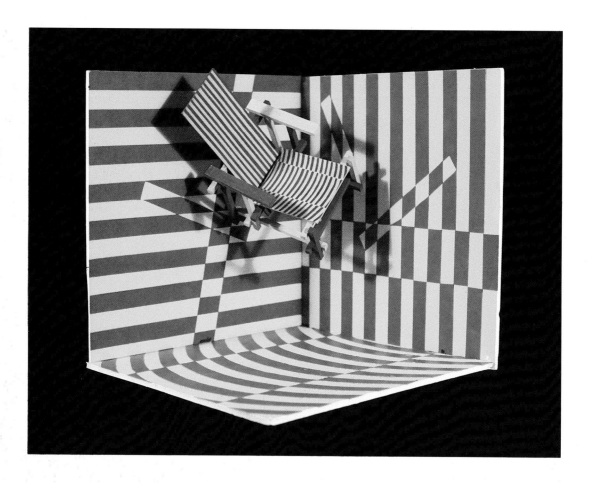

Figure 36

In Delaunay's case, the colours leave the painting, radiating from its surface. Different coloured energy approaches the observer, catches the eye, tearing the vision into the middle of the painting. Alternating between red and blue and underlying contrasts, the eye penetrates into an imaginary depth. This sort of flexible, direct, if unreal penetration of every position constitutes the new "space" that Delaunay praises so much.

As the first observer of his pictures, a painter knows how decisively the colour structure depends upon the eye and the function of seeing. Strictly speaking, Delaunay could only choose concentric structures for his painting. Concepts lead to consequences. Subsequent painters denied as far as possible the authorship of their pictures (Ernst, Pollock), because they would recognize no law of composition. That has consequences for the expression and character of colours: painters endeavour to let the colours speak for themselves.

This intention influences Josef Albers's life-work. In his *Interaction of Color* he reports how students overcome their personal dislike of certain colours by intensive use of them. They are free to choose any colour. In order to avoid any preferences, Albers uses the rules of *permutation* to organise the role-play exercises with fewer colours. The systematically planned sequence hinders the "director" in his free disposal of the actors.

Permutation is the cue that leads to Richard Paul Lohse (see cover for illustration of Lohse's *Thirty Vertical Systematic Colour Series with Red Diagonals*, 1940/1970). His constructive-systematic train of thought takes consistent steps towards equalising picture-media and picture-structures. In square *standard elements* Lohse overcomes the dual function of form and colour. The respective dimensions of these elements and their addition allow the development of series and group themes. The picture field emerges from these themes in its specific size and proportion.

Modular groups or serial sequences consequently spread out evenly over the entire field. Within this dense area, points of concentration or emphasis are avoided so that the eye can move freely. The whole surface should be easily grasped. Each painting that complies with Lohse's concept is based on *quantitative colour equality.* The balanced amount of the participating colours confirms the established format. Even so, rhythmic sequences and appropriate connections stimulate our imagination to widen the picture programme beyond the edges of the painting itself. In this respect, Lohse refers to his picture order as both *limited* and *unlimited systems.*

Early *Serial Orders* sometimes appear "dramatic" because the picture field seems stretched to the limit by extremes of light and dark colours. These variations in light intensity are reduced in the further development of the work. Their comparatively high intensity now connects the colours and relates them to the spectrum. Like the spectral colours, they continually follow each other and become stronger in the utmost complementary contrast. A smooth application of colour belongs to the character of light-colour: The paintings radiate energy, power and, let's say here again, "optimism", *joie de vivre.* Just as in Delaunay's *Sun and Moon* paintings, the light-temperatures are noticeably far apart, one certainly experiences warmer and colder elements in some areas of Lohse's paintings. The fluctuating temperature is integrated into the paradox-elastic space of the paintings.

Lohse includes *permutation* in the so far rationally substantiated picture-process in order to form relationships, even unforeseen relationships, between all elements of the same colour. For that reason it is difficult for the spectator to connect all places of the same colour in the picture field, or even to hold them together as groups. In his serial paintings Lohse considers an additional criterion. He shifts the phases of parallel *colour-chains* by at least two links. After that, identical colour elements never get close enough to optically "stick together" through assimilation. Each individual element retains its status in the entirety of the colour-field.

For Lohse, this continual presence of all colours is important in order to retain their balance of energy in the painting. On the other hand we recall that Albers respects the individual colours of a group in as much that he repeats them in perceivable intervalls. Both painters combine their artistic concepts with more generalised ideas. They consider their works as prototypes for new orders of human society. But Albers and Lohse do not lay claim to the ideas of pure spirituality or the absolute as Kandinsky or Mondrian did. However, this indication will have to suffice at this stage.

Ellsworth Kelly provides the final position in my sketch. His work begins with the use of commercially available coloured paper which he cuts up into small rectangles and distributes on a prepared grid according to the aleatoric method (i.e. principle of chance). From the start of the work process there is no relevant meaning of these so-called main-colours. While Kelly takes the coloured scraps of paper out of a box and sticks them on, one after the other, he conjures a picture "out of a hat". The juxtaposed colours follow the principle of statistic probability.

The experiences gained in the *Spectrum*-series, 1951 are fundamental for Kelly. The random distribution is more difficult, if the picture is made up of a lesser amount of colour elements. Kelly chooses pieces (fragments) from former collages that do not allow the visual formation of groups or figures. As the

searching eye is unable to establish any definite relationships between the elements, the positions of the colour-locations remain independent.

The use of a separate canvas or table for each colour authenticates Kelly's respect for the individuality of each colour element. The visible junctures between the neighbouring units underline their individual value within the arrangement. Kelly's next step is logical. He hangs his colour-tableaux wide apart on a wall or places different colour forms in defined distances beside one-another on a neutral background. No one colour can noticeably influence another, neither in a beneficial nor in a depreciative sense. Each colour stands and speaks for itself.

Later Kelly produced coloured paper-pulp himself and pressed it onto a paper base in parallel strips. This new method expands the world of colour objects. Surface-colours and volume-colours undertake new tasks in the field of colour art. With their specific material properties colour objects retain a palpable reality, very much in contrast to the light-orientated appearance that Yves Klein cultivated in his "trinity" of blue, red and gold and that Dan Flavin puts to effective use in his neon tubes.

Here we are confronted with colour bodies that quite naturally claim their place and demand our physical reaction. They need a certain size but not exaggerated dimensions. Our physical relationship with an object is decisive. If we can comprehensively perceive it and allow it to make an impression upon us, then a smaller version would also be suitable for a similar effect. Compared with the stability that Kelly's wooden or steel sculptures convey, an insecure, swaying feeling often overcomes us when confronted with one of the colour object-forms. Their outlines are also highly specific. They originate from the character of their colour, envelop it and yield to it. Kelly's works have left far behind the assignation of yellow, red and blue to triangle, square and circle introduced by the Bauhaus.

During the preparation of this lecture, I came across Theodor Hetzer's studies of Titian's Colour. His analytical insight was helpful to me because it is not obtained from contemporary art. The investigation of Titian's historical influence reaches to the turn of the 18th century, the time when my contribution sets in. Many of Hetzer's conclusions could apply to the painters I have dealt with, Rothko for example and Kelly. Let us demonstrate this with a quotation.

Towards the end of his life, Titian concerns himself with the powers of attraction of individual colours. He now knows that relationships reduce their specific effects. I quote: "Each colour is present and existent for the observer in a form that was never experienced before, as each one . . . works unimpeded with its full power, appears unimpaired by any consideration to the composition, to any principle or system or by any standards of taste or beauty."[17]

This summons up my introductory sentence that addressed our divided consciousness: the wish to achieve harmonious relationships or uniform moods, has the consequence of considering all colours as equal. Yet this contradicts the illustrative certainty that each colour has a special character. But it is this individual expression in particular that must be repressed by a visually balanced and sensually pleasant connection. This paradox can further challenge the creativity of the painter, but makes it more difficult to explain and discuss the artistic result.

At this point I will finish my sketch. My interpretation has laid a loose net of short lines over an endless field of artistic achievements. I hope it will survive in the course of further discussions. Its open mesh allows anyone who is interested to delve deeper into the many different areas.

Translation by Joanne Windaus

Notes

1. ALEBERS, Josef (1965) Op Art and/or Perceptual Effects. In: Yale Scientific. New Haven, Conn., November 1965, p. 2.

2. HESS Walter (1981) Das Problem der Farbe in Selbstzeugnissen der Maler von Cézanne bis Mondrian. Mittenwald: Mäander Kunstverlag, p. 158.

3. Philipp Otto Runge in: SCHAWELKA, Karl (1993) Quasi una Musica. Untersuchungen zum Ideal des Musikalischen in der Malerei ab 1800. München: Mäander Verlag, p. 212.

4. RUNGE, Philipp Otto (1982) Briefe und Schriften, edited and commented by Peter Betthausen. Müncen: Verlag C.H. Beck, p. 206.

5. RUNGE, Philipp Otto, op. cit., p. 179.

6. RUNGE, Philipp Otto , op. cit., pp. 126/7.

7. VAN GOGH, Vincent, in: Riedel, Ingrid ((1983),1989) Farben. In: Religion, Gesellschaft, Kunst und Psychotherapie. Stuttgart: Kreuz Verlag, p. 94.

8. SCHAPIRO, Meyer (⁴1958) Van Gogh. Köln: DuMont Schauberg, p. 18.

9. ITTEN, Johannes ((1961), ⁵1975) Kunst der Farbe. Ravensburg: Otto Maier Verlag, p. 131.

10. ITTEN, Johannes, op. cit., p. 131.

11. VAN GOGH, Vincent, in: Riedel, Ingrid, op. cit., p. 91.

12. KANDINSKY Wassily (⁸1965) Über das Geistige in der Kunst. Bern: Benteli Verlag, pp. 117-120.

13. LA MOTTE-HABER, Helga de (1990) Musik und bildende Kunst. Von der Tonmalerei zur Klangskulptur. Laaber; and SCHAWELKA, Karl (1993) Quasi una Musica. Untersuchungen zum Ideal des "Musikalischen" in der Malerei ab 1800. München: Mäander Verlag.

14. ADORNO, Theodor W. (1967) Die Kunst und die Künste. In: Ohne Leitbild. Parva Aesthetica, Frankfurt/M: Suhrkamp Verlag, pp. 163/4.

15. ROTHKO, Mark, in: Claus, Jürgen (1965) Kunst heute. Personen, Analysen, Dokumente, Rowohlt (rde), Reinbek bei Hamburg, p. 70.

16. ROTHKO, MarK, in: Claus, Jürgen, op. cit., p. 72.

17. HETZER, Theodor ((1935) 1948) Tizian. Geschichte seiner Farbe. Frankfurt: Vittorio Klostermann, p. 174.

From Black to White — Fragments

Colour itself is a complex phenomenon and colour education consequently deals with a multitude of different aspects. Colour can be approached from a strictly scientific point of view or in a purely subjective or spiritual manner. In between there are, of course, all the possible combinations of the two approaches. As a painter I am naturally interested in colour in all its ambiguity, because just this ambiguity of colour is an essential part of my own work. Colour's universality on the one hand and its highly subjective nature on the other, define the limits of the area I have in my possession.

As a vehicle of personal expression, colour can hardly be taught as a separate subject, but instead as a part of the whole apparatus of artistic expression. A student in painting has to resolve his or her relationship to colour on a very personal level. It is, of course, obvious that in the early part of his studies he must be acquainted with everything that is objectively known about colour and its perception. In addition I think that this basic knowledge of perception and colour forms the only path to a complete use of this instrument as a means of personal expression. This is why I can only bring some highly subjective views on how colour as a concept is integrated into my own pictorial thinking.

These views necessarily form a very fragmented approach to our subject matter because finally colour is but one part of the complex instrument a painter has to deal with, and it is bound in multiple manners to other elements of his artistic thinking as a whole.

I have a painter friend who insists that his paintings should only be viewed in daylight. Now, this is rather difficult in wintertime, at least in Finland. This meant that the gallery where he showed his work, had to have all artificial lighting put off. This somewhat troubled the viewers since they could hardly distinguish the paintings they had come to see - or possibly buy. I very much like my friend's idea. Paintings, colours, should have the right to wake up, to stay awake and to go to sleep again with the sun. This is one way that black meets white in painting.

According to the Hebrew conception, light, though gathered up and concentrated in the heavenly bodies, is not confined to them. Day rises, not solely from the sun, but because the matter of light issues forth from its place and spreads over the earth, at night it withdraws, and the darkness comes forth from its place, each in a hidden, mysterious way. There is something resemblant in a child's constatation: "Sometimes when the sun gets up in the morning, he sees that the weather is bad, so he goes where it is good."

Plutarch (a Greek historian of about 45-125) says that light gives birth to objects and makes them visible, whereas the black colour seems to produce shade and the impression of depth... "Everything we see through black seems to be hollow. That is why painters, when they want to give an object a volume, paint it white; when they want to achieve the effect of hollowness or depth, they paint it black." These few examples give us a glimpse of how differently light and darkness, white and black have been understood in the past or in the innocent consciousness of a little child, which, I think, is the same thing, since the history of mankind is somehow written in every human being.

Rudolf Arnheim points out that the existence of brightness and colour values belonging to the object itself is purely psychological. It seems that a medium value or common denominator of the various values exhibited by the object assumes that role. This concept is reflected in pictorial practice - found for example in medieval painting - of giving objects a uniform local colour and brightness, to which darkness is applied on one hand, and the

110 whiteness of the highlights on the other. Only the technique of the impressionists in the nineteenth century radically ignored the perceptual distinction of object values and illumination values by presenting any surface as a sequence of graded nuances and leaving to the eye the task of separating the properties of the object from those of illumination.

The symbolism of light probably goes as far back as the history of man. In perception darkness does not appear as the absence of light, but is an active counter-principle. The dualism of the two antagonistic powers is found in the mythology and philosophy of many cultures. Day and night become the visual image of good and evil. Black and white. Between these counterparts, or should we say extremes, is expressed the whole human condition. Black reposes on the basis of our consciousness as a kind of original, mythical beginning. A hindmost preposition of our existence and, as a matter of fact, its final goal. On the other hand black and white may have more subjective and detailed elements in our subconsciousness.

Just after the war at school, since - for understandable reasons - no new history or geography books were yet available we had to cover up or blacken with pencil all the passages that referred to the time before the war. History and geography had changed and I was troubled by what secrets lay under those beautiful graphite covered layers.

The black of coal belongs also to my childhood memories, and has since become an important part of my vocabulary. White symbolizes among other things virginity, purity. It tends to an other absolute, to a point where everything is in its right place, where absolute harmony reigns. Somehow the white of bone has always fascinated me. I do not, however, recall what kind of childhood experience could be behind this fascination, but on a more general level bone is associated with perishableness, again a reminder of the human condition.

Altogether, black and white represent the absolute limits of our visual perception, extremes between which stretches, not only what we see, but also our possibility to reach or at least seek that which is transcendent, above all categories. To my mind, this is the purpose of art.

In these northern latitudes the climate, the seasons have a particular sense and effect on the psyche of an individual. I felt and understood the importance of this inbuilt mechanism after having lived in very different climatic circumstances for a rather long time. I found out that this basic psychological structure could not be ignored. Here in the north the seasons are deeply connected to what colour as both perception and sensation means to us. To begin with summer, the luminous nights, abundant vegetation, then autumn with its blast of colours, that then are chased by the gloomy darkening nights, and shortening of the days. Finally the death of nature, the days becoming just a gray stripe in the horizon.

Then one morning you wake up and the snow has fallen during the night, commiserating the strangling darkness of nature with its luminous whiteness. The snow in winter and the increasing daylight create an almost unbearable lightness that then triumphally guides you to the spring with its wakening of colours. Summer again with its nightless nights.

This sounded as if it were taken from a tourist guide! Nevertheless, all this has a lot to do with how one relates to colour, both by exterior stimulus and inner response. As a matter of fact our sensation of colour is profoundly bound to the climate and its lighting conditions. This way colours become subconscious or archetypal concept. Anyway, this brings us to the complex question of the relativity of colour.

I remember an exhibition of 19th century landscapes in Paris. A catastrophe! How different the light of these paintings was from the light and colour that acted upon you in the Île-de-France, the cradle of impressionism! I just thought that these paintings were in the wrong place. They should have stayed home, bathed in the light of their place of birth.

In Matisse's line drawings the sensation of colour is present in the form of a tension he creates by the exactitude of his composition thus achieving warm and cool hues. Reinhart in his black paintings creates reds, blues, greens and so on by juxtaposing hues that separately taken we would call black, but seen side by side, give us the sensation of colours. These are startling examples of what Albers calls interaction of colour.

Huxley describes in *Heaven and Hell*, that the experience of seeing the stained glass windows in a medieval church possibly caused the people of that time hallucinatory experiences of the kind that in our days can be produced by strong drugs. People in those days scarcely had, with the exception of the sun, other sources of light than candles and torches. These few examples show that colour is relative in a somewhat broader sense than, for example, Albers thought. A painter has to consider the relativity, of not only colour, but of perception in general. Maybe a little the same way as Heisenberg considered it in nuclear physics.

Perception is not something independent from what is perceived, but affects it. Our capacity and sensitivity to perceive colours certainly alternates according to the stimulus available. I am thinking here of television or computer produced colours,

etc. Also signs and their colour symbols are a part of how we see and experience colours. In traffic lights or other communication systems red means "danger", "beware", "stop" or something similar. During the cultural revolution in China the colours of traffic lights were changed so that red meant: "go". We tend to think colours more and more as signs instead of sensations of experiences.

However, and despite of the many examples of colour's relativity, I tend to think that there is something constant in how we exerience colours. I think that colour should be regarded as something that still has its basic meaning in our subsciousness by the original perceptions about how nature works and acts upon us. Are the crops ready to be harvested, is it going to rain and innumerable other observations that man had and has to attentively make in order to survive.

Colour as a spiritual phenomenon has its roots much deeper in the human mind than it may now seem. And there is a common level of colour experience that is anchored in our collective memory. This could be based on our relationship with nature which has not altered essentially in the course of the history of mankind. Another painter friend of mine expressed this relationship to nature like this: "I catch myself observing flowers. Flowers that grow over the labyrinth of duties, inhibitions and enigmas. As if they remembered better than is convenable for human being, their ecstasy is more than the awakest, five senses could provide. I do not know what is sacred and what dedicates but I see how on corollas of these flowers, flowers that once again push me forwards, a divine functionality and entireness spreads."

Wundt's, Oswald's, Munsell's or others' attempts to build up a coherent, harmonious system of colours that could function the same way as the theory of musical harmony, has not worked out. The reason for this is that the formulation of a scientific theory of colour, which at first led to such aberrations as pointillism, has not had a permanent effect on artistic practice - the artist has discovered by now that he must rely on his sensibility and not attempt to particularize from laws of aesthetic effect.

I think that the conformities in music are so bound to cultural conventions and the history of music, that it is almost impossible to imagine something corresponding in painting. Every epoch creates its own conventions and preferences. These could be understood as some kind of doctrines of harmony of colour in the pictorial arts. I do not think however, that these doctrines or traditions can be approached from a theoretical point of view. But all these attempts to achieve a theory or system of colour harmony are in their own conceptual way beautiful, independent of their theoretical value.

Arnold Schönberg said that in music harmony is not a straight jacket, because harmony is, as a matter, of fact limited to each mood. Here we must observe that Schönberg's affirmations are made against a very solid and established musical praxis. This would be impossible in the field of the visual arts because of the lack of that kind of a solid base.

On the other hand, the similarities of colours and sounds have been studied without tending to an overall theory. For instance Kandinsky in his descriptions of the character of different colours and other factors of visual thinking, often used musical terms and Scrjabin tried to combine colours in a representation of one of his musical compositions. In fact, Kepler already stated that to find the true relationship of sensations is to unveil the similarity of these sensations in the realm of senses, to recognise it and bring it to light, with a definite primary notion of pure

harmony which rests deep in the soul of man. And Plotinus: "Beauty is the diversity tamed by the sense of unity".

Let us go back to colours. There cannot be a pattern that represents nothing. Any shape or colour has expression: it carries a mood, shows the behavior of forces, and thus depicts something universal by its individual appearance. We find numerous descriptions of the characteristics of colour for example from Goethe and Kandinsky. Goethe thinks that pure red has a high dignity and seriousness, because, according to his belief, it unites all other colours in itself. He called pure yellow "gay and softly charming" and blue "a charming nothing", empty and cold, conveying a contradictory sensation of stimulation and repose.

Kandinsky describes red like this: " Of course every colour can be warm or cold, but nowhere is this contrast as strong as in red. It glows in itself and does not radiate much vigor outworldly, achieving a manly maturity, a relentlessly glowing passion, a solid power in itself." Dark blue "sinks into the deep seriousness of all things, where there is no end", the lightest blue "achieves a silent repose" and "green is the most restful colour in existence, moves in no direction, has no corresponding appeal, such as joy, sorrow or passion, demands nothing". Green's passivity reminds him of "a fat, healthy, immovably resting cow, capable of eternal rumination, while dull bovine eyes gaze forth vacantly into the world."

The same kind of descriptions are found in the field of music. Kandinsky thought that especially music and painting had a profound connection. He also thought that Goethe meant something like that when he said that painting should also have its "basso continuo".

Kandisky imagined, in 1912, that it would really be possible to build a language of shapes and colours, a painting as a pure composition. An aim that Victor Vasarely much later claimed to have achieved in his "Planetary Folklore". Now we know that even if a far reaching part of the painting of our century was based on this kind of idea, this basis was only a marginal part of the complicated entirety that the art of painting of our century forms. This idea of "pure" colour as a basis of theory of painting has come back later in completely other forms, in conceptual art for instance.

Colour, form and content remain in the heart of this debate. I would like to conclude with a citation of Wolfgang Köhler: "When I see a green object, I can immeditely say the colour's name. I also know that the green colour is used to guide traffic, that it is the colour of hope. This does not mean, however, that the green colour itself could be deduced from this knowledge. I know that green as an independently existing sensorial fact, has obtained secondary significations and I am ready to admit the practical advantages of these achieved significations. The psychology of form also sustains in the same way the view that sensorial units have done a name, have become richly symbolic and have been given certain practical tasks, which does not prevent them from existing as such units before all these by-significations connected to them".

I sincerely think that painting deals with these kinds of units. We can reach the universal only by personal, subjective experience. The otherside, the transcendental on the other hand, cannot directly be expressed. There are no sacred colours and we can only express the invisible in visible form and the everlasting by perishable means.

The power of painting is not in its capacity to communicate exact messages, but in the fact that it gets in action a multidimensional movement in the conciousness of the spectator. For a painter colour means more than just an instrument. It has for him a trancendental value as well. Colour reaches deeper layers of our consciousness than a mere constatation.

A colour as an idea is a concept, whereas observed it becomes a prisoner of other colours. As Gauguin puts it: "Since colour itself is enigmatic in the sensations it causes in us, it cannot be used but enigmatically." Or Cezanne: "I try to communicate that which is the most enigmatic, that clings to the roots of existence, it can be found from the immaterial source of sensation." Anyway, colour as a phenomenon is so totally bound to our memory and experiences, that it is difficult to understand it as a separate element in the human psyche. All this is present in a painter's mind, consciously or subconsciously. Monet thought that he failed in attempting to capture light with colour on canvas (the series of paintings of the cathedral of Rouen) This shows the humility that a painter has towards light, that absolute. Absolute without which there is no colour. What then would be light without colours it generates? Probably something as absolute as is absolute black, darkness.

Things were not that complicated in Gian-Paolo Lomazzo's time, in the 16th century. In his book *Traité sur l'Art de la Peinture*, he says: "Colours in regard to one an other are friends or enemies. Because colours have a different character between them, they create a different impression in the spectator...Never put two beautiful colours next to each other, but put a dull one next to a bright one, in such a manner that they accentuate each other..."

David Burton

The Synchromist Theory of Color

The first decade of the twentieth century witnessed many extraordinary innovations in art, including the invention of several remarkable abstract and non-objective styles. Kandinsky, Matisse, Picasso, Delauney and others abandoned traditional pictorial representation in favor of abstractions that retained only slight allusions to real objects. In short order, even these minimal objective references were sublimated into non-objective amalgams of shape and color. Often, however, giving up the objective meant seizing upon the subjective. These great innovators looked deep within themselves to their own unique emotional and subconscious wellsprings for guidance and inspiration.

While we as educators can understand and encourage these subjective sources, it is very difficult to teach them. We cannot recreate the inner being of a Kandinsky or a Matisse that will in turn allow our students to produce a comparable work of art. To a large degree, their innovative *methods* remain hidden from us.

In that formative first decade of the century, two American artists, Morgan Russell and Stanton MacDonald-Wright developed an innovative approach to painting which they called "Synchromism". "Synchromism" sought no less than to resolve the paradox of creating three-dimensional form on a two-dimensional picture plane *entirely through the use of color.*

For us as educators, synchromism offers a particular advantage. It describes a fairly simple method which can help students construct color harmonies and use them effectively, particularly in abstract works of art. This enables students to produce complex color compositions based on rational choices while avoiding arbitrary guessing about what colors should go together.

Historical Background

Morgan Russell and Stanton MacDonald-Wright were both expatriate American artists when they met in Paris. Russell had been studying sculpture with Henri Matisse; MacDonald-Wright had attended the Sorbonne and several private academies. In 1911 they struck up a collaborative friendship and began studying color theory together under Percyval Tudor-Hart, who had worked out an elaborate analogy between color and music. Russell and MacDonald-Wright, both deeply interested in music, were immediately drawn to Tudor-Hart's theory. It would continue to influence them for years to come.

During this period, Russell and MacDonald-Wright also closely studied Chevreul's theories of simultaneous contrast, the optical theories of Helmholtz, and the color theories of Charles Blanc, Ogden Rood and Georges Seurat. Barbara Rose tells us, "From Chevreul they learned that adjacent complementary colors influence one another— when used in large areas, the colors are intensified and when used in small areas, they are blended by the eye into a neutral tone. From Rood they learned that the spectrum could be divided into harmonizing pairs and triads of colors which, corresponding to the dominant chord in music, could provide a tonal 'key' for a painting." (Rose, p. 91).

Both Russell and MacDonald-Wright were also greatly influenced by the Impressionist and Post-Impressionist artists. Cezanne held the pinnacle position in their artistic pantheon. MacDonald-Wright had bought four Cezanne watercolors when he arrived in Paris. Morgan Russell had borrowed a small Cezanne still life of apples from Leo Stein, and copied it several times. Russell credited Cezanne with helping him to discover "what was rhythm in color. It could be nothing other than the play of light and shadows. . . warm and cold light". (Levin, p.

12). It was Cezanne's interpretation of form as color that intrigued them and spurred them toward Synchromism.

Soon after their meeting in 1911, Russell and MacDonald-Wright began to develop an abstract approach to painting form. They started with the premise that form is intrinsically a three-dimensional property and cannot legitimately be represented in a two-dimensional medium, even through the illusionistic modeling of light and shadow. In a letter written to Andrew Dasburg in 1910, Morgan Russell had already asserted that "a painting should be a flat presentation of light and in this way will one preserve the flatness of the canvas and convey the sensations of mass and solidity." (Levin, p. 12). MacDonald-Wright and Russell held that pure *color* does in fact possess certain spatial qualities, notably the then-innovative idea that cool colors appear to recede away from the viewer and warm colors seem to advance.

Rousseau observes that "MacDonald-Wright and Russell were the only artists using such color juxtapositions (one strong primary against another); their use of color was very individual, even unique at the time." (Rousseau, p. 44), They reasoned that by precisely arranging planes of pure, strong color on the picture plane, they could create the impression of a truely tactile and spatial form, and thereby resolve the plane-space paradox."They rejected representational form altogether: the illusion of volumes was to be brought about only through the interrelation of colors (which were never to be isolated by an outline) or through modeling by the manipulation of lights and darks." (Davidson, p. 136). In this way, they "abstracted" Cezanne, raising his interpretation of color and form to a pure state, free of the object.

Willard Huntington Wright, Stanton's brother and a prominent contemporary art critic, wrote, "Their individual interpretation of Cezanne, however, little by little, showed them the method by which they might eventually open the door by their desires. Russell approached form through light, combining both qualities in a simultaneous vision. MacDonald-Wright approached light through form, regarding them as an inseparable and inevitable unity. Both painters expressed their vision in the purest gamut of colour which painting up to that time had seen. Colour with them became the totality of art, the one element by which every quality of a canvas was to be expressed. Even their lines were obtained by the differentiation of colours in the same way that tempo delimits sound." (Wright, p. 286).

In rejecting objective form, however, they also made the traditional principles of pictorial composition obsolete. Forced to invent a new way to deal with the picture plane, Russell and MacDonald-Wright conceived a theory of color harmonies based on an analogy between color and music. They came to this analogy naturally, both being as deeply devoted to music as to art. In a letter to Alfred Steiglitz in 1920, MacDonald-Wright pointed out "that he had studied music and its construction as extensively as as he had studied painting." (Levin, p. 47). At one time, Morgan Russell had considered conducting music as a career. Levin notes, "Russell adored music, particularly Beethoven's, and often studied a Beethoven score while working out color harmonies." (p. 44). Russell reportedly "used to sit with MacDonald-Wright when the two were in Paris in the early teens, listening to Beethoven and both painting compositions inspired by the music. . . . Russell's intent was to duplicate in his paintings the emotional intensity— the power and reverberation— of Beethoven's symphonies." (Kushner, p. 135).

116   The analogy between color and music did not originate with the Synchromists. Indeed, it boasts an ancient history. Aristotle suggested that the same ideal mathematical proportions underlie harmony in both color and music. Newton chose seven colors for his color wheel in order to correspond to the seven notes of the diatonic musical scale. Many artists throughout history have contrived various relationships between color and music. Most of these analogies make a simple, one-for-one match between a color and a corresponding musical note. Unfortunately, these analogies break down very quickly because the complexities of music quickly outstrip the simplicity of the analogy— until the invention of Synchromism.

Russell and MacDonald-Wright seized upon the music-color theories of their teacher, Percyval Tudor-Hart, who professed "a musical system of color harmony based on a purely psychological rather than physical group of equivalents." (Levin, p. 14). Tudor-Hart's color harmonies aimed at achieving *perceived* relationships rather than simply aligning the color spectrum with a musical scale. Tudor-Hart taught that "the twelve chromatic intervals of the musical octave . . . have corresponding sensational and emotional qualities to those of the twelve chromatic colors." (Klein, p. 102-3). However, Tudor-Hart's theories involved complex mathematical relationships rather than the intuitive instincts of a musician. He equated tone in sound to hue in color, pitch with luminousity, and sound intensity with color saturation. Such direct, almost literal, correspondences made for an interesting intellectual exercise but proved awkward in actual artistic practice. The Synchromists quickly moved beyond Tudor-Hart's formulaic restrictions.

The Synchromist Theory of Color

Artists of every generation reinvent new analogies between color and music. Typically, as Tudor-Hart had done, a color is assigned to each musical note, for example, red for *do*, orange for *re*, yellow for *mi*, and so on up the octave. Then, presumably, color "melodies" can be composed. However, the linear, temporal structure of music generally does not translate in any meaningful way into the simultaneous, spatial structure of art. The analogy quickly peters out.

The Synchromist theory of color begins with a standard twelve-color wheel, Yellow, Yellow-Green, Green, Blue-Green, Blue, Blue-Violet, Violet, Red-Violet, Red, Red-Orange, Orange, Yellow-Orange, and back to Yellow. It is then encircled by a musical scale of twelve tones arranged in a wheel, C, C#, D, D#, E, F, F# G ,G#, A, A#, B, returning back to C (of the next octave). The two concentric wheels are free to rotate within one another so that a variety of "keys" are possible.

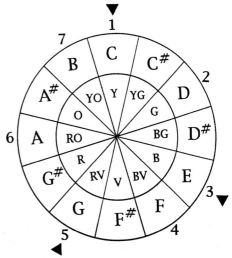

Figure 1: Tonic Chord in C Major

In music, combinations of harmonious notes, or chords, are formed by selecting notes separated by certain intervals. The key concept of the Synchromist color theory seized upon this idea. According to MacDonald-Wright, "The interval between the notes is the important thing." (p. 81) (He describes the natural notes, C, D, E, F, A, B of the musical scale as "degrees"). A tonic chord is made from the first, third and fifth degrees, or C, E and G. On the twelve-color wheel, the corresponding colors would be the first, fifth and eighth colors. Therefore, if yellow is the tonic color (corresponding to the first degree, note C), blue and red-violet, the fifth and eighth colors, make up the other two harmonious colors in this color chord, corresponding to E and G, the third and fifth degree notes.

Such a color chord comes very close to a color triad (the first, fifth and *ninth* colors). In his book, *Modern Chromatics*, Ogden Rood advocated color triads and near-triads as the most harmonious color combinations. (*Modern Chromatics* was a major influence on the European avant garde painters at that time, and MacDonald-Wright and Russell had studied it intently.) MacDonald-Wright points out in his *Treatise on Color* that the perfect balance of a triad is static and would cause a composition to stand still. (p. 84). As in music, a slight imbalance is needed to *progress* to the next chord, and to the next, and so on. The near-triads seemed prophetic to the Synchromists because they suggested a way to progress from color to color, and therefore, to construct a complete color composition. MacDonald-Wright, p. 90-91).

MacDonald-Wright describes two other color harmonies, both with the same interval spacing as the tonic chord. The second color harmony is the "dominant fifth" chord. Its first note rests on the fifth degree note or G. Progressing around the wheel, the intervals needed to make a chord are the seventh degree (B)

and the second degree (D). Staying in the yellow key, the resulting tonic chord, G B D, produces a red-violet, yellow-orange and green color harmony.

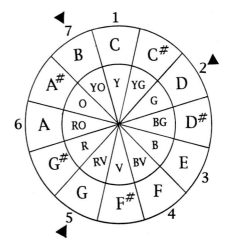

Figure 2: Dominant Fifth Chord in C Major

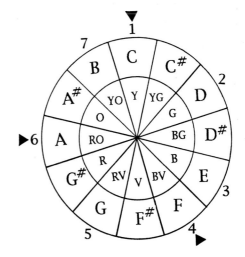

Figure 3: Subdominant Fourth Chord in C Major

MacDonald-Wright gives another color harmony based on the subdominant fourth degree. Remaining in the same yellow key, the musical chord starts on the fourth degree note, F, and progresses to A and C. The resulting color harmony is blue-violet, red-orange and yellow.

MacDonald-Wright also describes the harmonic minor key. Davidson observes, "As in music, minor chords could be formed that had a subtle air of sadness or unresolvedness. Thus colors, too, had certain emotional values." (Davidson, p. 136). In the minor scale, the notes progress C, D, E-flat, E, F, G, A-flat and B-flat. The middle degree in each chord is flatted, shifting it back one note (and one color). In this case, the minor tonic chord is C, E-flat, G, which in the yellow key, results in a yellow, blue-green and red-violet color harmony. The dominant fifth chord is G, B-flat, D, producing red-violet, orange and green as its color harmony. The subdominant fourth chord is F, A-flat, B, giving as its color harmony, blue-violet, red and yellow-orange.

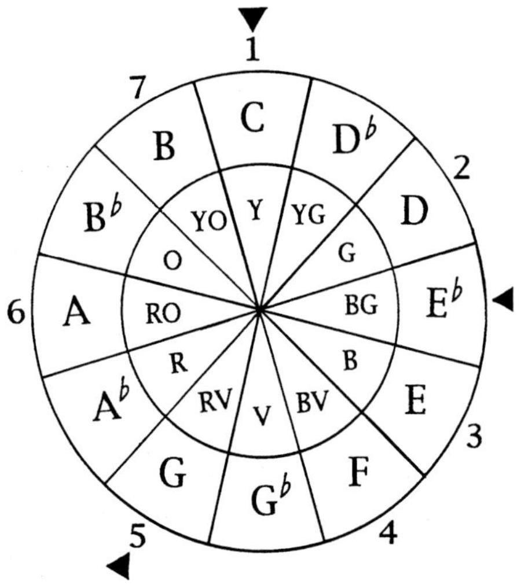

Figure 4: Tonic Chord in Harmonic C Minor

If the order of colors is reversed so that they move counter-clockwise (Y, YO, O. . .), the minor color harmonies are the same as the major color harmonies based on a clockwise color wheel (Y, YG, G. . .). That is to say, on the color wheel, the major and the minor color harmony chords are mirror reflections of one another.

The advantage of using color "chords" is not only in the selection of harmonious color combinations but in their progression. Just as a musician can construct a melody by making a harmonious progression of chord changes, an artist can progress through a painting composition from color "chord" to color "chord". Any color can be picked as the "tonic color" and it will produce logical and harmonious color "chords".

With regard to composition, MacDonald-Wright urged that the tonic chord be used for the main subject, the dominant fifth chord for the surrounding areas, and the sub-dominant fourth chord for subtle accents. "To utilize these chords correctly and for their greatest effect," he pointed out, "the colors which form them should be brought into close juxtaposition. For instance at a distance where the picture is seen only as several large masses, the tonic chord should be evident. Coming closer, the dominant (fifth chord) becomes plainer and at about the correct distance for viewing the canvas, the chord of the fourth should also make itself felt." (MacDonald-Wright, p. 95).

Although they shared the same artistic goals, MacDonald-Wright and Russell each developed their own unique painting style. Morgan Russell had studied sculpture with Henri Matisse, and he retained an architectonic solidity and mass in his paintings. They exhibit dense, opaque facets of bold colors and thick texture. Russell was particularly concerned that Synchromist painting possess a tactile quality.

Stanton MacDonald-Wright, on the other hand, developed an ethereal, feathery technique which blends colors imperceptably into one another, as light might reflect across a curved, shimmering surface. White played a prominent role in his work. Curiously, he compared white to the blending of all sounds played together, perhaps recalling that all the wavelengths of color blend into white light. He considered black to be akin to the silence between musical notes. (MacDonald-Wright, p. 98). Nevertheless, he described in detail the need to adjust the values of colors so that a composition would be balanced in tonality as well as chromatically.

MacDonald-Wright's subtle chromatic gradations presented a technical problem for him. When complementary colors are mixed together, they inevitably neutralize each other into a nondescript gray. To circumvent this dulling of opposed colors, MacDonald-Wright filled the area between them with a series of intermediate hues to produce a rainbow-like iridescence. He described this technique using the musical term *liason* (sic), defining it as "that element that stands approximately halfway between the extremes" (p. 99). *Liaison* is similar to the Renaissance painting technique *cangiante*, in which a succession of related colors produces a similar brilliant, iridescent effect.

Conclusion

For art educators, Synchromism provides a provocative method to pique the interest of students and stretch their imaginations. Musical chords provide a simple mechanism for generating color harmonies, and an immediate way to "test" unfamiliar color combinations— simply sound them out on an instrument. The harmonic quality of musical chords is instantly apparent, and can easily be translated into color harmonies that maximize contrast through near-triadic color combinations.

Perhaps as important as the color harmonies themselves is Synchromism's ability to compose with color, to extend color throughout a composition in a convincing, reasoned manner. Morgan Russell began his paintings from what he called "points of support", two or three focal points where the tonic color contrasts were most intense. (Levin, p. 24). He then proceeded outward, often joining his faceted planes into one or two sweeping curves that comprise the whole composition. Changes in tonality or in color harmonies allowed him to modulate the surface across the entire picture plane.

While the tonic, dominant and subdominant chords provide a coherent color scheme for a painting, they do not restrict the palette to a few colors. Rather, they direct the student's choice of colors. One color will suggest other colors that lead to harmonious color "chords". Two colors will point toward a third that will keep the color "chord" in the same color key. MacDonald-Wright encouraged artists *before beginning a painting* to work out several "octaves" in a given color key by adjusting their values and intensities. He also suggested finding the color harmonies for all seven notes of the scale in a particular color key. (MacDonald-Wright, p. 89). In this way, one is prepared to "play" each color "chord" as the opportunity arises in the composition. This encourages students to think in terms of color "chords" and overall color harmony rather than focusing on isolated or local colors.

A Post-Script

Synchromism was a short-lived movement. The active collaboration between Russell and MacDonald-Wright lasted less that three years, from 1911 until the outbreak of World War I in 1914 when MacDonald-Wright left Paris to live in London. Although they continued to correspond for many years, each artist began to drift away from Synchromism. After the war, Morgan Russell fell into a depression which greatly reduced his artistic production. He explained years later that after the war the spirit of radical experiment among the European avant-garde artists gave way to a more social and political conservatism in art. (Kushner, p. 144.) His own art eventually evolved into figurative works painted in a quasi-classical style.

MacDonald-Wright moved to New York in 1916, and then back to his native California in 1919. By 1920, he had also reverted to painting figurative works in a realistic style. He became interested in Oriental religion and Oriental art, and supported himself through teaching and technical work in the film industry. In the 1950's he returned to Synchromism and painted in that style again for several years.

As short-lived as Synchromism was, it had a significant influence on expatriate-artists living in Paris and on artists in New York (where MacDonald-Wright and Russell had several shows) in the first two decades of this century. Among the artists who embraced Synchromism were Thomas Hart Benton, Marsden Hartley, Andrew Dasburg, Morton L. Schamburg, Stuart Davis, Joseph Stella and Max Weber. All of them eventually developed their own unique styles, but each owed a significant debt to the lessons learned from Synchromism early in their careers.

References

DAVIDSON, Abraham A. (1974) The Story of American Painting. New York: Abrams.

KLEIN, Adrian Bernard (1930) Colour Music: The Art of Light. London: Crosby Lockwood & Son.

KUSHNER, Marilyn S. (1990) Morgan Russell. New York: Hudson Hills Press.

LEVIN, Gail (1978) Synchromism and American Color Abstraction, 1910-1925. New York: George Braziller/Whitney Museum of American Art.

MACDONALD-WRIGHT, Stanton (1967) The Art of Stanton MacDonald-Wright, and A Treatise on Color. Washington, D.C.: National Collection of Fine Arts, Smithsonian Press.

ROSE, Barbara (1967) American Art Since 1900: A Critical History. New York: Praeger.

ROUSSEAU, Kathy Brooks (1989) The Influence of Kandinsky and Synchromism on the Work of Georgia O'Keefe. Virginia Commonwealth University. Unpublished thesis.

ROOD, Ogden (1973) Modern Chromatics. New York: Van Nostrand Reinhold.

WRIGHT, Willard Huntington (1915) Modern Painting: Its Tendency and Meaning. New York: John Lane Co.

Wade S. Thompson

Color, Light and Temperature
A General Studies Component for Preparing Students for Fine Arts Painting

During the last several decades of teaching art and design courses within a public university setting, I have been involved in teaching and developing color courses for a wide variety of students. These color courses are most often located within the core curriculum or foundation studies sequence of courses in which students are required to enroll early within their undergraduate degree program. My experiences over the years have revealed a wide range of expectations within the content of the color course on behalf of both student and faculty members.

The attitudes towards color education and its relative importance within a visual arts program have changed, fortunately, towards the positive end. There seemed to me to be a period of time (specifically the 1960's and early 1970's) when color courses were often taught by reluctant faculty painters who were children of the abstract expressionist movement and had not themselves been trained specifically in color. Color for those faculty members was something based too heavily on chance and had it not been for the influence of Albers [1] and Itten [2], I suspect there may have been very little common ground at all amongst university color education courses. Albers and Itten did help to establish a dialog and "base line" reference that is commonly referred to by many current color educators within art and design programs.

Graphic design and digital imaging programs have become increasingly popular amongst students pursuing undergraduate degrees in the visual arts. Our world of information, based technology has initiated curricular changes within visual arts programs and has influenced the foundation and general studies components within many universities. Visual problem solving skills are often taught through the eyes of the designer and, I believe, often alienate the student pursuing avenues geared towards the fine arts. Ideally, the information and experiences presented in a foundation level color course would provide a common conceptual and experiential basis applicable to students pursuing most careers available within the visual arts. Realistically, however, I have found that this is not always the case. It seems that the parameters which are often established within the general studies color course are too restrictive to the painter; the design student is accustomed to working within established limitations which are inherent within the process of graphic communications, the painter much less so.

Many painting students intuitively reject classroom assignments which are in any media other than pigment and too often the information which is presented is abandoned and forgotten by the time they become involved in other studio arts classes. Within my role as a practicing painter and teacher, I have sought to develop within my color courses a sequence of practical exercises and assignments which more readily provide a visual springboard not only for those students pursuing design careers, but the painters as well. I have found that a sequence of exercises oriented towards developing perceptual sensitivity towards color through direct observation is often the most successful route for the painter to take. It is only a means to an end, however, and is meant to establish that previously mentioned springboard towards a personalized color manipulation.

Color, Light and Temperature

Students are often unaware of their own inherent ability to perceive a wide range of color variations within their own visual environment. Indeed, color students within their formative stages of development can be amazingly limited in their ability to categorize and make verbal notations of everyday fluctuations of color and light. Through disciplined observation of light and color in our natural world, the depth of their perceptual skills is increased. Within these formative stages, then, a structured sequence of problems which provide the necessary tools for analyzing and categorizing light and color into the two-dimensional format shall be discussed and presented.

The transformation of impressions of light and color into pigment or colored paper images can be accelerated and clarified through the application of contrasts of temperature. I define visual temperature essentially as the cold-warm sensation of particular hues as they relate one to another. I accept the overall notion of the expressive power of cold-warm hue contrast as exemplified by Itten [3], yet I reject any attempts to formulize or particularize these contrasts or sensations of temperature within overly rigid doctrine. The cold-warm response is largely a subjective one full of numerous influences which, from the creative standpoint, make it all the more useful and meaningful for the artist.

Therefore, color and light responses which are channeled through contrasts of temperature provide the formative artist/designer a means for not only creating color and light within an image, but also assist in attempts to structure form and space illusions within the image's picture plane. Unlike the color palette used by French Impressionist Monet in many of his landscape paintings in which light-dark contrast is subordinate to cold-warm, the student assignments to be discussed attempt to integrate hue, value (light-dark) and temperature contrasts. Additionally, all the assignments demand a holistic manipulation and organization of the elements within the image format which re-asserts issues of color relativity expressed by Albers.

Although the structured exercises presented are driven by specific goals related to temperature, the final choices are arrived at through trial, error and observation. Constant re-evaluation is demanded by the process whether executed in pigment or colored paper. The assignments are presented as an ongoing exploration, which, even within their constraints, allow for personal choices. Another important factor which adds to the value of utilizing temperature contrasts within image making based on observation is that it helps the students understand the difference between descriptive and interpretive color. Descriptive color within observation is concerned with recording local color (a red apple is articulated with pigment as being red, with tonal changes usually derived by adding white and/or black), whereas the interpretive use of color (such as allowing temperature contrast to override the local) fosters a much greater range of creative color choices.

The General Studies Component: A Sequence of Assignments

The sequence of assignments which shall now be discussed represent a final component of an entire series of color problems presented in a general studies color course. It must be made clear that although temperature contrasts and observed responses to color and light were a major emphasis within these particular exercises, one cannot disassociate other issues of color relatedness which combine to form an overall working knowledge and sensitivity towards color.

The first exercises within this series of student projects emphasize contrasts of temperature which work to create an illusionistic progression of space. These exercises are executed in cut colored paper mounted to illustration board with an image size of approximately six by eight inches. These are short duration exercises composed of horizontal bands of cut paper strips which require several days of classroom studio sessions to complete. One of the dominant color contrasts used to manipulate space is cool-warm, yet also involved are contrasts of scale and saturation. The color relationships utilized are not unlike those applied in traditional atmospheric or aerial perspective painting techniques [4]. However, the images are totally invented color progressions and not based (at this point) on observation.

Cool to warm contrasts are not predetermined in the sense of "warm advances and cool recedes." This relationship is often reversed and works as successfully when the cooler hues are placed within the foreground register of the picture plane. Whether a particular hue within a composition actually "feels" warmer or cooler relative to its neighboring hues can often initiate lively discussions amongst the students within classroom critiques. It begins to reveal to the students the subjective aspect of this particular response to color and substantiates color relatedness as an on-going process and discovery. In order for these spatial exercises to be successful, a number of inter-related visual components must be in action. Alternating light-dark contrasts must be combined with diminishing levels of hue, saturation and scale. Contrasts of temperature are embedded within all of the above.

An expansion of this exploration of invented space utilizing color and temperature relationships is continued within the next student assignment which is executed in acrylic pigment on illustration board measuring 9 x 12 or 10 x 10 inches. These are larger in scale than the preceding exercises and introduce volumetric form as an additional compositional device. Progressions of scale, temperature and saturation levels are combined with overlapping of volumetric solids as they progress into the picture plane. An acrylic on canvas diptych created by the author is used in the classroom to further illustrate and elucidate spatial progressions created, in part, by the progressive layerings of volumetric forms and temperature contrasts. The painting also

utilizes progressive layers of transparent and translucent films of color as a means for manipulating space.

The next classroom assignment provides an introduction to optical color mixing through problems assigned, again, in acrylic on illustration board with an image size of 10 x 10 or 9 x 12 inches. The objective in these assignments is to create a "push/pull" into the picture plane surface through contrasts of temperature, light-dark value and hue saturation levels. Additionally, another important component is optical color mixing which (from the appropriate visual distance) creates visual integrations of color which are determined through alternating patterns of hues. Since all of these contrasts of color must be obtained through visual mixtures and not actual physical mixtures of colorants, the images created by the students are very much process oriented. The final images are the products of a sequence of trial, error and adjustment and progress through numerous alterations and changes. Nineteenth century French Pointillist Georges Seurat and contemporary American painter Chuck Close are often used as a visual source which students can use as they develop their own particular methodology for creating optical mixtures of color.

The perceptual analysis of light and its inherent effect on surface color are next explored through a series of studies based directly on observation. The initial assignments within this series are executed in colored paper mounted to board. The immediate goal within the paper exercises is to "capture" the essence of light and color as observed within a particular quality of light and influenced by light source. Some of the light sources are natural and some are artificial. The advantage of utilizing colored paper as a means for perceptual analysis from an observed source is that description must be overridden by interpretation. The limited range of hue variations available within commercial color paper assortments forces the student to categorize observed data into color relationships of temperature and light-dark contrast. Attempts to duplicate local color in any precise manner are futile and forces the student to manipulate color as a relative force in which to build and establish light and color impressions. The fine arts student oriented towards painting takes the initial steps towards establishing a working visual color vocabulary.

The previous preparatory assignments in colored paper based on observation now lead into a new series of studies in pigment which become increasingly more specific in their goal to establish a vision of color and light. Figure 28 (page 99) presents an image based on an observed interior space within a classroom studio arts building. The students have been instructed to utilize their preceding experiences related to color, light and temperature and, within this assignment, to select an isolated part of a room within the interior structure of the building in order to establish a particular, if not momentary, response to observed color and light. The compositions are meant to reflect and communicate particular qualities of various light-color situations. Some compositions reflect interior spaces influenced by artificial light; some reflect the influence of natural light as it enters the interior environment.

The actual surface color of the interior spaces within the classroom building which the students are working from is white. Therefore, the example presented in Figure 28 represents one of many personal color choices which are interpretive in nature. Various times of day in addition to various light sources are transformed into individualized responses to color. Relative contrasts of temperature and light-dark are again emphasized, yet room for individual and intuitive responses are available and encouraged for each student. Responses to various impressions

of color quality are as wide and rich in the students' works as are those represented between a Vermeer painting such as *Lady in Blue Reading a Letter* with its serene color atmosphere and contemporary American painter Richard Diebenkorn's expressive interpretations of California light. The temporary and even momentary impressions of light and color within these environments demand the use of color memory and, again, the willingness to utilize color within an interpretive mode.

Another aspect of this assignment represented in figure 29 (page 99) is an extended version of the previous in which the analysis of color and light is executed through a comparative diptych. Two separate times of day and the inherent visual differences of light and color are articulated through a compositional source which remains constant. Although surface color remains unchanged, the effects of light create hue and temperature contrasts the student must analyze not only per each individual incident, but also comparatively. The level of sensitivity of each student and his or her ability to interpret accurately is challenged to a much greater extent within this dual-image approach. The effects of light and its inherent power to affect and change our perceptual responses to color and our environment becomes the overriding concern and is meant to introduce the concept of color transcendence.

Foundation Painting: Color and Light

The foundation painting class begins where the color design class left off. The initial sequence of painting assignments are meant to provide the beginning student a structured sequence similar to those experienced in the color design class. Additionally, however, the assignments as presented are also intended to introduce and encourage a level of experimentation which will begin to suggest to the student various image making options.

Initial paintings on canvas are initiated from observation, with similar concerns related to visual analysis of form and structure as related to drawing. Additionally, the studio exercises continue the visual response to color and light. The student is directed to transform the response to color and light into categorizations of light-dark, temperature and hue contrasts. These initial responses to the observed "data" are not meant to be descriptive in nature. The responses which each student manifests within each composition allows for individualized, personalized and expressive choices.

Figure 30 (page 100) is an oil on canvas painting representing an initial student exploration working within the familiar parameters of color and light. As indicated by this student canvas, descriptive concerns are transcended by concerns for color and generalized suggestions of form and space. The particular choices made by each student relative to these issues must be arrived at, still, through each student's own subjective "pool" of creative and visual responses. This allows for a wide enough range of interpretation within the parameters of the assignment to allow the student personal freedom to explore and to experiment. Experimentation through trial and error encourages the student to think and see within relative terms and to work within the compositional arena "holistically."

The exploration of painting through color and light also opens up to the student additional avenues and possibilities of abstraction. Students wishing to explore abstraction find it a natural transition from more formalist concerns of volumetric structure and space to concerns for surface, mark, shape and overall gesture. Those choosing this route most often maintain an overall sense of light, yet light and color transcend any concern for building volumetric form and space. Patches of color and shape create the overall impression of light contained within the paintings. The possibility of utilizing decorative "flat space" as an additional option within explorations of color and light can lead the student into expressionist mark-making and surface texture. Non-objective avenues of color exploration utilizing color and temperature contrast can evolve into geometric images still maintaining a sense of color and light. Repeated patterns of shape varying in levels of hue saturation, scale and cool-warm allow for a visual push-pull into and out of the picture plane space.

In 1961 Johannes Itten wrote: "The end and aim of all artistic endeavor is liberation of the spiritual essence of form and color and its release from the imprisonment of objects". The sequence of classroom exercises discussed and presented here represent an attempt to guide students through a continuum of learning which will gain them insight into the ultimate transcendent nature of color. Color and light can provide a student a number of rich avenues for creative exploration and it can confront the student with issues of content and meaning which exist within many related aspects of visual art. Whether the student chooses, eventually, to work naturalistically or totally non-objectively, an experiential basis has been formed to provide insight into the creative possibilities of color.

Notes

1. ALBERS, Joseph (1968) Interaction of Color. New Haven, Connecticut: Yale University Press.

2. ITTEN, Johannes (1974) The Art of Color. New York: Van Nostrand Reinhold.

3. ITTEN [2] p. 48.

4. CARPENTER, James. Visual Art: A Critical Introduction. New York: Harcourt Brace Jovanovich, p. 90; DAWSON Philip (1977) Design. Englewood Cliffs, New Jersey: Prentice-Hall, p. 236; and ELLIOT BEVLIN, Marjorie (1988) Design Through Discovery. New York: Holt, Reinehart and Winston, p. 59.

5. Itten [2] p. 95.

4

Environment

Galen Minah

Reading Form and Space
The Role of Color in the City

Color in architecture, in architectural drawings and in the facades and interior spaces of built projects, has been a characteristic focus in work from the early 70's at the birth of Post-Modernism through the current Late Modernist and Deconstructivist phases which dominate the architectural media. The most published architects in the last fifteen years have been highly skilled in graphic abilities, some being accomplished painters and graphic artists, whose most memorable work is not their buildings but their splendid presentations. Michael Graves, Zoe Zenghelis, Zaha Hadid, the models of Frank Gehry, and the bright red follies for Parc La Villette in Paris by Bernard Tschumi are familiar to every architecture student. The current wave of interest in color began when Robert Venturi sanctioned American subculture, ignored the restraints on color from early modernism and used color in architecture as imagery in much the same way as roadside advertising.[1]

Much of the work of the 90's, particularly the recent work of Peter Eisenman and Bernard Tschumi, architects associated with the Deconstruction movement in architecture, have used theories of language and meaning as arguments for their conceptual design in which ambiguities, contradictions, and multiple meanings are translated through their interpretation into architectural form. Color is strongly integral as a component of this form-language, but its rationale is often part of the designer's own subjective language of color.[2]

In academic circles there are personalities who are noted colorists, such as Robert Slutsky at the Department of Fine Arts, University of Pennsylvania, and John Hejduk at Cooper-Union in New York City, who have been influential in stimulating an interest in color among architecture students, but their teaching is often very esoteric, and related strongly to their own ideas developed through their painting.

Although color has been used in the architecture of the last 20 years, color theory as part of an objective methodology for design in which color becomes part of a conceptual understanding of architectural form in the design process, or is used as a critical tool for evaluation, seldom enters architectural design studio education.

It is important to look more closely at the formative period of the early Modern Movement, particularly at the attitudes toward color and architecture, and examine the ways in which color was incorporated in the theory, teaching, and production of those times.[3] A schism in approach to design education known as the "Norm vs. Form Debate" took place during the Deutsche Werkbund Exhibition of 1914. "Norm" represented the belief in the development and refinement of prototypes in architecture and industrial design; and "Form" represented the creative sovereignty of the individual artist.

This controversy carried into the early years of the Dessau Bauhaus. Johannes Itten was an artist and color theorist who sided with the artistic, anti-authoritarian 'Form' side of the argument. Itten established a very important teaching document in his book *Art of Color*, which is still used in teaching color theory to artists and architects. Itten taught the basic design course at the Bauhaus, in which his teaching methods were subjective, very inner-directed and focused on individual creativity. Itten was interested in how personality could be revealed through color exercises, and had a somewhat mystical approach to color and design. His anti-authoritarian beliefs often clashed with the strongly rational approach of Bauhaus director and architect Walter Gropius. When Gropius proclaimed his support for professors in the industrial production and craft design faction of the Bauhaus, Itten resigned.

He was replaced by Laszlo Moholy-Nagy, a Hungarian artist with constructivist leanings who took over the basic design course. Moholy-Nagy practiced "programmed art", and was well known for his "telephone pictures" which were executed by calling color specifications to a factory supervisor who then produced the work of art in enameled steel.[4] Moholy-Nagy fitted in very well with Gropius's rational objectives, and he became a powerful influence in the Bauhaus.

At the same time, Neue Sachlichkeit, or "New Objectivity", emerged as the intellectual basis for design theory in the late 20's. New Objectivity practitioners sought to make the design process a highly rational one, stressing materiality, economy, and function, and divesting designed artifacts of any ideal implications. New Objectivity was the foundation for many early twentieth century movements in design such as Suprematism and Neo-Plasticism or DeStijl.

The Dutch De Stijl movement was an important accomplishment in the use of color as a tool in theoretical approaches to architectural form. The best known members of this movement were the artists Piet Mondrian and Theo van Doesburg, who became the prime spokesman for the movement, and Gerrit Rietveld, an architect who produced some of the only built objects of this period. Their lofty goal was "to work through the arts to achieve an ideal future when all walls that separate men would be broken down, society integrated and capable of constructing an urban environment of abstract forms."[6]

These artist-architects saw the three-dimensional properties of mass and volume as antithetical to their movement, and they attempted to counteract and destroy these formal characteristics through the use of color. Their methodology was to use primary colors, white and green planes of color defined by black borders, displacing corners and the boundaries of floors and ceilings with these color planes, thus changing the volumetric characteristics of architectural space. In its place, one experienced floating planes of color, some advancing, some receding, dissolving all the references to cubic volume and becoming an assemblage of spatial effects created by color juxtapositions.[7]

De Stijl was a dramatic development in the use of color as both an integral part of the design process and as a tool for the creation of a new spatial experience. No other movement had employed color as a conceptually spatial idea to this extent and none had recognized and used in practice the de-structuring capability of color.

Other movements employing color as a basis for their conceptual design were Constructivism, in which color played a symbolic role[8], and Expressionism. The Expressionists were artists and architects who saw their creative role as a calling to save society through their inspired artistic achievements. Color for the Expressionists was powerfully emotive and highly individual and subjective, as seen in the architecture of Hans Poelzig and Hans Scharoun.[9]

Le Corbusier was influenced by De Stijl, particularly in his use of color in Pessac Housing of 1929. With the artist Ozenfant Le Corbusier established Purism, which among other influences, brought machine aesthetics to the attention of contemporary architects. The color white was a dominant theme in the architecture influenced by Purism particularly in the 1930's; later, white surfaces and structural members became a characteristic of the International Style. Mies van der Rohe and Walter Gropius were influenced by the Le Corbusian theories, but their work was characteristically restrained in the use of color except for the qualities of color and texture in unadorned materials such as steel, glass, concrete, masonry and stone. Color was considered ornamental and thus superficial when applied purposely.

Gropius and Mies came to the United States as teachers in the late 30's, and their influence in architectural education is still felt in the design studios of professors today, who were students of these two men. This accounts in part for the continuation of their attitudes about color in U.S. architectural education today.

Except for the teaching of the early Bauhaus and the brief emergence of color in the movements described above, color theory and teaching has been considered supplemental to the mainstream of architectural education. Architecture students in the United States have few courses in color theory or studios which focus on color in architectural design. Rarely is a course offered in which color in design and the relationship of form and color to architecture is the focus of the instruction.

An exception to this is the course offered by Christopher Alexander at the University of California at Berkeley, in which Alexander's pattern language is expanded to employ the use of color by studying cultural precedents for the use of color in various spaces based on functional similarities.[10]

Color in student work, for the most part, remains a matter of individual expression most often influenced by journal graphics and high quality photographs of built projects in which the coloration is often exaggerated. A student's involvement with color at the University of Washington Department of Architecture is entirely elective. Occasionally students from fine arts who matriculate for a professional degree in architecture have some knowledge of color theory, but often color remains a matter of individual taste. Color issues are rarely discussed in a design studio review, and then almost never on an objective basis.

The challenge is to bring color theory into a conceptual framework where its relevance is part of the design process. This challenge has become the point of departure for these investigations in color-form interactions, and the subject for a number of graduate architectural design studios. Color theory is used in these classes as a conceptual design tool to expand the means for clarifying the figural or hierarchical nature of building form. Color theory is also used in the analytical or interpretative phase of the process as a critical tool in examining the integral relationships between the parts and the whole.

Formal analysis, a theoretical framework which has influenced architectural education, is currently taught in several influential schools of architecture in the U.S. Douglas Graf, of Ohio State University, is the leading theorist in the field. Graf defines analysis as a process of "loosening" a building into its constituent pieces and relationships.[11]

The object of analysis is interpretation, or 'making sense' out of visual phenomena. This methodology can be applied to two-dimensional as well as three-dimensional phenomena. Formal analysis in architecture begins with the plan. Through diagramming, one 'loosens' the building into constituent elements, reducing the plan to the micro components of point, line, plane, and volume. The diagram presents these constituent parts both as objects and as a set of dynamic relationships between the objects. These diagrams are compared to buildings or parts of buildings which share a similar diagram and display a similar diagrammatic relationship, but may be unrelated in type, function or cultural circumstance. These comparisons give the analyst a wider field of reference from which to draw interpretive strategies. As Graf states, "the process wrests the building from the tangible world of the specific and deposits it as fragments in the intangible world of the general."[12]

Figure 1
Michael Graves, line rendering of the
Portland Building

grammatic strategies. As with the formal analysis of buildings, a color field can be named using the same terminology as architectural forms: center, perimeter, figure, and ground. For example, an abstract painting can be analyzed, diagrammed, and interpreted in much the same way as a work of architecture, although color juxtapositions become the only formal elements.

Most formal analysis dismisses color as transitory or treats it as a specific issue in the analysis of form. The preferred media for analytic studies are black and white drawings and photographs for elevational and perspectival studies. When color is introduced it is not used in the critique of building form. Color, however, is a powerful factor in the reading of form, as seen in the work of the De Stijl movement, and it is a major factor in clarifying the figure-ground relationships. Diagramming techniques used in formal analysis reveal the order of figure-ground, and these can be amplified by color studies.

It is also clear that the perception of spatial phenomena is due in part to color contrasts, through juxtaposition of color surfaces, and to the effects of atmospheric perspective upon color. Certain color phenomena such as these fall into categories that are recognizable and thus generalizable. These categories can be represented as part of the 'familiar' and 'general' world of color interactions, and can also be represented through dia-

Since we understand the architectural diagram by means of black and white, solid and void, we neglect atmospheric reality in which color is the variable which complicates and enriches the experience of figure/ground and solid/void. Color has the capacity to clarify the figural components of form or confuse or obfuscate these elements causing multiple readings of architectural form.

An example of the interaction of building form with color is the Portland Building in Portland, Oregon, by Michael Graves. If we compare the architect's line rendering of the building which portrays a clear cubic mass with delineated parts with the actual building (Figure 1), there are substantial differences. The actual building's colors reveal another interpretation of the nature of the building. Here the cubic volume appears to bracket a second volume which appears as a dark mass in the center of the building. Thus the actual volumetric characteristic of the building appears quite different from the drawn work (see figure 31, page 101).

The work which follows is a composite of experiments, observations, and student projects from a number of design studios taught by me, beginning in 1980, at the University of Washington. The students were graduate students in the professional degree program in architecture.

The course began with a number of short exercises which would familiarize students with 'color effect'. These exercises usually included an experimental exercise in the studio followed by observations in the field. Field observation focused upon the color effects in the built environment. The second half of the quarter, students designed a building or redesigned an existing building on a site within the context of the city. The student was asked to include color decisions in the conceptual phase of the project, using the earlier experimental work as a reference in this process.

The city of Seattle, Washington was always the laboratory for these studies. A city is an ideal environment for color research of this kind, since the complexities of urban form contain a multiplicity of color contrasts, involving numerous site specific color decisions over time. The palette is relatively stable, with change occurring over long periods. The opportunities for studying the color juxtapositions of figure/ground in relationship to the spatial juxtapositions of solid/void, and how color clarifies or obfuscates these juxtapositions are abundant in the urban environment, and the scale of these juxtapositions ranges from building detail to regional view. The city also provides a spatial dimension where the effects of atmosphere and foreshortening in distant views may be studied relative to objects at close proximity.

The first investigation was to explore the spatial effect of color and create optical illusions using this effect in three-dimensional form. Students constructed 3"x3" paper cubes with single planes of color on their faces. Through color juxtapositions and the spatial effect created by these juxtapositions students were asked to arrange these cubes in space and photograph them from a point of view which would create an optical illusion, misrepresenting the actual positions in space which the cubes occupied. It was interesting to note in these exercises the power and ambiguous characteristic of black. Black can be figural either as a solid or a void, and can easily deceive the eye as to its actual position in space. A black object in front of a lighter background can advance dramatically toward the viewer, or appear as a void in the background.

In the next exercise students were asked to find and photograph examples of the spatial effect in the urban environment with particular attention to the figure/ground interactions. These examples were numerous, and the variety of spatial effects observed were apparent in large spatial contexts as well as in fine detail. For example light columns in slight relief on a darker background appeared from a distance as free-standing columns. Warmer colored buildings appeared closer to the viewer than cooler buildings at approximately the same distance. The tops of towers from street level could deceive the eye as to their actual positions in space if color contrasts were present.

In these initial studies we noticed specifically two factors which affected color in urban settings: the importance of daylighting and climatic conditions on the perceived color effects within the city; and the dominant presence of highly saturated colors in the environment. These two factors became subjects for further study in later design studio courses.

To understand the context of the studies which follow, a profile of the site city is necessary. Seattle, Washington is one of the youngest large cities in the United States. It was first settled in the 1850's and grew rapidly when the railroad arrived in 1885. As a port city, Seattle grew as a rough and ready frontier town with lumber, fishing, and shipping as the primary industries. Seattle served as the departure and arrival point for the gold rush in Alaska. The city, like Rome, grew on seven hills; one of the hills was completely leveled at the turn of the century to stimulate the direction of growth of the Central Business District and its earth used to make a harbor island. Water and mountains on two sides of the city give it a unique setting, but also have determined its predominant linear north-south growth pattern which was exaggerated in the 1960's by a north-south interstate highway through its urban center.

Large bedroom communities have grown up east of the city, accessible by floating bridges over Lake Washington, a long north-south lake east of the city. There are spectacular views from the hills within the city, and Seattle is one of the few urban environments in the United States where mountains and water are such a dominant part of the perception of the urban environment. The weather is often cloudy and overcast during the winter and spring, creating an ambient gray sky and dramatic lighting through clouds. Seattle has a reputation for being a rainy city, but the rain is most often a light drizzle. Temperatures are moderate all year long, with cool wet winters and warm summers.

To study the effects of daylighting and climatic conditions upon color in Seattle, we first photographed color samples on bright and overcast days to observe colors which changed significantly with these conditions. We also photographed single family residential areas that had a variety of color juxtapositions and could be viewed from a distance. Photography was done in differing weather conditions, and at different times of the day. From these exercises we observed the changes in the reds in the urban environment, particularly brick, in sunshine and under overcast skies. In sunshine, the red-orange hues dominated, usually making the building figural as the reds advanced when contrasted against a cooler field. On overcast days, the reds became dull and cool and retreated into the background, changing sometimes from figure to ground spatially.

Blues, on the other hand, became vibrant and appeared more saturated on overcast days. This also was true of hues that contain blue such as blue-green, red-violet, etc. Yellows also became vibrant on overcast days, and colors with yellow components such as green could alternate between blue-green and yellow green in differing light conditions. Guided by these initial observations, we photographed a number of buildings and objects in the red, blue and yellow range of colors on sunny, overcast and rainy days.

Another investigation focused on highly saturated colors on buildings within the city to observe their spatial effect. Of particular interest was to see how atmospheric perspective changed these colors and what spatial effects occurred at varying distances. Observations were made in different lighting conditions and these were photographed. Saturated reds and yellows were the most obvious colors on buildings observed. Both reds and yellows advanced dramatically from every point of view and seemed to be less affected by atmospheric perspective than the surrounding buildings. The strength of highly saturated colors, particularly on large surfaces such as building facades is obvious from this study, and these colors have an ability to exaggerate the spatial effect, advancing toward the viewer in nearly every example we observed.

An example of a well known urbanscape demonstrates the ways that methodologies employed in formal analysis are useful in discussing the relationship between color and urban form. The Mall in Washington, D.C., is a clear example of ordered relationships in a clear hierarchical system. The plan reveals a focus on the Capitol Building at one end of the grand axis of the Mall. The Capitol, in turn, is reinforced by flanking institutional buildings, each a figural building in itself. The Capitol Building becomes a stronger figure as the focus of two large converging avenues, Pennsylvania and Maryland. The Washington Monument, on the Mall, further defines the axial relationship with the Capitol Building, provides a central focus in the Mall, and enforces an axis to the White House perpendicular to the Mall. The monument takes on a pivotal role as the intersection of two axes and the counterpart to the central figures at the ends of these axes. Along the avenues are key governmental buildings, each taking a place in the hierarchical pattern established by the Mall, the Capitol Building, the White House, and the Washington Monument.

The Capitol Building, the White House, and the Washington Monument are all white, achieving figural status against the darker landscape, and advancing spatially. Against the sky the contrast is softened and makes the buildings appear to float in space. White also reveals detail in shadow often making the building appear larger than it really is. Buildings with a combination of very large scale contrasted with repetitive small scale elements make the building appear larger, exemplified in the drawings of the French neoclassical architect Ledoux. Many of the flanking institutional buildings are off-white, giving them equal status with one another, but of lesser rank than the primary buildings.

In contrast to the relatively flat, concentric form of Washington, D.C., Seattle is a linear city flanked by two large natural bodies of water and several hills. The street system is a grid. The grid is

an egalitarian planning system since each block is the same, unlike the combination of the radial and orthogonal systems in Washington. In a grid, hierarchy is possible through an intervention which breaks the repetitive pattern. Central Park in New York City is an example of this as is Savannah, Georgia. Other interventions are created by superimposing another system over the grid as in the cities influenced by Beaux Arts planning such as Philadelphia, Chicago and Washington, D.C.

In comparing the planning of governmental and major institutional buildings in Seattle to Washington, D.C. there is little similarity. In Seattle most institutional buildings are treated no differently within the grid from commercial buildings, occupying the same block pattern. There is no hierarchical intervention such as a central park, a mall, or a purposeful axis. The plan of the city reveals little information about where the governmental buildings are and how they achieve their status. In fact, they have no separate status: they occupy the same sized blocks as the commercial buildings, and have no plazas nor any special height.

A photograph of Seattle reveals a concentration of skyscrapers in the central business district where commercial, governmental and institutional buildings are located. The towers themselves are dominated by one massive black building, the Columbia Center, the highest tower in the city. The coloration is designed to show minimal shadow and little detail, thereby creating a black monolith of great power within the city. The figural strength of this building is not because of its height alone or its position in the city but by its color.

However, it is really only another commercial office tower, which in most American cities are really background buildings in terms of their civic importance. The Seattle City Hall huddles at its feet directly adjacent to the Seattle Public Library which is also dwarfed, as are the court houses and the Art Museum a few blocks away.

In a design studio focusing on color and urban form, students were given a building design project in the Central Business District near the Columbia Center. As a sketch problem, students made a large painting from photographs of a view of the Columbia Center in its urban context. Each student was asked to change the color scheme of the Columbia Center and paint an overlay to be attached to the original painting. It was interesting to see how the center of gravity of skyline comprised of all the towers together was changed when the Columbia Center was light gray or silver and softened by the skyscape.

In the second part of the quarter, students were given a building design project for an office tower on a site in the Central Business District near the Columbia Center. The new tower was not as high as the Columbia Center but would be in a prominent position in front of the Columbia Center when viewed approaching the city from the east, west or south. The students were asked to select color schemes for their new towers which approached the figural status of the Columbia Center.

The most interesting resulting design was a white tower which used color to exaggerate its own height and stood as a strong counterpoint to the black tower (figure 32, page 102). A more neutral color scheme would have joined other neutral towers and become part of the background. A dark tower would become one of the family with the Columbia Center and other dark towers, but a smaller sibling.

Another design project in the vicinity of the Columbia Center addressed the new county jail, built adjacent to the major north-south freeway and just on the edge of the Central Business District at the south end of the city. As one approaches the city from the south, the jail becomes a gateway building. The new jail is a block away from the Columbia Center and near City Hall and County Courthouse. The jail is designed to look like a neutral beige office building. Through clever coloration, dark concrete panels give the appearance of large glass windows; however, at the base of these panels is a five inch slit which is the only real window to the cells behind. At night these slits become visible, and the building becomes a looming dark object with eerie thin slits of light, contrasted to the lofty, fully lit office towers.

Tight security is required when prisoners are moved from the jail to the county courthouse two blocks away. To provide this security a high skybridge extends from the top floor of the jail across a street over an entire block at the roof of an adjacent building, across another street, and into the courthouse. The bridge, intended to be innocuous and to avoid notice, instead becomes a figural foreign object, and thus a sinister intrusion into the fabric of the city.

Students were asked to select a point of view from photographs which included the new jail and bridge with the city behind. A mural of this view was painted by the class. This exercise gave the students experience in mixing the grays and beiges which make up much of the urban palette. The students were then asked to take a point of view about the relationship of a jail to the commercial center of the city, and express this point of view in coloristic terms. This was recognized as an abstract exercise, knowing that a project like this in reality would need to consider more than one point of view.

Many students chose to accept the institution for what it was without disguising it. These projects made the building more

Figure 37

Figure 38

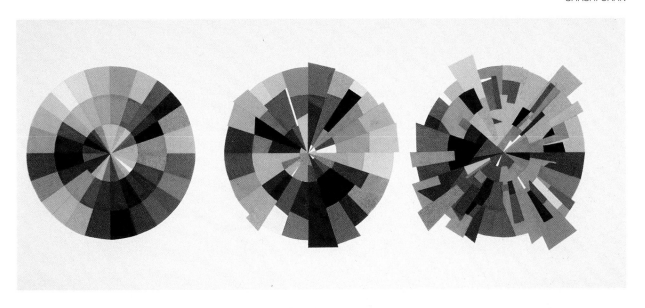

Figures 39 and 40

Figure 41

Figure 42

Figure 43

Figure 44

Figure 45

figural in nature and treated the dark concrete panels as planes of color rather than disguised as windows. Most solutions attempted to break the dominant scale and figural nature of the bridge with varying planes of color. Some experimented with hues complementary to the warm grays and browns of the surrounding buildings for the purpose of creating a color harmony with the urban context, but appearing as clearly distinct from the other buildings. The most unusual design was done by a student who abstracted the pattern of windows from the surrounding towers, and in bold black and white rectangles, de-structured the cubic volume of the jail into a collage of fragments which blended with the rectangular patterns of the windows in the surrounding buildings (figure 33, page 102).

In all these exercises, students used an analytical process to explore the relationship between their designs and the larger urban context. As part of this process, they made color decisions that would clarify the formal and spatial properties of the designed buildings. This inevitably led to a broader understanding of how color contrasts and, in particular, the spatial effect of color, become components in figure/ground and the perception of three dimensional space. The students also learned that color is part of the experiential nature of architectural awareness, and that its relevance in the design process is one of clarifying, complementing and enhancing rather than as an independent study.

Formal analysts feel it is impossible to fully 'know' a building. It can only be understood as a group of diverse abstractions. Likewise, it is impossible to fully 'know' a city, but the complexities and ambiguities which characterize the 'reading' of form and space are truly enriched by the diversity of color, giving great variety to the creative interpretation of the city.

Notes

1. MINAH G. (1984), Color Language. In: Arcade, Seattle, p. 3.

2. EISENMAN P. and TSCHUMI B. (1989). In: Deconstruction, eds. Papadakis, Cooke and Benjamin, New York, pp. 154-191.

3. FRAMPTON K. (1992), Modern Architecture, A Critical History. London.

4. Ibid., pp. 124-126.

5. Ibid., pp. 130-132.

6. TROY N. (1983), DeStijl Manifesto. In: The DeStijl Environment, Boston, pp. 5-6.

7. Ibid., p. 83.

8. CHERNIKHOV J., The Harmony of Colors. In: Deconstruction, op. cit., pp. 56-59.

9. PEHNT W. (1973), Expressionist Architecture. London, pp. 34-47.

10. ALEXANDER C. (1981), The Linz Café. New York, Vienna.

11. DRAL JOURNAL (1986), New York, pp. 43-44.

12. Ibid.

Harold Linton

Color, Light, Form And Space

After authoring my first text, *Color Model Environments*, in 1985 with Van Nostrand Reinhold and several books since about color in architecture and design for various publishers, I have become known to my colleagues in academia as a publishing surfer. It is said that surfers spend their lives searching for the perfect wave - in the same way that teachers of design spend theirs searching for the perfect text. And sometimes, it seems that books on the subject are nearly as numerous as waves in the ocean.[2,3,4,5,6]

However, prior to the publication of *Color Model Environments*, texts for foundation studio courses in three-dimensional design focused on an achromatic approach to the development of curriculum content, i.e., concepts, theory, vocabulary, design process and general sensibility toward materials. For me, Tom Porter and Byron Mikellides' *Color For Architecture*,[7] in the mid 1970's as well as Lois Swirnoff's, *Dimensional Color*,[8] in the late 1980's have contributed pedagogical direction, insight and enthusiasm for the role of color in three-dimensional art and design foundation curricula. Recent texts such as *Basic Visual Concepts and Principles*[9] by Wallschlaeger/Busic-Snyder and several more have recognized the relation of color and light to three-dimensional foundation design experience and integrate color theory and application within their content.

If *Color Model Environments* has played a small role in fostering the integration of color and light sensibilities in three-dimensional foundation curricula, the hope for my latest publishing project, *Color, Light , Form and Space* currently under consideration with Van Nostrand Reinhold, is to broaden and deepen the understanding of the visual elements of design particularly color and light in foundation programs. A growing interdisciplinary design dialogue among the fine arts and architecture seems to embrace the future of educational and professional practice reflecting a sense for strong technological emphasis in art and design professions, a media explosion within the communications industries, and as we view the eve of an interactive and highly visual information age, certain impact on our home and work environments.

A fully engaged foundation design exposure today should also underscore aspects of an interrelated two and three-dimensional exploration. This would include the role of computer visualization, video presentation, photographic methodologies, reprographic technologies along with traditional approaches to media exploration such as additive and subtractive form manipulation, an understanding of modeling and materials, and the related processes of graphic search and refinement.

The three-dimensional studio, and foundation curricula in general, continue to be challenged to meet the requirements of preparing students for the consequent visual and cultural diversity in art and design practices through a holistic view of the language and experience of design, i.e., design theory, design precedent, design process, media exploration and a breadth of view in studio discussion and critique. Student examples of design selected for this presentation evolved within a three-dimensional foundation color course in which color and light are integrated with previous elements and processes of 2-D foundation studio experience.

The viewpoint maintained throughout the course is that an awareness of the vocabulary of design and the fundamentals of color and light are basic to all personal explorations of form and space in two and three-dimensional design, and that incorporation of these elements, including knowledge of the properties of materials, lends direction and support to individual expression.

I have included examples of student work to reflect a relationship between the visual and physical properties of dimensional form and to support the following criteria for the role of color in three-dimensional design education:

- To experience the qualities of color and light and their combined effect on form in planning and practice. Studies of the perception of color and form are by students under the direction of Franz Zeier, Zurich School of Art and Design and students under the direction of Lois Swirnoff, U.C.L.A.

- To understand the structure and planning of color as a fundamentally rational and visual process interwoven in the act of design. Studies of linear structures and perception of space are by students under the direction of myself, Lawrence Technological University.

- To utilize drawing as a means of furthering an analysis of the qualities of form and composition in the design process. Studies of pattern on volumetric forms in harmony with their environment are by students of Jean-Philippe Lenclos, National School for Decorative Arts in Paris.

- To acquaint one with the special possibilities of color materials and their methods of application in three-dimensional design. Models of sculptural wall planes in acrylic sheet with transparent color laminates and internal lighting, are by students under the direction of myself.

It is my belief that attempts should be made to adapt suitable methods of design representation to background goals - of fully appreciating any idea that satisfies the initial criteria of a design problem. Although the materials used in three-dimensional design will differ from those used in actual construction, they provide the designer with the tactile experience of shaping physical space and thereby influence the quality of form it replicates. Within the frame work of a creative and developing design dialogue, design tools can be harnessed to serve each individual in his/her pursuit of unique concepts of form and space.

Studio Projects
A Spatial Interpretation of a 2-D Composition[10]

The project as presented to the students is to create a spatial interpretation of interconnected three-dimensional forms developed from a two-dimensional graphic composition. Students are asked to research a composition created by a prominent 20th century artist, the artist's cultural background and aesthetic beliefs to be used for the three dimensional interpretation. The three-dimensional version is to be executed in model form and accompanied by a constructed, scaled, and titled reproduction of the original painting or design.

At Lawrence Technological University, one of my architecture students poses the question of what a painting by Ad Reinhardt might evolve into in the third dimension if allowed to open his palette and geometry. Views taken from around the student composition reflect an evolution of dynamic geometry and spatial construction lurking behind the facade of Ad Reinhardt's dark and rectilinear reduction. In another student work, Mondrian is reinterpreted in planar terms where the geometry is skewed and the grill is given a fragmented, trellis-like interpretation.

As a visiting artist, I had an opportunity to share this problem with students at The Art Academy of Cincinnati. The first example following Georgia O'Keefe uses painted and fabricated metals. Another one based on the work of Sonia Delaunay applies paint to cardboard tubing. A color still-life installation with heat sensor further stretches the nature of interpretation, while another Cincinnati student works from the origin of graphic design.

Color Space Collage[11]

The following study helps to further the relation of two-dimensional and three-dimensional design methodologies and extends the study of color and light in three-dimensional space. The problem begins with a color collage of a fixed dimension (e.g. 4" x 3" subdivided by 1" squares) from color papers and images found in advertising such as magazines, posters, and newspapers. The mosaic of one inch color squares is then used as the subject in the following transformations.

First, a contour line drawing is made directly from the original collage color study. This becomes a "floor plan" for an axonometric drawing (again in contour line) of imaginary form and space. The axonometric contour drawing is used as a vehicle to re-explore the relationship of collage (which itself explores the nature of juxtaposition) to a visual environment and to the consequent architectonic/sculptural environment through an imaginary labyrinth that begins and ends with the colors and images found in magazines, newspapers, and posters.

It is worth noting that once a conclusion is reached, class discussion of the project may suggest change and impact all of the four stages, thereby requiring revisions to the line drawings and color collages. Students discover that dimensional effects are possible through an understanding of the principles of design including contrast and color interaction.
- The contrast of bright against dark, with the exception of black.
- The contrast of pure colors or black and white against grayed colors.

Figure 1

- The contrast of warm colors against cool colors.
- The contrast of detail, texture and micro structure against a plain or film surface.
- The use of perspective to distinguish near from far distances.
- The implied use of highlights and cast shadows.
- The use of easily recognized objects, which, because of familiarity and relative size, will give mental clues to their spatial positions.

Color-Space Facade[12]

A relatively simple entryway facade is selected as the subject matter for this visual transformation exercise in color and form. Five separate compositions will be created reflecting an evolution from drawing through relief construction and visual transformation in color.

The first step is a simple black and white line drawing of the facade showing important shape elements of the facade - exclusive of small decorative elements, detail, texture or shadows (figure 1).

The second step assigns each shape element a value on a scale

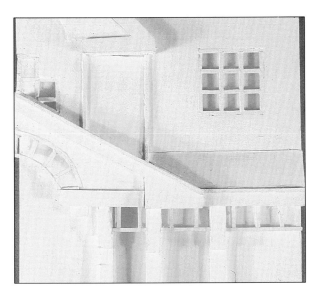

Figure 2

Figure 3

of 1 to 10 (light to dark). For example, lighter values are applied to the shape elements of the facade closest to the viewer while darker values are applied to elements further away (figure 2).

The following three steps involve the construction of a low relief construction and accurate representation of the facade as it was originally designed by the architect using 1/8" or 1/4" thick foam core. The layers correspond to the values in step 2 such that the closest element would be the lightest value and the element furthest away would be the darkest (figure 3).

In the fourth step, color is used to enhance the sense of depth and to indicate change of materials. No attempt is made to duplicate colors used by the architect in the original facade; rather, to develop their own scheme using a range of hue, value and chroma (figure 34, page 103).

In the final relief, color is used in such a manner to minimize the visual/physical depth of the facade and alter the form as much as possible. The design should no longer look like an architectural facade or a place of entry, but should become instead, quite abstract (figure 35, page 103).

Re-Rietveld Chair[13]

Gerrit Rietveld's famous Red and Blue chair of 1918 is the subject of this two stage problem. In the first stage, a scale model of Rietveld's Red and Blue Chair is constructed of basswood. Color is applied in such a manner to completely alter the perception of the chair as a three-dimensional Mondrian painting - so that it is no longer at home in the Schroder house and no longer a statement of the De Stijl ideals: geometric purity and simplicity, the use of primary colors with neutral colors, and the composition of a unified 'whole' from individual elements or components.

In the second stage, an environment is created to contain the chair and reinforce the new color/design concept of the chair, similar to the relationship that existed between the Schroder house and the Red and Blue Chair - an environment that creates a metaphor or further states the concept developed for the chair. The background container is viewed as a means to enhance perception and communicate a vision of the chair, its environment, and new color-form meaning - introducing aspects of lighting design and illumination where appropriate (figure 36, page 104).

Professional Directions

The capacity of color to evoke, imply and conjure up magical illusions that exist in an imaginative mental space - as demonstrated by the students' work - is also demonstrated by the following artists and designers. Like the cosmic space of a Kandinsky or a Pollock, or the atmospheric space of a Klee, Miro, Rothko, or Newman - the concept of spatial experience in abstract art is very much part of our cultural heritage.

Today, designers and artists who work with color at the scale of the built environment are redefining their art not as a narrow, arid and reductive modernism, but as a rich, varied capacity to birth new images into an old world. The new generation of designers who have matured slowly, skeptically, privately, and with great difficulty, have had to struggle to maintain conviction in an art that the media and the public said was barely alive.

The inspiration for significant environmental color works does not lie within the literal material properties of the physical environment as pigment on walls and ceilings, but behind the proverbial looking-glass of consciousness, where the depth of the imagination knows no limits. By calling attention to the spatial qualities of architecture through immersing an environment in a volume experience of colored light or by embedding the physical attributes of a structure in a spatial layering of pigment, environmental color works today do not ignore the fundamental assumptions of modernism - which precluded any regression to the conventions of illusionism and representation, but stress originality, individuality and synthesis which are marks of quality in color works today - as they have always been.

Serious colorists of the Nineties are an extremely heterogeneous group - some far more lyric and abstract while others embrace narrative and topical forms. Their aesthetic, which synthesizes tactile and optical qualities, defines itself in conscious opposition to all forms of mechanical reproduction which seek to deprive (by flattening out) the color-space concept of its unique 'aura'. It is, in fact, the enhancement of this aura, through a variety of means, that color work in three dimensions now self-consciously intends - either by emphasizing the involvement of the designer/artist's hand, or by creating highly individual visionary images that can not be confused either with reality itself or with one another. Such a commitment to unique images necessarily rejects seriality as well.

These original and individual interpretations of "allover" structure point to the wide number of choices still available with visual as opposed to physical rendition of our environment. For in submitting itself to the supporting role that decorative styles inevitably play in relationship to architecture, painting, sculpture, interior design and graphic arts, the environmental colorist renounces its claim to autonomy.

The imagery of those committed exclusively to colorist traditions in the design and fine arts, an inner world of stored images ranging in modernism from Itten to Lewitt, is entirely invented; it is the product exclusively of the individual imagination rather than a mirror of the ephemeral external world of objective reality. Even when such images are strictly geometric, as in the case of designers and artists like Carlos Cruz-Diez, Jean-Phillipe Lenclos and David Barr, they are quirky and sometimes eccentrically personal interpretations of geometry — always asymmetrical or skewed, implying a dynamic and precarious balance, the opposite of the static immobility of the centered icon, emblem or insignia. The rejection of symmetry and of literal interpretations of "allover" design, such as the repeated motifs of Pattern Painting, defines these colored environments as exclusively projects referring to space in front of and within, rather than beyond the angles and points of reference contained by the physical geometry.

These artists and designers are equally committed to a distinctively humanistic art that defines itself in opposition to the a priori and the mechanical: A machine can not do it, a computer can not reproduce it, another artist can not execute it. Nor do their forms of art and design in any way resemble graphic art, advertising, bill-boards, etc. Highly and consciously structured in its final evolution (often after a long process of being refined in preliminary drawings, paper studies and model experiments), these environments are clearly the works of rational planning, painstaking research and experimentation with high conceptual content.

As organizational and informational aspects of two and three dimensional design, the elements of color and light are not only an aesthetic force but also a language. Their potential power can stimulate or relax, alter the appearance of size, shape and form, and change our perception of space and movement. Those who work creatively with color and light require a thorough understanding not only of their resources and expressive potential, but of the manner by which they may be ordered harmoniously to convey a vision in its most effective form.[14]

Notes

1. LINTON Harold (1985), Color Model Environments. In: Color and Light in Three-dimensional Design, New York: Van Nostrand Reinhold.

2. ROCHON, Richard and LINTON, Harold (1991), Color in Architectural Illustration, New York: Van Nostrand Reinhold.

3. LINTON, Harold and STRICKFADEN, Roy J.(1991), Architectural Sketching in Markers, New York: Van Nostrand Reinhold.

4. LINTON, Harold (1993), Color Consulting. In: A Survey of International Color Design, New York: Van Nostrand Reinhold.

5. LINTON, Harold and SUTTON, Scott (1993), Sketching the Concept, New York: Design Press/McGraw-Hill.

6. LINTON, Harold (1994), Color Forecasting. In: A Survey of International Color Marketing, New York: Van Nostrand Reinhol.

7. PORTER, Tom and MIKELLIDES, Byron (1976), Color For Architecture, New York: Van Nostrand Reinhold.

8. SWIRNOFF, Lois (1990), Dimensional Color, New York: Van Nostrand Reinhold.

9. WALLSCHLAEGER, Charles and BUSIC-SNYDER, Cynthia (1992), Basic Visual Concepts and Principles, Dubuque, Iowa: W.M.C. Brown Publishers.

10. LINTON, Harold (1994), Basic Design Two Syllabus (Semester System), Southfield, Michigan: Lawrence Technological University.

11. LINTON, Harold (1988), Basic Design Two Syllabus (Quarter System), Southfield, Michigan: Lawrence Technological University.

12. RUDY, Gretchen and MARTIN, Rochelle (1993-94), Color Space Facade, Southfield, Michigan: Lawrence Technological University.

13. RUDY, Gretchen (1993-94), Re-Rietveld Chair. Based on the original Rietveld Red and Blue Chair of 1918, Southfield, Michigan: Lawrence Technological University.

14. LINTON, Harold (1991), Color Consulting. In: A Survey of International Color Design, New York: Van Nostrand Reinhold, pp. 125-126.

Shashi Caan

Color from the Ground Up
Teaching Architects Color

It is time to reconsider the basic visual elements of three-dimensional design in architecture. Current architectural/interior design practice starts with developing a distinctive form to which, if considered at all, color, texture and patterns are applied more as an afterthought. Contemporary design education which emphasizes form over more intimate visual details is responsible for the present generation of designers who create tonal gray environments devoid of sufficient visual interest to enliven the human spirit, resulting in a discomforting sensory deprivation. The design process must be reversed, starting with color and light, to utilize their full potential. This will bring a rejuvenation and new hope to our built environments.

Recent design history, especially the Bauhaus and its modernist legacy, has produced a fragmented rather than an integrated design education. The intellectual focus on the purity of line and form denies the potency of more emotive and sensual qualities offered by colors, textures and patterns. The modernist dictum 'Form follows function' was modified by Peter Blake, a contemporary architect and author, to 'Form follows fiasco'. 'Less is more', as stated by Mies van der Rohe, and so aptly rebutted by Venturi to 'Less is a bore', clearly excludes certain elements - like color - from architectural discussions. Whatever one's philosophical position regarding form and purity in architecture, unquestionably form is but one of the vital ingredients necessary to impart in a complete design education. Therefore, to breathe fresh life into stagnant built environments, designers must be provided with a heightened awareness of the interrelationships among the fundamentals of light, color and form and how to skillfully manipulate these elements together. The issue is not to propagate a specific style or to create particular forms but to respond to basic human needs by generating a visually more exciting, stimulating and satisfactory built environment.

Traditionally in architecture little consideration is given to color, patterns and textures and color is a last consideration. In order to understand the potential of color as an architectural element, it seems reasonable to begin an architectural project with color (in relation to the site as well as proposed structure) as the initial element. By changing from form to color as a starting point, the spaces generated will be different and have an inherent sensitivity and freshness, whilst advertently injecting sensory stimulation in the built world around us.

In the physical world, the hierarchical order of light, color and form, starts with light. Without light, we have no color or form, without color, we have no form.

To elaborate further, without light there is darkness; we are unable to distinguish color and forms of objects. With light, lightness and darkness constitute shade and shadow. Simultaneously, we see color. It is this information rendered by color; the surfaces, planes, volumes and voids, which are made perceptible to us only through the visual information of the edges defining boundaries of objects. The edges in three-dimensional space are made via the color change of the surface. The eye and mind achieve distinct perception through comparison and contrasting. If mankind were not capable of seeing the full visible spectrum of color, with its thousands of incremental subtleties, the visual information would be restricted to the interplay of lightness, shadow and darkness; or alternatively, tonal grays, from white to black.

There is a need for a new impetus in our built environment which addresses the human element and therefore caters to our basic sensory needs of visual, tactile, olfactory and auditory stimulus. Partially attributed to our technological advances which have resulted in more sedentary lifestyles and diminishing kinesthetic input, our contemporary spaces also reflect the emphasis on architectural intellectualization and theorizing, at the cost of neglecting colors, textures and patterns, which are a basic and perhaps more sophisticated human need.

Without resorting to specialist help from any one of the various related industries, i.e. environmental specialists, perceptual analysts, etc., designers have at their disposal the three basic design elements of light, color and form. When these elements are manipulated and integrated creatively, they make balanced statements that result in dynamic, and exciting, as well as stimulating spaces.

The following outlined visual process 'color makes form' is a reversal of the standard process of making architecture through the exploration of form. In order for this reversal to be considered, it is mandatory that a visual literacy be developed for color within 3-D, which is comparable to that of the existing awareness of form. 'Color makes form' is, therefore, a development of the process by which a visual literacy can be imparted to the architectural designer, regardless of the designer's experience. It is also proposed that this process be considered for implementation as part of the required design learning within any art/ design academic institution.

The educational methodology for the teaching of color starts with a visual documentation of the site and context, followed by comprehensive color analysis which takes into account light and air. Using alternate composition formats, the proportions of hue, contrast of light and dark, scale, shape and size are emphasized.

This analysis then, hypothetically, allows for intelligent design decisions regarding proportion, scale, size, shape, materials, patterns, and textures to be used in a new design project. Most importantly, it allows the designer the capability of manipulating the mood or required ambiance.

It should be noted that this process is set up as a tool to help the designer as an aid towards incorporating color in the design process with a more objective and meaningful approach. It is not intended as a dictate or recipe for colors of additions, but to help the architect with decision making.

By emphasizing color, this process does not imply that form should be considered last. It simply sets up criteria for color which is equivalent to the requirement for form.

Those of us who are designers and architects give form to our surroundings and deal with the human mind as well as the senses. One of the skills of the visually literate designer has to be the ability to represent and abstract a three dimensional world on the two dimensional plane. Conversely, the designer has to appreciate a three dimensional object or space from a two dimensional rendition.

To give the designer a better understanding of that visual literacy, the following images represent a method of visually recording, analyzing, digesting and generating new images and objects using the fundamental design elements of light, color and form without actually putting a pencil to paper.

154 *See page 137-144 for figures relating the following text.*

Contextual Color

The first phase of a contextual color study is the visual recording of the site, like this image of the mid-block space of Paley Park, New York. This particular image has been deliberately abstracted to allow for the full evaluation of color, texture, light, dark mass and void, without being influenced significantly by the formal aspects of the space. Different images that similarly obliterate form in favor of color, texture and light may be developed for other spaces (figure 37).

Visual Analysis: Color Sentence

Colors are isolated from the visual recording and matched as closely as possible to generate bar compositions. Referred to as color sentences, they represent, in their differences, the variations the eye observes when scanning the space (figure 38).

With the aid of color sentences, a new and personal language of sketches can be generated. These color sketches easily make evident the visual information constituting our environmental ambiance (ie. heavy/light, big/small, dull or bright). This type of color sketching can take place without generating any particular form or conventional drawing (figures 39 and 40).

Color makes form

Utilizing the visual recording and color analysis, the process can be used to generate conceptual forms that can be seen as inspiration for form to be placed within this interior space of Grand Central Station, New York (figure 41).

Visual analysis: Color sentences

Color Sentences prepared for Grand Central Station that delineate hue, value, chroma, proportion and light encountered in this space (figure 42).

Sketching 'Magic Squares' (Klee)

Alternatively, 'magic squares' can be prepared by using language acquired in preparing color sentences. By relating the colors in two perpendicular directions, the composition with its changing scales and layering furthers a more comprehensive understanding of the design elements as the basis for making conceptual forms (figure 43).

Conceptual forms

Using the language of earlier sentences and compositions, conceptual forms can be generated that reflect the context in terms of color, proportion, scale and quality of light. These conceptual forms, because of their derivation, are in harmony with the original context and will lead to a more permanent form (figure 44).

Making form

By starting out with the analysis and manipulation of light, color and texture, a form can be made that in its volumetric representation is harmonious in the space (figure 45).

Research

Christopher A. Willard

Surface Film Colour
Perception and Painting

In 1911, psychologist David Katz published the results of his studies in which he originally planned to pursue all phenomena of colour perception. The German original was translated into English in 1935 as *The World of Colour*. In one series of observations, Katz noted the special appearance that colours took on when he viewed them through the eye of a spectroscope — he described the appearance as filmic and non-localized. Additional empirical observations with both the spectroscope and an aperture (a screen with a small hole in it through which a colour is viewed) allowed Katz to assemble a list of properties he considered characteristic of this filmic appearance. The film colour: had an indefinite localization; it extended into space [toward the viewer]; it appeared to have a spongy texture; one perceived one could reach into it; it was localized in a bi-dimensional (Martin would later argue tri-dimensional) plane; it maintained a frontal-parallel position to the viewer; it was relatively smooth without major wrinkles.

"The spongy texture of the spectral colour," Katz wrote making further distinctions, "was not of such a nature that it could be referred to as a voluminousness or as a colour-transparency." Thus to signify colours evincing these apparent properties Katz employed the taxonomic heading of "Flächenfarben," or "film colour" in English, and positioned its definition opposite to that of a definition of colour as a property of a surface. Excepting a very brief aside on the attitude of the painter who attempts to reproduce the world, in none of Katz's discussions do we find a conceptual link between film colour and colour interactions found in two-dimensional configurations, a bridge I will delineate in this paper.

However his listing of filmic attributes allows us to re-examine a host of historically ambiguous descriptions of two-dimensional colour appearances that seem to hint at film colour — the decorative term 'bloom' for example or the statement supposedly relayed in conversation by Seurat, "Painting for me is the art of hollowing out a surface." (Kahn, 1891)

My focus lies beyond a recognition of film colour in an aperture mode to the non-iconic elements of 2-dimensional surface colour combinations that may provide the stimuli for a perception of the film. My goal in differentiating the types of stimuli used to create the filmic mode of appearance is to define an area for further research specific to colour education, and to describe an historical outline for the filmic illusion in two dimensional art. There are also what I propose to be two constants for the production of film. These are 1) a strong contrast and/or near assimilation of hues, and 2) a repetition of elements in the design.

Relatively few colour theory and psychological literature writings speak specifically about film colour. Descriptions predating Katz that focus on the relationship between an interaction of colours and film colour are virtually nonexistent. More frequently found are observations of surfaces where colours presented as small elements may be seen to mix optically, albeit the effects of the optical mixes are equivocally described.

In 1873, Charles Blanc notes in *Grammaire des Arts du Dessin* that a mutual penetration of colours in the 'mélange optique' can confound the eye and cause colours to vibrate at certain distances. He writes: "If at a distance of some steps, we look at a cashmere shawl, we generally perceive tones that are not in the fabric, but which compose themselves at the back of our eye by the effects of reciprocal reactions of one tone upon another."

Von Bezold noted both the spreading and spatial effects that enlivened colours mixed "...otherwise than upon the palette...."

Remarking in 1876 upon patterning with intervals of different colours he says: "Whenever these intervals are made use of, they do not indeed enter the composition as two different colours, but only as modifications of the same colour, so that the whole surface appears as if it were animated by a sort of low relief."

Regarding the assimilation of colours, as when coloured ornaments are executed upon a neutral ground or upon a ground the colour of which is closely allied to that of the ornament itself he suggests if: "...the surfaces were allowed to touch each other without some special means of separation, a mixed colour would be likely to result at the boundary lines, and the various parts of the ornament, instead of being sharply defined, would present the appearance of passing gradually into each other." With hues of greater contrast he writes: "It has previously been shown that designs executed in two different colours cannot be seen distinctly at the same time, and that the difficulty increases with the increase of the distance in the spectrum between the two colours. The line of contact of two coloured compartments of this kind must therefore invariably appear to be blurred...."

Decorative designers mention proto-film conditions frequently especially in reference to observing shawls and carpets where by technique and pattern lend to optical mixes of colours at various distances. In *Principles of Decorative Design*,1882, Christopher Dresser cites a mingling of colours for which he says he can offer little beyond pointing out what should be studied. He writes: "This principle however I cannot pass without notice — namely, that the finest colour effects are those of a rich, mingled, bloomy character."

Dresser's attempts to define 'bloom' using analogies occur throughout the book, for example: "Imagine a luxuriant gar-den, the beds in which are filled with a thousand flowers, having all colours of the rainbow and imagine these arranged as closely together as will permit of their growth. When viewed from a distance the effect is soft and rich, and full and varied, and is all that is pleasant."

In viewing Indian shawls, scarves and table covers, Dresser writes: "...observe the manner in which small portions of intense reds, blues, yellows, greens, and a score of tertiary tints, are combined with white black and gold to produce a very miracle of bloom." And further on: "By the co-mingling of colours in the manner just described, a rich and bloomy effect can be got, having the general tone of a tertiary colour of any desired hue."

Dresser confronts the reader's possible perplexity in understanding the effect the term 'bloom' describes. He prefaces his chapter on carpets with the caveat, "I hope that my language does not appear mystical..." He needn't have been too concerned however, the term bloom, as applied to optical mixtures of primaries was often used by other decorative designers, Owen Jones, for example, in *An Attempt to Define the Principles which Should Regulate the Employment of Colour in the Decorative Arts...* dating 30 years earlier and presented publicly at the Society of Arts in London.

The tri-dimensional aspect of the filmic illusion was straightforwardly offered by Robert Beaumont in a chapter concerning contrast and harmony of colours in woven design. He writes: "Colours of contrasting qualities and tones undergo two modifications when juxtaposed; first they alter in depth, and, second, in nature of hue."

Also examining mutual interactions of colour and their modes of appearance was Ogden Rood who published his findings in

Modern Chromatics with Applications to Art and Industry,
1879 (French edition available in 1881). He posits than when
colours are placed side by side in lines or dots and viewed from
a distance: "...there is a stage in which the colours are blended,
though somewhat imperfectly, so that the surface seems to
flicker or glimmer... This communicates a peculiar brilliancy to
the surface, and gives it a certain appearance of transparency;
we seem to see into it and below it."

The odd, often filmic effects of optical mixture, at least in the
works of Seurat, were contemporarily seen. Félix Fénéon specu-
lated at length about the reasons for Pointillism and wrote of
the atmosphere of Seurat's painting *La Grande Jatte* as "...trans-
parent and singularly vibrant; the surface seems to flicker."

In 1922 we find the second controlled examination of film colour by psychologist Mabel Martin. In this study she attempted to
confirm Katz' description of film as well as any other intermediary modes of appearance. Her hypothesis was that many distinctions of filmic colour may occur between surface colour and
film colour which she explored in a series of experiments using
apertures. Important here is the mode she termed 'bulky colour.' Bulky colours, she writes, are colours with a tri-dimensional and partially transparent appearance. In other words, the
colour fills the space and yet the viewer can still distinguish the
object through the colour. Katz uses film and volume colours to
describe the same appearance. Martin also allows that bulky
colour is one phenomenological mode of appearance derived
from the original Katz would call film colour, with which I am in
accord, thus my general use of film rather than bulky colour.
On the other hand, perhaps Martin's descriptions of bulky colour better fit with the effects found in painting. In viewing film
colour in painting we usually also see the design of the painting
as within or somewhat behind the semi-transparent film. Martin

described six categories of bulky filmic appearance intermediate
between surface and film colour. These were: 'soft surface' described by one observer as a 'Very soft, velvety surface'; 'veiled
surface' described as a "Surface with a slight film over it";
'fogged surface' described as a haze of "...indefinite depth and
uncertain localization"; 'immersed surface' as "Something with
haze in front of it...," and yet 'More haze than surface' and
lastly a 'substantial haze' and a 'cloudy haze.' Martin's work as
an important follow up to Katz presents in her words: "...the
gradual break-down of a visual object. We begin with the coloured surface of a determinate thing, and we end up with a
sheer quality of colour that is not the colour of anything."

However, the underlying physiological bases of the perception of
colour interactions with possible filmic effects were yet to be
explored. In noting the appearance in painting, J. Carson
Webster in *The Technique of Impressionism: A Reappraisal*,
1944, hypothesizes the effect is a post-retinal action. He sup-
poses: "...it is possible that in some paintings...something in the
way of a 'delusive blend' of colours takes place, in which a few
touches of colour in an area seem to give a tinge of that colour
to the whole area...when touches of two colours are set side by
side, it is not retinal fusion, but rather a kind of mental
averaging..."Webster argues that the effect is not based in the
eye but occurs through a non visual averaging that takes place in
the mind.

Before presenting contemporary viewpoints regarding the physiological factors in a perception of film colour, I wish to diverge
chronologically for a moment to the position taken by Joseph
Albers. I mention Albers in that his exercises have held a prominent position in colour education. Further, his use of the word-
ing "film colour" is pertinent to my subject. In Chapter nine of
Interaction of Colour he notes the middle mixture between

two colours loses its opacity and can "... appear as a thin, transparent, translucent layer between the eye and an object, independent of the object's surface colour." Although he describes a filmic mode of appearance using terms such as transparent, translucent, frontal, as a colour without spatial localization in certain instances, and lists physiological filmic events such as atmosphere with a bluish hue, or reddish hue in the evening, when assigning the problem to practical exercises, he equates film colour with transparency. His fixed conception of film colour maintains influence, for example John Gage in *Colour and Culture*, 1993, relays per Albers (incorrectly so) that Katz actually means transparency when using the term film.

Faber Birren in 1976 was one artist and colour theorist who predicted the potentials of Katz' work when applied to artistic effects beyond perceptual transparency. He writes: "The work of Katz and others led me to formulate principles of colour expression which I believe are new to the art... [of colour]." Birren apprehends film as a fog or the sky and extended into space, likewise extending into or beyond the painting rather than a haze in front of the picture plane.

Present day psychologists have worked toward a clearer understanding of the filmic mode of appearance colour can take. A filmic appearance of colour can be seen or produced in ways other than with the spectroscope: in looking at the sky or into fog, by covering a portion of a bipolar point of vision with a nearer opaque surface, by the use of a semi-transparent material over a surface colour, in the looking at the visual grey after closing one's eyes. I should note here too that when gestalt psychologists or vision researchers look at film colour, many make no differentiation between the forms of film colour, the filmic appearance of colour in an aperture mode is examined for a more primary level of colour vision processing as a substitute for illusions created by contrast and assimilation effects in two dimensional patterning.

Jacob Beck defines film colour as "colour perceived as an expanse of light in a bi-dimensional plane without objective reference." (Beck, 1972) He suggests, based on the continuing use of an aperture to create the filmic experience, that "Optically, the stimulus for a film colour consists of an area of uniform luminance and chromaticity separated by a sharp contour from an area of lower luminance." Fabio Metelli, on the other hand, (Metelli, 1974) outlines filmic illusions as variations of transparency. Of course I am attempting to broaden this definition to include patterns of hues not seen within an aperture and tending toward a mode of appearance differing from strict transparency effects. I have incorporated Metelli's two original distinctions of transparency into three perceptual types of film colour to help clarify distinctions I have made in this paper. These are: 1) the physically filmic mode, for example air or colour perceived through an aperture; 2) the perceptually filmic mode, meaning a depiction of film as with utilizing a middle mixture of opaque papers, and 3) the retinally filmic mode, meaning the film results from viewing stimuli that does not necessarily depict any filmic illusion.

It is problematic to move from the theoretical to the practical in regard to film colour. Film colour can involve distinct illusory phenomena — that of perceived transparency, the spreading or Bezold-Brücke effect, optical mixture of contrast and of near assimilation, to name a few. Observations also show it is often difficult to predict which colour interactions will produce filmic illusions. Dorothea Jameson notes that we probably can set up a quantitative formula for filmic appearance, and determine receptive field sizes as well as the prime viewing distance from the painting, and still this will not indicate whether a spreading of hue or a filmic illusion will occur. The process of our perceiving a filmic illusion involves both retinal and post retinal pathways although I hesitate to make the separation.

Inhibitions and excitations of the retina may exist in at least 13 levels along the synaptic pathway. Responses from one level may influence other levels in a variety of ways through inhibition, excitation, averaging and lateral interactions, yet many of the exact processes have not been firmly established. A perception of film colour most likely includes aspects of both the trichromatic and opponent process functions of colour perception. Further, the additive and subtractive mixture theories play roles in our perception of the coloured stimuli. Floyd Ratliff has suggested these theories are not so polarized when we perceive paintings, but in effect one colour theory involves both optical mixture and an interaction of colour, yet pointing out conditions may emphasize one or the other.

On the other hand, Ellen Marx proposes we designate a third category termed 'optical synthesis' to describe the interplay of the two mixture systems. If the hue of film colour created by optical mixture is, as some suggest, an averaging of the hues in the stimulus, our discussions of film colour will want to include the types of colour mixtures so that we may begin to explain the perceptual aberrations in seemingly constant colour mixture rules. Exact colour stimuli that cause filmic modes of appearance as well as the aspects of the film are areas that require a great deal more practical experimentation. I believe I am safe in saying no process of a perception of film can exist as a function of the retina only. I also may be on solid ground in suggesting that components of wide spectral differences falling on a large receptive field of the eye may induce a spreading and often filmic illusion. This particular idea was also expressed by von Bezold and by Dorothea Jameson.

The depth perception present in observations of film colour is also an area of great controversy. The way in which spatial and spectral information is mediated by one or more systems in the visual path continued to be explored. Studies have shown that certain ganglion cells may primarily process spatial and contrast information while others process movement and directional information. Lastly, we may note that uniformity and repetition is often a harder optical focus for the eye. Jameson and Hurvich have examined repetitions of colour and line suggesting one can see: "...a line pattern present, and simultaneously...the mixture of these lines with their adjacent image areas."

A perception of film through interactions of colours utilizes visual processes that also make distinctions about types of information while reconciling them into a complete organization. Livingstone has shown how our visual system is composed of three types of pathways, one that transmits information regarding border contrasts and other high resolution static form, one that transmits colour and grey information, and one that transmits movement and stereoscopic information. Regarding film colour, her findings suggest that when colour borders are equiluminant or where strong luminance contrast exists, a vibration takes place as one system can process the shapes, but the movement system cannot account for the borders and is unable to signal either movement or position. 'Hence,' she writes "...it seems to jump around, drift or vibrate on the canvas." She notes colours integrated into a fine pattern that appear to bleed or blend probably lie beyond the resolution threshold of our colour perception system. Thus I return to the two elements I suggest as the basis for promoting a filmic illusion: high contrast of hue or near assimilation of hue and a repeating element of design.

I mention that other artists, some in the groups 'N' and 'T' in Italy during the early 1960's and others exploring 'Optical Art,' infrequently stumbled upon filmic effects, Richard Anuszkiewicz for example. One of the first American artists, if not the first, who purposely explored Katz's ideas in painting was Vincent Longo. Focusing on Katz's 'subject visual grey' as a filmic experience, Longo made paintings during the 1960's that approached the metaphoric experience of looking when one's eyes are closed, in other words, as a non-localized grey. The works are somewhat akin to an aperture form of colour appearance. Literal apertures were constructed by James Turrell and Robert Irwin.

Longo was also influential in introducing Katz's ideas to other artists. One such artist, Sandford Wurmfeld, is now directly pursuing the creation of film colour in painting. His paintings involve near assimilation and contrast of hues, and transparency illusions that interact to create a haze of film colour. Although we perceive the surface design of the painting, duration in viewing and the optical mixing of the colours quickly generates an illusion of non-surface localized colour. In my works, I have attempted to use contrasts and repetitions of ramping colours to create an optical blur. This blur, or coloured Mach banding, also acts as a stimulus for a filmic haze. Photographs cannot duplicate the filmic effects found in actual viewing of the paintings and with all the works viewing distance, size of the receptive field and luminance play key roles in the perception of the filmic mode of appearance.

Film colour is a subtle and complex phenomenon and in this paper I have stressed only a few of its aspects. We now have, as educators, the occasion to introduce the concept of film colour to students for their analyses. As artists we have the opportunity to investigate a relatively unexplored phenomenon in a ground breaking role. Further, explorations of film colour allow us the possibility to refine our empirical creation working jointly with recently available insights of vision researchers, psychologists, and neurobiologists. In ending, I will return to David Katz to remind us:

"We must constantly emphasize the fact that visual sensations … are not physical 'reals' but are rather hypothetical constructs … one would emphasize anew the methodological necessity for a position which takes natural colour-experience as its starting-point."

Acknowledgements

I wish to thank Dorothea Jameson, James Gibson and Floyd Ratliff for their comments on the physiological and psychological aspects of this paper; and Sandford Wurmfeld and Vincent Longo for discussing their paintings and lending images.

References

ALBERS, J. (1963) Interaction of Color. New Haven: Yale University Press.

BEAUMONT, R. (1912) Color in Woven Design, Being a Treatise on the Science and Technology of Textile Colouring Woollen, Worsted, Cotton and Silk Materials. 2nd ed., London: Whittaker.

BECK J. (1972) Surface Color Perception. Ithaca: Cornell University Press.

BEZOLD, W. von, (1876) The Theory of Color; in its Relation to Art and Art-Industry. (trans. S.R. Koehler). Boston L. Prang.

BIRREN, F. (1976) Color Perception in Art. West Chester: Schiffer Publishing Ltd., 1986.

BLANC, C. (1872) Grammaire Des Arts Du Dessin. (trans. K.N. Doggett). New York: Hurd and Houghton, 1874. pp. 145-169.

DRESSER, C. (1873) Principles of Decorative Design. 4th Edition, New York, 1882.

FÉNÉON, F. (1886) Les Impressionnistes en 1886. In: Impressionism and Post-Impressionism 1874 - 1904. (trans. L. Nochlin), Englewood Cliffs: Prentice Hall, 1966, pp. 108-110.

GAGE, J. (1993) Color and Culture: Practice and Meaning from Antiquity to Abstraction. Boston: Little, Brown and Company.

ITTEN, J. (1961) The Art of Color. New York: Reinhold Publishing Corporation.

JAMESON, D. and Hurvich, L. (1975) From Contrast to Assimilation: In Art and in the Eye. In: Leonardo, vol. 8, Spring, pp. 125-131.

JONES, O., (1852) An Attempt to Define the Principles Which Should Regulate the Employment of Colour in the Decorative Arts, with a Few Words on the Present Necessity of an Architectural Education on the Part of the Public... (Read Before the Society of Arts, April 28, 1852), London: G. Barclay.

KAHN, G., (1891) Seurat. In : Seurat in Perspective. (ed. N. Broude) New Jersey: Prentice Hall, Inc., 1978.

KATZ, D. (1911) Die Erscheinungsweisen der Farben und ihre Beeinflussung durch die individuelle Erfahrung. In: The World of Colour. New York: Johnson Reprint Corporation, 1935.

LIVINGSTON, M.S. and Hubel, D.H. (1988) Art, Illusion and the Visual System. In: Scientific American, vol. 258, pp. 78-85.

MARTIN, M.F. (1922) Film, Surface, and Bulky Colors and Their Intermediates. In: The American Journal of Psychology, vol. 33, no. 4, pp. 451-480.

MARX, E. (1981) Couleur optique. rpt. Optical Color and Simultaneity. (trans. G. O'Brien), New York: Van Nostrand Reinhold (1983).

METELLI, F. (1974) The Perception of Transparency. In: Scientific American, vol. 230, no. 4, pp. 90-98.

RATLIFF, F. (1992) Paul Signac and Color in Neo-Impressionism. New York: The Rockefeller University Press.

ROOD, O.N. (1879) Student's Text-Book of Color; or Modern Chromatics with Applications to Art and Industry, New York: D. Appleton and Co. 1908.

SIGNAC, P., (1921) From Eugäne Delacroix to Neo-Impressionism.In: Ratliff, F.(1992) Paul Signac and Color in Neo-Impressionism. (trans. W. Silverman), New York: The Rockefeller University Press.

WEBSTER, J.C. (1944) The Technique of Impressionism: A Reappraisal. In: The College Art Journal, November, no. 4, pp. 3-22.

The Pleasantness of Bi-Colour Combinations of the Four Unique Hues

At the beginning of this century E. Bullough (1907) published the paper *On the apparent heaviness of colour. A contribution to the aesthetics of colour*, which was the first of a long series of works about the weight of colours and the pleasantness of colour combinations. Bullough's idea was that the spatial arrangement of two colours had to obey the gravity principle, in the sense that the heavier colour had to stay in the lower part of a display and the lighter colour in the higher part. With this arrangement one gets a balanced combination which therefore appears natural and pleasant. The weight of the single colours has to be carefully evaluated in order to generate balanced and pleasant combinations. Nevertheless a heavier colour can be put in the upper part of the display, provided its area be reduced in comparison with that of the lighter colour. The influence of hue, value, chroma, and other colour characteristics, has been studied with regard to the apparent weight of colours, and related to the pleasantness of colour combinations by a number of researchers (J.D. De Camp, 1917; M. Monroe, 1927; C.D. Taylor, 1930; M. Carr Payne, 1958, 1961; E. Pinkerton & N.K. Humphrey, 1974; K.R. Alexander & M.S. Shansky, 1976). The warmth of colour was also associated to its weight (B. Wright, 1962).

On the other hand J.E. De Camp (1917) observed that the influence of colour of an object on its apparent weight is relatively small. C.J. Warden & E.L. Flynn (1926) started very early to analyse the effect of colour on apparent size and weight, and later Moon & Spencer (1944a, 1944b, 1944c) handled the problem of area and other related aspects in a systematic and quantitative way. Pope (1944) argued against their assumptions, considering them either incorrect or at least open to question, and recommended his colour system as a more useful instrument to analyse colour harmony (see also E. Heila, 1988).

The effect of area in colour balance seems to have been first considered by G. Fiels (1845) but from a different perspective which was later expanded by Munsell himself (1911): to arrange a pleasant combination, the relative areas of two colours had to be adjusted in such a way that a neutral gray can be obtained mixing the two colours in the same proportion on a spinning disc. This concept of harmonious balance about the neutral colours received special emphasis by many researchers and artists up to our days (among others, Morris Dunlop & Hammond 1982; Morris & Dunlop, 1987).

Another approach to the study of colour combinations is centred on the analysis of the affective values of the single colours. In the quoted series of works it was assumed that a balance between two colours depends on the weight of the single colours: here too the pleasantness of a bicolour combination is considered a linear function of the pleasantness of the single colours, and therefore the pleasantness of the whole can be predicted from the characteristics of the single components. Although experimental studies on colour preference go back to J. Cohn (1894), the work by Guilford and colleagues put the modern basis for quantifying the affective value of single colours (J.P. Guilford, 1931) and of colour combinations (E.C. Allen & J.P. Guilford, 1936; J.P. Guilford & P.C. Smith, 1959). Other authors tried to model the relationships between hue, value, saturation and single colour pleasantness on the one hand (R.D. Norman & W.A Scott, 1952, a review; G. Smets, 1982) and colour combination harmony on the other hand (G.W. Granger, 1953, 1955a, 1955b, 1955c; K.O. Goetz & K. Goetz, 1974a, 1974b, 1975).

A further kind of approach to single colour pleasantness and colour combination harmony made use of semantic differential response and factorial analysis (B. Wright & L. Rainwater, 1962; J. Hogg, 1969a, 1969b; L. Sivik & A. Hard, 1974, 1989; L. Sivik

& C. Taft, 1989, 1992), and, more recently, of multidimensional scaling (D.J. Polzella & D.A. Montgomery, 1993).

According to K.E. Burchett (1991), who tried to reduce to six the categories under which colour harmony is examined in nine books on colour, the role of colour systems appears to have always obtained a special position in the treatment of colour combination pleasantness. It is rather well known that the main colour systems devised until our days are primarily concerned with colour notations and colour combination theory (G. Dumarest, 1957): just to mention the most known systems applied to colour harmony, one can recall Munsell (1991); Ostwald (see: W.C. Granville, 1944; E. Jacobson, 1948), Abbot (1947), Mueller (1944, 1946, 1948; also: W. Spillmann ed., 1987), Coloroid (Nemcsics, 1980).

Our work took into account the theories by Abbot and Mueller, and the development of their ideas, promoted by Spillmann (1983), is the core of our hypotheses.

Lightness vs Whiteness and Blackness

Leaving aside for the moment the problem of hue and saturation, the role of lightness in determining the pleasantness of colour combinations has been always considered critical: the results of the experimental aforementioned works can be divided into three sections, those in favour of the decisive relevance of lightness (M. Carr Payne Jr, 1961; B. Wright, 1962; K.R. Alexander & M.S. Shansky, 1976) those against (E. Pinkerton & N.K. Humphrey, 1974; D.J. Polzella & D.A. Montgomery, 1993) and those neutral (Bullough, 1907; G. Smets, 1982; R.H. Morris & W.L. Dunlap, 1987). An interesting observation, put forward by J.M. Pieters (1979) on the basis of his experimental results, stresses the joint effect of hue and

lightness harmony which changes with saturation in harmony. This consideration leads us to reconsider a recent theory in which not the simple lightness of colours, but their natural 'lightness' plays a major role (already H.J. Eysenck, 1941, emphasised the importance of the "luminosity factor" of the different wavelengths in determining the pleasantness of the single colours).

Abbott (1947) and Mueller (1948), almost contemporarily, proposed that colour combinations of different hues can be harmonious if the colours correspond to the natural lightness ratios of hues (i.e. to their relative brilliances found in the spectrum. As regard to this concept, M. Monroe already in 1926 was speaking of an "inherent brightness of the chroma", as a relevant factor determining the colour apparent weight). The statement means that two colours of different hues are "corresponding" as regard to their natural lightness ratios if the lighter the hue the lighter also the colour in the combination (and the darker the hue, the darker the colour). For instance, in a 'correspondent' combination, one particular red must always be chosen darker than a particular yellow with which it is combined, because the red hue is naturally darker than the yellow hue.

On this basis, Mueller built a chromatic test to evaluate the artistic predisposition of people: the aim of his test was to differentiate the gifted persons from the non artistic ones. In fact those who liked the inverted combinations, i.e. the combinations in which the lightnesses were reversed in comparison with the natural lightness of their hues, were supposed to be artistically poor. The interest of this view was that lightness and hue were not considered independent variables, but interacting factors.

W. Spillmann, pupil and co-worker of Mueller, recognised that the idea of inter-relating hue and lightness was very interesting, but he realised that sometimes correspondent combinations appeared not so nice as expected, while inverted combinations could sometimes look quite agreeable. Therefore he proposed a modification of the theory, incorporating the concepts of whiteness and blackness together with that of lightness (W. Spillmann, 1983, 1985).

The new formulation then, which referred to the Natural Colour System as devised by Hering (1874) and implemented by the Swedish NSC Company, comprehended three kinds of bi-colour combinations: a) the 'correspondent' combinations in which the colour of the naturally lighter hue appears whiter and less blackish than the colour of darker hue; b) the 'distinct inverted' (or simply 'inverted') combinations, in which the colour of lighter hue appears blacker and less whitish than the other colour; c) thirdly, the 'vague inverted' combinations, in which one colour is both whiter and blacker than the other colour. Moreover, in the natural colour system it is still possible, and apparently also necessary, to take into account the different lightness levels: thus also lightness, in addition to whiteness and blackness, should be reversed to make a distinct inverted combination.

The theoretical predictions put forward by Spillmann were that correspondent combinations had to always appear agreable, while the vague inverted combinations had to always look unpleasant and disharmonious; the distinct inverted colour combinations normally show an unusual appearance, not appreciated by most people, but the prediction is that sometimes they can be considered attractive by subjects who like novelty and extraordinariness.

Such hypotheses have been tested for a limited number of colour combinations, both with adult and young subjects (O. da Pos & G. Fabrizi , 1988; G. Fabrizi & G. Vigliocco, 1988; O. da Pos, 1992b), with positive results.

The Experiment

This experimental research is limited to heterochromatic bi-colour combinations in which only the four unique hues are coupled together. The main hypothesis is that, in any case, independently from the hues involved, correspondent combinations have to be judged more positively than the vague inverted ones, and that the distinct inverted combinations have to be generally rejected, except in special cases.

Material

For each hue pair, the three correspondent, distinct inverted and vague inverted combinations have been prepared using sheets of paper supplied by the NCS Company (Sweden). Good correspondence between nominal and real notations was achieved by assuring a good natural illumination and a standard colour adaptation of the observers, who were facing a whitish wall near a window open toward north sky.

Helson and Lansford (1970) studied the pleasantness of object colours observed against a uniform coloured background and under different illuminations. Their results did not evidence relevant differences when the role of the two colours was reversed. Similarly, in a previous research, da Pos & Fabrizi (1988) had the same results when the figure/background function of the two component colours was inverted. Therefore in this experiment the two colours of each combination were arranged in a six square (5 x 5 cm) checkerboard, and pasted over a white rectangular (15 x 20 cm) cardboard (Fig. 1) to neutralise the figure/background salience.

The total number of bi-colour combinations was 18. Table 1 lists all the combinations used in the experiment. Beside the NCS

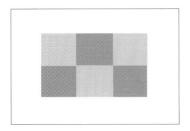

Fig. 1 - Display with the two colour combination.

notation of the component colours, their lightness (Y) is also registered following the Svensk Standard SS 01 91 03 (1982).

Very little agreement can be found in the literature about the role of lightness contrast in conditioning the pleasantness of bicoloured combinations (see J. Cohn, 1894, and J.T. Metcalf, 1927, just to quote two early divergent positions in the subject, and R.H. Morris & W.L. Dunlap, 1987, D.J. Polzella & D.A. Montgomery, 1993, for a more recent debate): therefore we reported also the lightness contrast value of each combination according to the formula: $C = (Ya - Yb) / (Ya + Yb)$ for a successive comment.

TABLE 1. - The 18 bi-colour combinations used in the experiment.

N°	1st Colour NSC Notation	1st Colour Lightness (Y)	2nd Colour NSC Notation	2nd Colour Lightness (Y)	Lightness Contrast	Comb Kind
1	40 60 B	09.35	20 70 G	20.06	0.364	C
2	40 60 B	09.35	20 70 Y	39.83	0.620	C
3	10 60 B	29.80	20 70 R	13.15	0.388	C
4	40 60 B	09.35	20 70 R	13.15	0.166	I
5	10 60 B	20.90	20 70 G	20.06	0.021	I
6	10 70 B	24.44	30 60 Y	31.41	0.125	I
7	30 50 B	17.85	20 70 G	20.06	0.058	VI
8	20 60 B	20.90	10 80 R	16.69	0.112	VI
9	30 50 B	17.85	20 70 Y	39.83	0.381	VI
10	40 60 R	08.00	20 70 Y	39.83	0.665	C
11	20 70 R	13.15	10 60 G	39.41	0.500	C
12	30 50 R	17.31	20 70 Y	39.83	0.394	VI
13	10 80 R	16.69	20 60 G	26.69	0.230	VI
14	10 70 R	24.80	30 60 Y	31.41	0.118	I
15	20 70 R	13.15	40 60 G	10.23	0.125	I
16	20 70 Y	39.83	30 50 G	22.13	0.286	VI
17	30 60 Y	31.41	10 70 G	28.45	0.049	I
18	20 70 Y	39.83	40 60 G	10.23	0.591	C

Subjects

One hundred persons, aged between 20 and 60 years, 45 male and 55 female, took part in the experiment. All had normal colour vision. In the collection of the data, the whole group was randomly divided into four subgroups of 25 subjects each, for a successive comparison of their results. In fact we also wanted to control how many subjects could be considered optimal for such kind of research.

Procedure

There are many different methods to rank a series of stimuli according to some perceptual criteria. The pair comparison method is one of the most used when the number of stimuli is not too large; otherwise a direct estimation can be used. In analogous previous studies (Fabrizi & Vigliocco, 1988) very similar results were obtained by the two methods. A third way to scale stimuli which have a common attribute varying in degree of intensity is the ranking method in which the observer directly disposes the stimuli in a subjective sequence. The 'ranking' method has been also called the 'arranging' method by J.E. De Camp (1917), who expressed his personal preference for the pair comparison method which he considered more scientific. In fact this method assures a careful consideration of all the possible comparisons between the stimuli, and for this reason it has been widely used in psychological research.

Because of the length of the task, the subjects were singularly tested in four sessions, separated by three relaxing periods of different length, according to the needs.

All the 153 possible pairs, one at a time, were kept by the hands of the experimenter in a vertical position, a few centimeters be-

N°	NCS Notation	Lightness (Y)
1	20 70 Y	39.83
2	20 70 R	13.15
3	20 70 B	15.99
4	20 70 G	20.06

TABLE 2. - Single hue colours.

tween one card and the other, and randomly shown to the subjects at a distance of about 50 cm from their eyes. For half the subjects the orientation of the cards was reversed, in order to compensate for the right/left anisotropy of the display. Subjects had to report in a short time which combination they preferred. The same task was performed as regard to the single four unique hues: all the possible pairs made of the colours listed in Table 2 have been shown to the subjects for their preference choice.

Results

The raw data were analysed according to Brunoro's method (1980). The resulting scale of preference for all subjects is shown in Tables 3-4. For each pair of hues, the three correspondent, inverted and vague inverted combinations have been grouped, keeping unaltered their order with respect to the main preference scale, and shown in Table 5. The results of the male subjects are shown in Table 6, and Table 7 shows the results of the females; male and female subjects are compared in Table 8 as far as the preference for different hue combinations is concerned.

TABLE 3 - General scale of preference for the 18 bi-colour combinations obtained by means of the pair comparison method: the distance between the combinations is described by z points, and is normalised in a scale starting at point zero.

N°	1st Colour NSC Notation	2nd Colour NSC Notation	Z Scale	Normalised Scale	Rank	Kind
1	40 60 B	20 70 G	-0.382	0.000	1	C
2	40 60 B	20 70 Y	-0.270	0.113	2	C
3	10 60 B	20 70 R	0.162	0.544	13	C
4	40 60 B	20 70 R	-0.165	0.217	6	I
5	10 60 B	20 70 G	0.012	0.394	10	I
6	10 70 B	30 60 Y	0.286	0.668	17	I
7	30 50 B	20 70 G	0.210	0.592	15	VI
8	20 60 B	10 80 R	0.004	0.386	9	VI
9	30 50 B	20 70 Y	0.053	0.436	12	VI
10	40 60 R	20 70 Y	-0.219	0.163	5	C
11	20 70 R	10 60 G	0.033	0.415	11	C
12	30 50 R	20 70 Y	0.176	0.560	14	VI
13	10 80 R	20 60 G	-0.016	0.367	8	VI
14	10 70 R	30 60 Y	0.444	0.827	18	I
15	20 70 R	40 60 G	-0.236	0.146	4	I
16	20 70 Y	30 50 G	-0.055	0.327	7	VI
17	30 60 Y	10 70 G	0.225	0.607	16	I
18	20 70 Y	40 60 G	-0.264	0.119	3	C

TABLE 4 - General order of preference for the different bi-colour combinations.

Preference Order	Comb. N°	1st Colour NSC Notation	2nd Colour NSC Notation	Lightness Contrast	Normalised Distances	Comb. Kind
1	1	40 60 B	20 70 G	0.364	0.000	C
2	2	40 60 B	20 70 G	0.620	0.113	C
3	18	10 80 R	20 60 G	0.230	0.119	C
4	15	10 70 B	30 60 Y	0.125	0.146	I
5	10	40 60 R	20 70 Y	0.665	0.163	C
6	4	40 60 B	20 70 R	0.166	0.217	I
7	16	20 70 Y	30 50 G	0.286	0.327	VI
8	13	10 80 R	20 60 G	0.230	0.367	VI
9	8	20 60 B	10 80 R	0.112	0.386	VI
10	5	10 60 B	20 70 G	0.021	0.394	I
11	11	20 70 R	10 60 G	0.500	0.415	C
12	9	30 50 B	20 70 Y	0.381	0.436	VI
13	3	10 60 B	20 70 R	0.388	0.544	C
14	12	30 50 R	20 70 Y	0.394	0.560	VI
15	7	30 50 B	20 70 G	0.058	0.592	VI
16	17	30 60 Y	10 70 G	0.049	0.607	I
17	6	10 70 B	30 60 Y	0.125	0.668	I
18	14	10 70 R	30 60 Y	0.118	0.827	I

Preference Order	Comb. N°	1st Colour NSC Notation	2nd Colour NSC Notation	Lightness Contrast	Normalised Distances	Kind
Red - Green						
4	15	20 70 R	40 60 G	0.125	0.146	I
8	13	10 80 R	20 60 G	0.230	0.367	VI
11	11	20 70 R	10 60 G	0.500	0.415	C*
Blue- Green						
1	1	40 60 B	20 70 G	0.364	0.000	C
10	5	10 60 B	20 70 G	0.021	0.394	I
15	7	30 50 B	20 70 G	0.058	0.592	VI
Yellow - Green						
3	18	20 70 Y	40 60 G	0.591	0.119	C
7	16	20 70 Y	30 50 G	0.286	0.327	VI
16	17	30 60 Y	10 70 G	0.049	0.607	I
Blue - Red						
6	4	40 60 B	20 70 R	0.166	0.217	I
9	8	20 60 B	10 80 R	0.112	0.386	VI
13	3	10 60 B	20 70 R	0.388	0.544	C*
Blue - Yellow						
2	2	40 60 B	20 70 Y	0.620	0.113	C
12	9	30 50 B	20 70 Y	0.381	0.436	VI
17	6	10 70 B	30 60 Y	0.125	0.668	I
Red - Yellow						
5	10	40 60 R	20 70 Y	0.665	0.163	C
14	12	30 50 R	20 70 Y	0.394	0.560	VI
18	14	10 70 R	30 60 Y	0.118	0.827	I

TABLE 5. - Order of preference of the different hue combinations. C* = unexpected positions.

N°	1st Colour NSC Notation	2nd Colour NSC Notation	Z Scale	Normalised Scale	Rank	Comb. Kind
1	40 60 B	20 70 G	-0.381	0.000	1	C
2	40 60 B	20 70 Y	-0.266	0.115	2	C
3	10 60 B	20 70 R	0.109	0.490	13	C
4	40 60 B	20 70 R	-0.256	0.125	3	I
5	10 60 B	20 70 G	0.008	0.389	8	I
6	10 70 B	30 60 Y	0.254	0.635	17	I
7	30 50 B	20 70 G	0.200	0.583	15	VI
8	20 60 B	10 80 R	0.075	0.456	11	VI
9	30 50 B	20 70 Y	0.017	0.398	9	VI
10	40 60 R	20 70 Y	-0.225	0.156	6	C
11	20 70 R	10 60 G	0.032	0.413	10	C
12	30 50 R	20 70 Y	0.123	0.504	14	VI
13	10 80 R	20 60 G	0.088	0.469	12	VI
14	10 70 R	30 60 Y	0.479	0.860	18	I
15	20 70 R	40 60 G	-0.262	0.119	4	I
16	20 70 Y	30 50 G	-0.011	0.370	7	VI
17	30 60 Y	10 70 G	0.239	0.617	16	I
18	20 70 Y	40 60 G	-0.226	0.155	5	C

TABLE 6. - Scale of preference for the 18 colour combinations obtained by the male subjects.

N°	1st Colour NSC Notation	2nd Colour NSC Notation	Z Scale	Normalised Scale	Rank	Comb. Kind
1	40 60 B	20 70 G	-0.388	0.000	1	C
2	40 60 B	20 70 Y	-0.276	0.112	3	C
3	10 60 B	20 70 R	0.206	0.594	13	C
4	40 60 B	20 70 R	-0.094	0.293	7	I
5	10 60 B	20 70 G	0.015	0.402	10	I
6	10 70 B	30 60 Y	0.315	0.703	17	I
7	30 50 B	20 70 G	0.218	0.606	15	VI
8	20 60 B	10 80 R	-0.052	0.335	9	VI
9	30 50 B	20 70 Y	0.085	0.473	12	VI
10	40 60 R	20 70 Y	-0.219	0.169	4	C
11	20 70 R	10 60 G	0.035	0.423	11	C
12	30 50 R	20 70 Y	0.227	0.614	16	VI
13	10 80 R	20 60 G	-0.102	0.286	6	VI
14	10 70 R	30 60 Y	0.422	0.810	18	I
15	20 70 R	40 60 G	-0.218	0.170	5	I
16	20 70 Y	30 50 G	-0.093	0.295	8	VI
17	30 60 Y	10 70 G	0.216	0.603	14	I
18	20 70 Y	40 60 G	-0.299	0.089	2	C

TABLE 7. - Scale of preference for the 18 colour combinations obtained by the female subjects.

	Male		Female	
	Comb.N°	Kind	Comb.N°	Kind
Red - Green				
	15	I	15	I
	11	C	13	VI
	13	VI	11	C*
Blue- Green				
	1	C	1	C
	5	I	5	I
	7	VI	7	VI
Blue - Red				
	4	I	4	I
	8	VI	8	VI
	3	C*	3	C*
Blue- Yellow				
	2	C	2	C
	9	VI	9	VI
	6	I	6	I
Yellow- Green				
	18	C	18	C
	16	VI	16	VI
	17	I	17	I
Red - Yellow				
	10	C	10	C
	12	VI	12	VI
	14	I	14	I

Table 8 - Scales of preference for the different hue combinations as a function of sex. C* = unexpected positions.

A scale of preference has been also derived for each subject, and from the whole population six subgroups have been extracted through a cluster analysis. Subjects are considered to belong to one particular subgroup when their scales of preference are highly correlated, i.e. they make very similar choices. The scales of preference of each group are shown in Tables 9, and Table 10 shows an overview of the preferences of the different subgroups with respect to each pair of hues. Table 11 exhibits the preference scales of the different groups of subjects with regard to the single hues.

Discussion

The first comments regard the congruence of the results with the general hypothesis: it is possible to affirm that the data are

TABLE 9. - Order of preference of the six subgroups.

Group A 17 Sogg			Group B 13 Sogg			Group C 10 Sogg			Group D 9 Sogg			Group E 9 Sogg			Group F 8 Sogg		
N°	Col.	Kind	N°	Col.	Kind	N°	Col.	Kind	N°	Col.	Kind	N°	v	Kind	N°	Col.	Kind
10	RY	C	16	YG	VI	15	RG	I	15	RG	I	1	BG	C	2	BY	C
2	BY	C	14	RY	I	4	BR	I	8	BR	VI	15	RG	I	10	RY	C
18	YG	C	5	BG	I	18	YG	C	4	BR	I	5	BG	I	9	BY	VI
16	YG	VI	17	YG	I	1	BG	C	13	RG	VI	18	GY	C	15	YG	C
1	BG	C	6	BY	I	10	RY	C	1	BG	C	7	BG	VI	4	BR	I
9	BY	VI	9	BY	VI	2	BY	C	3	BR	C	10	RY	C	12	RY	VI
12	RG	VI	8	BR	VI	13	BR	VI	11	RG	C	2	BY	C	1	BG	C
15	RG	I	11	RG	C	8	BR	VI	5	BG	I	16	YG	VI	3	BR	C
4	BR	I	13	RG	VI	9	BY	VI	7	BG	VI	4	BR	I	8	BR	VI
17	YG	I	2	BY	C	3	BR	C	18	YG	C	11	RG	C	11	RG	C
6	BY	I	1	BG	C	16	YG	VI	2	BY	C	13	RG	VI	16	YG	VI
13	RG	VI	12	RY	VI	5	BG	I	10	RY	C	12	RY	VI	15	RG	I
14	RG	I	3	BR	C	11	RG	C	17	YG	I	17	YG	I	6	BY	I
7	BG	VI	18	YG	C	12	RY	VI	6	BY	I	9	BY	VI	13	RG	VI
11	RG	C	7	BG	VI	17	YG	I	16	YG	VI	3	BR	C	17	YG	I
5	RG	I	10	RY	C	6	BY	I	9	BY	VI	8	BR	VI	14	RY	I
8	BR	VI	4	BR	I	7	BG	VI	14	RY	I	6	BY	I	5	BG	I
3	BR	C	15	RG	I	14	RY	I	12	RY	VI	14	RY	I	7	BG	VI

Group A N°	Kind	Group B N°	Kind	Group C N°	Kind	Group D N°	Kind	Group E N°	Kind	Group F N°	Kind
Red - Yellow											
10	C	14	I	10	C	10	C	10	C	10	C
12	VI	12	VI	12	VI	14	I	12	VI	12	VI
14	I	10	C	14	I	12	VI	14	I	14	I
Blue - Green											
1	C	5	I	1	C	1	C	1	C	1	C
7	VI	1	C	5	I	5	I	5	I	5	I
5	I	7	VI	7	VI	7	VI	7	VI	7	VI
Blue - Yellow											
2	C	6	I	2	C	2	C	2	C	2	C
9	VI	9	VI	9	VI	6	I	9	VI	9	VI
6	I	2	C	6	I	9	VI	6	I	6	I
Green Yellow											
18	C	16	VI	18	C	18	C	18	C	18	C
16	VI	17	I	16	VI	17	I	16	VI	16	VI
17	I	18	C	17	I	16	VI	17	I	17	I
Red - Green											
15	I	11	C	15	I	15	I	15	I	11	C
13	VI	13	VI	13	VI	13	VI	11	C	15	I
11	C	15	I	11	C	11	C	13	VI	13	VI
Blue - Red											
4	I	8	VI	4	I	4	I	4	I	4	I
8	VI	3	C	8	VI	8	VI	3	C	3	C
3	C	4	I	3	C	3	C	8	VI	8	VI

TABLE 10. - Order of preference for the different hue combinations according to the six subgroups of subjects.

Colour	From Combinations	General Ranking	Male Scale	Female Scale
Green	75	0.000	0.085	0.000
Blue	85	0.155	0.132	0.249
Red	88	0.142	0.000	0.327
Yellow	91	0.560	0.631	0.576

TABLE 11 - Scales of preference for the single hues. The first scale is derived from the preferences for bi-colour combinations; the second from the pair comparison of all the subjects; the third and fourth are related to the male and female subjects.

in very good agreement with the theory, with only two exceptions. Looking at the Tables 5, we see that in 16 cases the correspondent bi-colour combinations come before the vague inverted ones, while in other two cases they come after. From Table 5 it appears that only the females show this incongruity for both combinations while the male are anomalous only for one of them. In the case of the Blue - Red combinations, we could say that the difference between the natural lightnesses of the two hues is not very large (see Table 2) and therefore the concepts of correspondence and inversions applied to these two hue combinations might not be employed in a very strict sense.

The other faulty Red - Green combination cannot be explained in the same way, because the difference in lightness between the two hues is quite substantial, at least according the measures given by the NCS Company. This seems to be really an exception to the theory, although it is shown only by the females (Table 8). The positions of the inverted combinations are usually in the lower part of the scales, as it is expected; nevertheless for some particular hue pairs they appear in the upper part of the scales: this happens for the already mentioned Red - Blue and Red - Green pairs, but also for the Blue-Green pair.

In a previous research (da Pos, 1992a) a comparison has been made between people of different cultures and age (the bi-colour combinations were made of the Green and Blue hues), and it emerged that in South Brasil, and still more in India (Delhi) inverted combinations are better appreciated than in Italy (Venice and Milan). Moreover (da Pos, 1992b), among Italian children, the inverted combinations (always with the Green and Blue hues) are differently appreciated by different groups of subjects, ranking from the top to the bottom position, without substantial changes in the other kinds of combinations. As far as the lightness contrast is concerned, we can see from Tables 4 and 5 that it does not play an essential role, although highly contrasting colours usually are better appreciated than those showing low contrast. Therefore our results are not in favour of the theories which emphasise the role of lightness contrast in determining the pleasantness of colour combinations and agree with the recent findings by D.J. Polzella & D.A. Montgomery, 1993.

Looking at Table 5, the different hue pairs appear preferred in the order: 1) Red - Green (23 [4+8+11]); 2) Blue - Green (26); 3) Yellow - Green (26); 4) Blue - Red (28); 5) Blue - Yellow (31); 6) Red - Yellow (37). This order is not very decisive, because it depends on the specific nuances which have been combined. Nevertheless it shows that the presence of Green generally makes pleasant combinations, while the yellow makes the combinations less agreable.

If we look for the sex differences in Table 8, we realise that the two sexes are almost perfectly identical in their preference for the colour combinations, with the only exception, already mentioned, of the low appreciation of the correspondent Red - Green combination by females. On the other hand, the two sexes seem a little different as regard to the preference for the single hues (Table 11): males seem to prefer Red and Green while females Green and Blue, and both dislike Yellow.

If we randomly divide the whole group of subjects in four subgroups, and derive the scales of preference for each subgroup, these scales appear extremely highly correlated (between 90% and 95%): this means that we could have obtained the same main results from a smaller group of subjects, i.e. 25 instead of 100. Nevertheless, the large number of subjects we examined allowed us to perform some further interesting investigations. By a cluster analysis, we obtained six subgroups of a relatively large number of subjects who have the characteristics of being highly correlated inside each group (correlation between 45% and 90%), i.e. they showed almost the same preferences. Their average scales of colour preference are listed in Table 9, and in Table 10 we can see the main differences between the six subgroups: the group B appears the most special in comparison with the others.

For almost all kinds of hue combinations, the pleasantness scale of this subgroup is different from that of the other subgroups. On the contrary, the other subgroups reveal very little differences: the group A shows an inversion VI/I for the Blue - Green combinations, with the inverted combination at the bottom of the scale; the group C shows the same inversion in the Red - Yellow and Blue - Yellow combinations, the group E shows a VI/C inversion in the Red - Green and Blue - Red combinations with a stronger preference for the correspondent combination, the same is true for the group F with another inversion I/C in the Red - Green combinations. On the whole the differences are not large, except for group B, and it should be interesting to see if there are other personality traits correlated with these differences in colour preferences.

A number of unpublished experiments have evidenced no correlations between colour preferences analysed according to this methodology and results derived from different personality tests. Future experimental results may be more comforting: for the moment the research on colour preferences does not seem to support the claim of those personality tests which use colour preference as a diagnostic tool of personality.

References

ABBOTT A. G. (1947) The color of life. McGraw-Hill Book Company, Inc., New York & London.

ALEXANDER K.R. Shansky M.S. (1976) Influence of hue, value, and chroma on the perceived heaviness of colors. In: Percept. & Psychophysics,19, pp. 72-74

ALLEN E.C., Guilford J.P. (1936) Factors determining the affective values of color combinations. In: Am. J. of Psychol. 48, pp. 643- 648.

BRUNORO G. (1980) Il metodo della comparazione a coppie per la misura degli atteggiamenti. Liviana, Padova.

BULLOUGH E. (1907) On the apparent heaviness of colours. A contribution to the aesthetic of colour. In: Brit. J. of Psychol., 2, pp.111- 152.

BURCHETT K.E. (1991) Color Harmony Attributes. Col. Res. & Appl., 16, pp. 275-278.

CH'HUANG-FANG Lo (1936) The affective values of color combinations. In: Am. J. of Psychol. 48, pp. 617-624.

COHN J. (1894) Experimentelle Untersuchungen ueber die Gefuehlsbetonung der Farben, Helligkeiten und ihre Combinationen. In: Philos. Stud.,10, pp. 562-603.

DA POS O., Fabrizi G. (1988) An experimental contribution to colour harmony theory. In: Proceedings of AIC Interim Symposium on colour and environmental design, Winterthur(11) , pp. 1-5.

DA POS O. (1992) Colour combination pleasantness with surface and projected colours. Paper presented at the Princeton ISCC - AIC Interim Meeting 1992a.

DA POS O., (1992b) An experimental research into children preferences for colour combinations. Atti e Memorie dell'Accademia Patavina di Scienze Lettere ed Arti, 103, pp. 51-63.

DE CAMP J.E. (1917) The influence of color on apparent weight. A preliminary study. In: Journal of Experimental Psychology, 2, pp. 347-370.

DUMAREST S. (1957) Les donnees objectives fondamentales du probleme de l'esthetique chromatique. In: Meyerson Ed., Problemes de la Couleur. Sevepem, Paris, pp. 207-226.

EYSENCK H.J.(1941) A critical and experimental study of colour preferences. In: Am. J. of Psychol., 1941, 54, 385-394.

FABRIZI G., Vigliocco G. (1988) An experimental investigation on two colour combinations. In: Proceedings of AIC Interim Symposium on colour and environmental design, Winterthur, (11a), pp. 1-6.

GOETZ K.O., Goetz K. (1974a) Color attitudes of art students and university students: I. imagined colors. Percept. mot. Skills, 38, pp. 63-70.

GOETZ K.O., Goetz K.(1974) Color preferences of art students: surface colors. In: I. Percept. mot. Skills., 39, pp. 1103-1109.

GOETZ K.O., Goetz K. (1975) Color preferences of art students: surface colors. In: II. Percept. mot. Skills., 41, pp. 271-278.

GRANGER G.W. (1953) Area balance in color harmony: and experimental study. In: Science, 117, pp. 59-61

GRANGER G.W. (1955a) An experimental study of color harmony. In: J. of Gen. Psychol., 52, pp. 21-35.

GRANGER G.W. (1955b) Aesthetic measure applied to color harmony: an experimental test. In: J. of Gen. Psychol., 52, pp. 205-212.

GRANGER G.W. (1955c) The prediction of preference for color combinations. In: J. of Gen. Psychol., 52, pp. 213-222.

GRANVILLE W.C. (1944) Colorimetric specification of the Color Harmony Manual from Spectrophotometric Measurements. In: J. Opt. Soc. Am., 34, pp. 382-395.

GUILFORD J.P. (1931) The prediction of affective values. In: Am. J. of Psychol., 43, pp. 469-478.

GUILFORD J.P., Smith P.C. (1959) A system for color-preferences. In: Am. J. of Psychol., 72, pp. 487-502.

HEILA E. (1988) An Artist's Preference for the Pope Color System. In: Col. Res. & Appl., 13, pp. 260-263.

HELSON H., Lansford T. (1970) The role of spectral energy of source and background color in the pleasantness of object colors. In: Applied Optics, 9, pp. 1513-1562.

HERING E. (1874-1964) Outlines of a theory of the light sense. Trad.: Hurvich L. & Jameson D., Harvard University Press.

HOGG J. (1969a) A principal components analysis of semantic differential judgements of single colors and color pairs. In: J. of Gen. Psychol., 80, pp. 129-140.

HOGG J. (1969b) The prediction of semantic differential ratings of color combinations. In: J. of Gen. Psychol., 80, pp. 141-152.

JACOBSON E. (1948) Basic Color. An interpretation of the Ostwald Color System. Paul Theobald, Chicago.

METCALF J.T. (1927) The pleasantness of brightness combinations, In: Am. J. of Psychol., 38, pp. 607-623.

MONROE M. (1927) The apparent weight of color and correlated phenomena. In: Am. J. of Psychol., 36, pp. 192-206.

MOON P., Spencer D.E. (1944a) Geometric formulation of classical color harmony. In: J. Opt. Soc. Am., 34, pp. 46-60.

MOON P., Spencer D.E. (1944b) Area in color harmony. In: J. Opt. Soc. Am., 34, pp. 93-103.

174 MOON P., Spencer D.E. (1944c) Aesthetic measure applied to color harmony. In: J. Opt. Soc. Am., 34, pp. 234-242.

MORRIS R.H., Dunlap W.P., Hammond S.E. (1982) Influence of chroma on spatial balance of complementary hues. In: Am. J. of Psychol., 95, pp. 323-332.

MORRIS R.H., Dunlap W.P. (1987) Influence of value on spatial balance of color pairs. In: Am. J. of Psychol., 114, pp. 353-361.

MUELLER Ae. (1944) Das ABC der Farben. Zurich.

MUELLER Ae. (1946) Schweizer Farbenkombinator, Winterthur.

MUELLER Ae. (1948) Die moderne Farbenharmonielehre. Chromos, Winterthur.

NEMSICS A. (1980) Colour harmony in architectural space. In: Periodica Polytechnica. Budapest, 24, pp. 79-99.

NORMAN R.D., Scott W.A. (1952) Color and affect: a review and semantic evaluation. In: J. of Gen. Psychol., 46, pp. 185-223.

PAYNE, M.C. Jr. (1958) Apparent weight as a function of color. In: Am. J. of Psychol., 71, pp. 725-730.

PAYNE M.C. Jr. (1961) Apparent weight as a function of hue. In: Am. J. of Psychol. 1, 74, pp. 104-105.

PIETERS J.M. (1979) A conjoint measurement approach to color harmony. Percept. & Psychophysics, 26, pp. 281-286.

PINKERTON E., Humphrey N.K. (1974) The apparent heaviness of colours. In: Nature, 250, July 12, pp. 164-165.

POLZELLA D.J., Montgomery D.A. (1993) Dimensions of color harmony. In: Bull. of the Psychon. Soc., 31, pp. 423-425

POPE A. (1944) Notes on the problem of color harmony and the geometry of color space. With reference to articles by Moon and Spencer. In: J. Opt. Soc. Am., 34, pp. 759-765.

SIVIK L., Hard A. (1974) Outlines of a theory of colour in combination. In: Man-Environment Systems, 9, pp. 217-228.

SIVIK L., Hard A. (1989) On studying color combinations. Some reflections and preliminary experiments. In: Goteborg Psychol. Rep. 19 (2), pp. 1-38.

SIVIK L., Taft C.(1989) Semantic variables for judging color combinations. An analysis of semantic dimensions. In: Goteborg Psychol. Rep. 19 (5), pp. 1-22.

SIVIK L., Taft C.(1992) Colour combinations and associated meanings- semantic dimensions and colour chords. In: Goteborg Psychol. Rep. 1, pp. 1-25.

SMETS G. (1982) A tool for measuring relative effects of hue, brightness and saturation on color pleasantness. In: Percept. mot Skills, 55, pp. 1159-1164.

SPILLMAN W.(1983) Colour order systems and environmental colour design. In: Fargrapport F 26, AIC Midterm Meeting - The Forsius Symposium, Stockholm 1983.

SPILLMAN W. (1985) The concept of lightness ratios of hues in colour combination theory. In: AIC Mundial Couleur '85, MonteCarlo 1985.

SPILLMAN W. (1987) Color Order and Aesthetics: the oeuvre of Dr. Aemilius Mueller. The Bertha and K. Leubsdorf Art Gallery, Hunter College, New York.

SVENSK STANDARD SS 01 91 03, CIE Tristimulusvarden och trikromatiska koordinater for fargproverna i SS 01 91 02. SIS Standardiseringsgrupp, Stockholm, 1982

TAYLOR C. (1930) Visual perception versus visual plus kinaesthetic perception in judging colored weights. In: J. of Gen. Psychol. 4, pp. 229-246.

WARDEN C.J., Flynn E.L. (1926) The effect of color on apparent size and weight. In: Am. J. of Psychol., 37, pp. 398-401

WRIGHT B. (1962) The influence of hue, lightness and saturation on apparent warmth and weight. In: Am. J. of Psychol., 75, pp. 232-241.

WRIGHT B., Rainwater L. (1962) The meaning of color. In: J. of Gen. Psychol, 67, pp. 89-99.

an Janssens

The Impact of Colour Research on Design Practice and Education

A large amount of research on colour has been carried out during the last twenty years both in Sweden and elsewhere. Most of the research has dealt with the physical properties of colour and the physiological and phenomenological aspects of colour vision and colour perception. The research has, to a lesser degree, treated colour as a property of the built environment and, to an even smaller extent, the influence of colour on humans. Part of this knowledge is now in the process of being compiled on the initiative of the Swedish Council for Building Research and the Colour Science Foundation.

However, there seems to exist almost no research about how the presumed users of this knowledge, that is the specialists, like architects, interior designers, and colour consultants, have benefited from the large amount of colour research. Nor is it known to what extent the research findings have penetrated the educational process at the schools of architecture and interior design. Search of colour literature on this issue.

The aim of the present study was to investigate the actual knowledge about the results of colour research; the existing myths and beliefs about colour; the everyday choices of colour and coloured materials, and the motives behind these choices. This was studied amongst experts like architects, interior decorators and master house painters, as well as amongst the teachers and students at the schools of architecture and interior design. In order to widen the basis for analysis, the study will also be carried out in a cross-cultural context, including a comparison between Sweden and the United Kingdom. This will make it possible to evaluate the national strategies in research implementation; to compare the outcome of different educational curricula; and to separate individual and cultural factors in the final analysis.

Background and Problems

Considerable research, not least in Sweden, has been carried out to identify various salient colour dimensions and to construct a unified nomenclature of colour. Swedish researchers have been highly successful in establishing a coherent language based on colour perception, known as the NCS, the Natural Colour System. Environmental designers are supposed to be familiar with the system, especially since the NCS has a strong communicative potential in the design process. One aim of the study was to investigate the actual knowledge of practitioners and students concerning the NCS, and the extent to which the system is used in everyday colour choices.

Perceptual studies have demonstrated that various properties of colour may influence the perception of the built environment. Colour may be used to change (for instance) the apparent size, shape, warmth, complexity, coherence, and social value of an interior. Part of this is considered to be common knowledge, while other results are less well known. A second aim of the study was to investigate what actual knowledge exists amongst practitioners and students as concerns these perceptual properties of colour.

Recent psycho-physiological research has demonstrated that colour might influence the activation state (stress level) of the nervous system. In a study where two rooms of totally different characters were created, the one with many colours and patterns, the other grey and monotonous, it was shown that colours and patterns stimulated the electrical activity of the brain. In contrast, pulse rate was lower in the complex room, which might be interpreted as a compensatory response to visual overstimulation. In another study, red colours were shown to have an activating influence, while blue colours decreased the activation level of the nervous system.

It has been claimed that time should pass faster in a red as compared to a blue or green space. It has further been claimed that people would tend to feel warmer in rooms decorated with reds, yellows, oranges and rich browns, and conversely people would feel cooler when rooms are decorated in blues, greens, and pale neutrals. However, in series of laboratory studies, these claims have not been verified. Thus, there is good reason to doubt the existence of any colour influence on experienced time and temperature comfort. A third aim of the study was to investigate the extent to which practitioners and students make assumptions about physiological colour effects, whether these assumptions are correct, and eventually will influence their own design work.

Colour has been used for therapeutic purposes to induce mood changes in depressive or anxious patients. It has been claimed that specific colours may induce specific moods, that certain colours may have a positive effect on criminals; on patients suffering from Parkinson's disease; and on the intelligence development of children. Evidently studies of this kind suffer from a lack of experimental control. There are simply too many factors at work to enable any firm conclusion about the relative importance of colour. The fourth aim of the study was to sample the existing myths and beliefs about colour amongst both practitioners and students in order to elaborate a plan for future more critical research within this area.

Almost every year since the end of the 19th century there has been some study concerning colour preferences, the best known made by Eysenck, who compiled over 20 000 colour preference ratings previously carried out in diverse experiments and concluded that people prefer colours in the following order: blue, red, green, violet, orange and yellow. One of the most striking features of the results concerning preferences is the consistency from one individual to another, from group to group and cross-culturally. However, in some instances cultural differences have been found. One aim of the study was to chart the everyday choices of colours and coloured materials amongst practitioners and students and investigate the motives for these choices.

Methods

The study was carried out by means of interviews of experts (architects, interior designers, master house painters, and colour teachers) and questionnaires to students of architecture and interior design. In addition, an appraisal of educational curricula was made.

Figure 1 : The Study
Sampling of questions
Pilot study (questions tested by colour experts and researchers)

Interviews with colour practitioners (on their work offices)
- 20 architects
- 20 interior designers
- 20 master house painters

Interviews with colour teachers at six schools
Appraisals of educational curricula
Questionnaires to (first and final year) students at design schools
- 3 schools of architecture
- 2 schools of interior design
- I school of art
 (to be repeated in the United Kingdom)

On the basis of the problem areas presented above, the existing knowledge was compiled and transformed into an extensive interview form. The form was presented to colour researchers for comments, and after due corrections, used in interviews with 20 architects, 20 interior designers and 20 master house painters, randomly selected from the member lists of the professional associations in southern Sweden. Besides colour related questions, there were questions on background, including age, education, occupational standards, and individual response patterns.

The environmental design experts (practising architects, interior designers and masterhouse painters) were interviewed at their work offices, thus giving the interviewer the opportunity to make an inventory of available colour literature and other facilities. In general, the respondents also presented some relevant design projects, illustrating the colour work at the office. In our sample, all of the house painters, most of the architects and half of the interior designers were men. The ages of the respondents varied between 32 and 65, with a median of 46 years, and most of them had been practising their occupation for at least ten years.

On the basis of the results from the interviews with the experts, a questionnaire was developed and distributed to six schools for environmental designers: three schools of architecture, two schools of interior design and one school of art. The questionnaires were administered by the colour teachers to first year and final year students, giving the opportunity to gather additional information concerning the educational impact. In total, 228 students answered the questionnaire. Of the student respondents half were men and half were women, with an age span between 18 and 45, and a median of 24 years. The individual data were supplemented by an appraisal as concerns colour nomenclature

systems, colour perception, and exercises in colour design. This appraisal was done in collaboration with the teaching staff.

In order to be able to compare the outcome of the interviews of the practising design experts with the results of the questionnaires for the students, identically formulated questions were posed to all respondents. Both interviews and questionnaires started with background information on the respondent, emphasising job descriptions for the experts and educational curricula for the students. A rough disposition of the questions is given in figure 2.

Figure 2: Questions

Block I   -The respondent's background
          -Description of work office (experts) and educational situation
          (students)

Block 2   -Description of the creating process and colour design work
          -Expectations (first year students) and results of colour education
          (final year students)

Block 3   -Attitudes towards colour research
          -What is expected from colour research
          -What are the sources of colour research information
          -How does one to be informed about colour research

Block 4   -What is known about colour research:
          -Perceptual properties of colours
          -Physiological and psychological effects of colours
          -Preferences of colours

Block 5   -What is known about NCS (Natural Colour System)

Other   -Comments on the enquiry

Results: Design Practice
Environmental Design and Colour

The act of creating, including colour design, is a lonely process. All architects, half of the interior designers and more than one quarter of the house painters were alone in the initial creating phase of common design projects. Colleagues and other engaged persons were only sometimes involved at the end stage of larger projects. The interviews revealed the design work to be mostly an intuitive and often spontaneous act, rather than a conscious and rationally structured process. Architects often started from a more or less elaborated concept, based on a dominating idea or the formal conditions of the project, thus stating the "general tone" for the work, emanating in the colouring's "falling into place". Interior designers worked sometimes under more or less strict conditions, imposed by the head architect for the project. This was also the case for most of the house painters. External colour specialists were consulted only very rarely.

The design process was affected by the size of the office. In larger offices, many employees had clearly defined working fields, giving room for specialisation and delegating of specific tasks. Colour design might be such a task for a skilful colour designer. Smaller companies, on the other hand, offered more comprehensive opportunities for all, including all kind of tasks for most employees. In general, small offices spend proportionally more time on colour design than large companies do. Asked for specific time quantities, architects estimated their factual colour design time to be as little as two hours per week, while interior designers estimated it to be about 15 hours, and master house painters one hour per week only.

Two colour design strategies could be discerned. The one often applied in smaller offices involved colour consciousness under the entire design process. The other, mostly employed in larger companies, dealt with colour problems at the end of the design process, more or less as a "finishing touch". Almost all respondents wanted more time during the design work for colour questions.

The most important factor to the colour design work seemed to be the nature of the project. Public environments required completely different approaches in this respect as compared to private dwellings. In general larger projects received proportionally less time for colour design questions than smaller projects. Discussions with actual users or clients could demand a great deal of compromising from many parts, especially when it came to colour. Total creative freedom for designers was extremely rare. Environmental colour appeared to be one of the last unclaimed fields in this respect. A severe drawback for the serious colour design was the total contract work system. Elaborate colour designs were sometimes mutilated by the contractors into insensitive renderings of the original intentions. A wider possibility for interfering and correcting on the building site was wished for.

Design Experts and Colour Research

The investigation of attitudes towards colour research, as described here, is one of the crucial topics in this study. The interviews revealed a general positive feeling towards the results and the potential of scientific work in the field. All the interior designers and most of the architects were positive, although some of the latter feared that overly general preference studies might be interpreted as directions instead of guidelines. Master house painters were somewhat more sceptical towards scientific work and tended to rely more on their own practical experience.

Asked to recall known colour research or researchers, two thirds of the architects and half of the interior designers could state names or projects. Tangible results could be named by only a few. Common knowledge was generally limited to somewhat vague descriptions of particular research, mostly on preference and perception studies. Master house painters had difficulties in relating research work.

As to the importance of literature as a source of colour research information, only one tenth of the respondents related to specific literature on colour. Specialist handbooks and scientific reports were rarely named, and they were often several years old. Articles in designers' magazines and newspapers were read more often, even in Danish and German publications. An obvious search for relevant information apparently occurred only in direct connection with demanding colour tasks. Inspection of the bookshelves of the designers confirm the poor literature picture. If asked for good examples of readable literature, only some minor publications were mentioned. Generally, the need for a good handbook on colour was stressed. Nearly one third of the architects and interior designers did sporadically attend courses or conferences on colour. Although many found this type of information useful, the time and high costs were regarded as discouraging. Most appreciated presentations were combinations of theory and practice, that is, lectures combined with practical exercises.

Own professional education as an information source for colour questions was mentioned by only a few. Especially architects complained about their basic education. Most of their knowledge had been gained in the field, with both success and failure.

Knowledge of the NCS (Natural Colour System) was studied by some general and some specific questions covering the origin and potential of the system. All respondents knew about the NCS system and used it on a daily basis in almost all colour projects. The offices generally had a manual or colour sample album. They used the system in one of two ways. Either they departed from an inner picture, completing it gradually with corresponding samples from the system, or they used it directly as a design tool, using the colour samples in the design process, matching colours until a satisfying result was reached. The last method was mostly used by master house painters, but also by interior decorators.

All respondents were pleased with the potential of the system as a means of colour communication. Many found the colour samples too expensive and some complained about the severe discrepancy between small colour samples and large painted surfaces. A proof painting in full scale was recommended by many.

More specific knowledge about the theoretical and practical properties of the descriptive system was less well spread amongst the designers. Only half of the architects, one third of the interior designers and one of ten house painters could describe satisfactorily the system's theoretical background or its descriptive components and produce a fair notation of a given colour. Although many of the respondents knew of several other colour descriptive systems, the NCS was the only one used in daily design work.

The interviews also contained a number of questions on specific colour research results. An inventory of more or less actual research projects founded the basis for an examination of the knowledge in this respect. Nine questions were grouped into the three fields of research, mentioned above. Knowledge of perceptual properties of colours was generally good. Almost all respondents were aware of bright colours increasing the perceived size of rooms and decreasing the perceived weight of objects. Physiological and psychological effects of colours on humans were less known. The ability of affecting the perception of pleasantness and warmth in rooms by reddish colours was misjudged by more than half of the respondents. Also some misleading reports on effects on the convalescence of patients in greenish hospital rooms were accepted by half of the respondents. Knowledge of colour preferences was equally poor. Only one third of the designers was aware of the fact that blue is the most preferred colour, that men prefer dark colours more than women do and that so called complementary colours do not always harmonise when put together. Analysing these knowledge questions, one feels inclined to say, with some exceptions, that most of the answers were pure guesswork. Calculation of a knowledge index by summarising all answers, indicated only minor differences between the three professional groups, revealing a more categorical opinion of the architects, whether they were right or wrong.

Other background variables, such as age, gender or professional experience, could not be shown to have any effect on the attitudes towards colour research or knowledge of specific research results.

Results: Design Education
Design Education and Colour

Colour is by all involved considered to be an important subject matter in the education of environmental designers. This point of view has nevertheless little influence on the educational situation at the studied schools. As many practising designers complained about colour training in their earliest professional education, a comparison with the educational situation of today can be useful in many respects.

The interviews with responsible teachers and scrutiny of educational curricula in six design schools showed that rather little time was spent on colour related subjects, especially in schools of architecture. In general, at the beginning of the education, a block of more or less theoretical lectures, combined with some practical training, was provided. During the following years the students were supposed to incorporate, more freely, their colour knowledge into the educational design projects.

Schools educating interior designers spent more time on colour related subjects, as compared to schools of architecture. They treated colour more as an individual subject with their own teachers, giving opportunity to a both broader and deeper penetration of the subject. In schools of architecture, at the initial stage, the departments of theoretical and applied aesthetics (Formlära) were responsible for colour education. Here, due to time scarcity, colour was often integrated into other related subjects, thus obstructing a more thorough treatment of the colour subject itself. Handbooks and compendia were mostly oldish. Information on colour research results was very rare at all schools.

The teachers expressed positive attitudes towards colour research, most so at the schools of architecture. The more artistic oriented teachers in the schools of interior design and art took a somewhat more sceptical stand as to the ability of science to provide generally applicable knowledge.

The students' perception of their colour education was studied by means of questionnaires and examined at two educational stages. One questionnaire was distributed to first year pupils, revealing their expectations and hopes. Another, but similar questionnaire, was given to final year students, examining the results of four years of design education. The questions, mostly formulated for multiple choice answers, were based on the results of the interviews with the practitioners and followed roughly the same grouping of questions.

Students who intended to become architects had generally a more technical background, with less previous humanistic/artistic subjects than those who studied interior design and art. The latter had also more previous colour education and spent more of their leisure time with colour related work and hobbies.

The expectations of the newly-fledged students on their colour education were significantly higher than the turn out after four years. Both more theoretical and practical items were expected than provided. On the average, colour-related subjects were taught less than one hour per week, while several hours were expected. Considerable differences between the architecture schools and the other schools were found. Architecture students assessed the average time, spent on colour issues, to be less than 2% of the total time of education, interior designers to more than 10%, artists considerably more. Student projects at architecture schools were only seldom presented with careful colour accounts, more often at schools for interior designers. Interior design students also dealt with colour questions during the entire project work, from start to finish, while architecture students often tended to skip colour problems until the final stage of the design process.

More than half of the students admitted that they had never read any literature on colour outside school. One third of the respondents read a little and only five percent had read several works. Interesting colour programmes on TV or video were mentioned by one fourth of the students, but titles were hard to recall. External colour courses and conferences were occasionally attended by less than half of the students, architecture students being the least active.

Design Education and Colour Research

Information about colour research results turned out to be disadvantaged. Consequently, only one third of the students could relate any colour research work and only one fourth of them could name specific results or names of researchers. No particular differences in this respect between first and last years students could be discerned. Asked about preferences for information sources on scientific work, most of the students chose colour lectures and courses, followed in descending order by articles in magazines, handbooks, TV- and video programs and finally research reports. Most students found questions about human perception and the effects of colours upon well-being of greatest importance for future research, along with questions on topics of ecology and work environment.

Students' knowledge of the NCS was studied through four questions. Half of the students had heard about the system and one quarter of them had used it occasionally, naturally more of the students in their final year. Questions about the number of parameters used in the system, and about the notation of a given colour, resulted in satisfactory answers by less than every fourth student.

The students' general attitude toward colour research was studied through two questions. Almost all students felt colour research to be meaningful and opposed to the assumption that colour is only a matter of taste. Half of the students did not fear that colour research would become a threat to the creativity of the designer, although one third expressed some scepticism in this respect. The questionnaires even contained a number of questions on specific colour research results. They had the same content as the questions in the interviews with the practitioners. The answers show a similar pattern as for the professionals. The knowledge of perceptual properties of colours was generally good. Almost all students were aware of bright colours increasing the perceived size of rooms and decreasing the perceived weight of objects. For the other questions, the results were less persuasive. Even here, one feels inclined to say that most of the answers were pure guesswork. No significant differences in this respect could be shown between first and last years students or between the six schools.

Female students reported a generally higher colour activity in their leisure time, they were more familiar with the NCS-system and they answered more correctly on the nine knowledge questions. Other background variables, such as age or previous experience, could not be shown to have any effect on the attitudes towards colour research or knowledge of specific research results.

Design Practitioners and Students, a Comparison in Colour Knowledge

The results of the two related studies can be summarised in rather negative terms. In spite of the great importance of the colour subject for environmental design, certified by all participants, factual knowledge seems in many cases to have been replaced by personal experience and individual preferences. Neither practitioners nor students in environmental design were aware of most results of actual colour research work. Although many of the professionals complained about their own colour education, not much seems to have been improved in this respect. The ill-treatment of the colour subject at the schools is continued in the everyday design work of the practitioners. Too little time of the design process is spent on colour questions, as reported by both the practitioners, teachers and students. It seems as if only minor increases in knowledge level are reached

during design education. The most devoted pupils continue their search for colour knowledge and spend more time on colour training and presentations, than their less motivated colleagues do. This pattern is probably continued during the entire career of a designer. Persons interested in colour know more on the subject, read more and attend more courses and conferences, spend more leisure time with colour work, and are also inclined to reflect more on colour in their design work. These persons are more often female.

There are obvious differences between general architecture and interior design. Colour seems to be more important and respected as a subject in the interior design world. More time is spent on colour questions, both in education and in design practice, at schools and offices, working with interior design.

Master house painters have a different situation. Neither in their education, nor in their practical everyday work, are they overwhelmed with colour research results. Only very rarely do they read about research work in their own professional magazines or in more common literature. But many of them express clear positive feelings about scientific work, especially if research results can be helpful in arguing with clients.

Conclusions

The information problem is obvious. Colour research is too unknown to design students and practitioners. Most of them seem eager to learn more about the subject. Relevant and useful results are present. How to improve knowledge? From our results, it can be concluded that designers do not read very much. Many prefer spoken information, like lectures and courses, to written reports. Thus this must be provided for to an even greater extent. But also handbooks are asked for, presenting facts in intelligible and useful ways. All efforts must be put on improving this state of affairs. Most effect is gained when the written word is accompanied by illustrative pictures. Much work is lately being done translating scientific research papers into more common and readable magazines and books. Maybe still more has to be done. But mostly, school education must be improved. More time for the colour subject must be accompanied by a more conscious treatment of knowledge on people's perception of everyday colour situations and the impact of the coloured environment on their well-being.

This project was supported by a research grant from the Swedish Council for Building Research.

Stephen Coonan

An Appraisal of the Quest to Find a Viable Method of Colour Photography

When we take colour photographs today, the longest delay, once the subject has been selected, is in picking up the camera and switching it on. Although you may wait hours or days for your prints or slides, the actual processing time is now, at most, about half an hour. Focus, light measurement, and exposure level and film advance are now automated and take just fractions of a second to complete.

This differs greatly from the situation a little over 100 years ago. People's understanding of the nature of light and its effect on certain chemicals in the 1890's was based - as ours is today - on a few major scientific discoveries. A brief resumé follows.

Newton's discoveries of the 1650's included the dispersion of white light into its 'component' colours and its reconstruction through additive synthesis. Moving to the early 1800's, Thomas Young applies the wave theory of light to sets of sensors within the eye which are sensitive to blue or green or red. In the 1860's, Helmholtz modifies Young's theory on the sensitivities of the sensors. Maxwell demonstrates additive synthesis from three primaries and goes on to show a colour picture by an indirect method of photography and triple projection with the aim of demonstrating colour vision. Louis Ducas du Hauron predicted in a series of articles, patents and books, almost every form of colour photography which was to be invented. Much of his work was in collaboration with Charles Cros. du Hauron originally supposed the additive colours to be Blue, Yellow and Red, but later revised this to Blue, Green and Red.

Turning from the physical to the chemical approach, Seebeck discovered, in 1777, that silver chloride adopted the colour of light falling on it. It was upon these foundations that the search for colour photography was based.

In the mid-1800's, Becquerel and Niepce de St. Victor met with marginal success with the silver chloride method, but 'fixing' the images to make them permanent caused problems as ambient light destroyed the pictures. However, some of their results were shown as historical curiosities at the Crystal Palace Exhibition in London in 1898. This would suggest a life-span of 40 years, which, even with careful storage, is longer than some so-called permanent colour processes to be derived later.

For some of his experiments, Becquerel had used the highly-reflective base plates normally used for Daguerreotypes, and it has since been shown that, in part, the colour had been formed by the phenomenon of interference. Some of the attempts to resolve the problems of colour photography were absolutely ingenious, while others were totally fraudulent. A short description of some honest ones may be appropriate.

Interference is the key to the Lippmann process of 1891. The camera used a modified plate holder in which the photosensitive side of the plate was placed in contact with a layer of mercury. During the exposure, light passed through the glass base of the plate and through the transparent emulsion to be reflected back along its path by the mercury. This caused constructive and destructive interference which formed a pattern of 'standing waves' within the processed emulsion. When the plate was viewed by reflected light, falling at a suitable angle, a positive colour image was seen. If Lippmann had had access to a laser at that stage, Holography might have been discovered then.

In 1895, F.W. Lanchester patented a camera which focused the image on a grating consisting of fine parallel opaque lines. The image of the object and grating was then projected by a second lens to the photographic plate. Between the second lens and the focal plane, a prism dispersed the light into spectra which filled the clear spaces of the image of the grating, thus introducing colour to the image of the subject.

Using positives made from separation negatives, R.W. Wood used successive contact exposures onto one plate to introduce diffraction grating patterns to appropriate areas of the image. In this way, the entire photograph was reproduced as a pattern of diffracting lines. When placed in a special viewing apparatus, a colour image was seen.

Not everything went smoothly, of course. One worker, when making up chemistry for a colour process, observed: "The precipitate in the dish and on the back of the paper, when dry, exploded on the slightest touch." Photography is full of surprises!

Frederick Ives utilised du Hauron's concept of a 'one shot' colour camera and viewer. From the early 1890's, his Photochromoscope camera and Kromskop viewers and projector adapters were available commercially. While his early cameras used a 'repeating back' to make the three successive exposures, he also devised a 'one shot' camera which could make the blue, green and red separations simultaneously on three plates. It was through this work that Ives noted that the filters suggested by Maxwell were not entirely suited to the photographic analysis of the additive colours.

Louis Ducas du Hauron, in his 1868 patent, suggested that the three taking filters of Maxwell's experiment could be replaced by one plate of glass "....covered mechanically by grains of three colours...."

James W. McDonough of Chicago, protected by three patents in 1892, a devised method for making photographic plates by first applying an adhesive to one surface of the glass and then ran-

domly covering it with minute transparent particles of shellac which were dyed red, green or blue, thus producing an irregular mosaic pattern. The particles were either applied to, or were subsequently coated with, a sensitive photographic emulsion. This became known as the 'dusting-on' process.

When the plate was placed in the camera with the 'particled' side towards the lens, the image-forming light would pass through the particles - or perhaps pixels in todays terms - before reaching the photographic emulsion. In this way, the blue, green and red separations could be made simultaneously on one plate.

Although unable to produce a photograph in true colours by this method as late as 1896, McDonough's work did not pass unnoticed, and from his dusting-on method the highly successful Lumiere Autochrome process evolved in 1904, to be followed by others, the most notable being the Agfa Farbenplatte in 1916. du Hauron had further proposed that "....the coloured rays can be ruled either mechanically or chemically...."

Dr. (later Professor) John Joly patented a process in 1894 which was the precursor of almost all of the additive methods of colour photography which have served in one form or another to the present day. The fundamental concept in this approach was that a glass plate the size of a standard photographic plate should be ruled with thin lines (200 lines per inch was suggested) of equal width of alternate red, green and blue transparent dyes.

The 'screen' was placed in the camera with the ruled side in front of and in intimate contact with the emulsion side of a black-and-white photographic plate. The separation was made in the same way as outlined for McDonough's proposal. There were two important differences - (1) the image was in lines, and (2) the plate was processed without the screen in position.

When the positive was re-positioned with the ruled plate, as when the photograph was first taken, a colour picture was seen. Any changes of luminosity of colour within the subject would be represented in the picture by the ability of the photographic emulsion to reproduce them as differences in density. These density differences modulated the transmission of light through each line of dye. The final product was a lantern-slide or transparency.

Theories are often accepted as sacrosanct laws, particularly if presented in an educational context and often, it seems, when the subject relates to colour. There appears to be an unwillingness to question fundamentals. Perhaps if theories are considered to be merely concepts waiting to be proved and laws as concepts not yet disproved, our understanding of colour might reach new levels.

Ives, Joly and others were prepared to take on the gurus of colour science.Ives had expanded on Maxwell's method of colour photography and found that different sets of dyes were required to analyse subject colours during photography from those required to synthesise the positive image at the projection stage. However, although noting the need for a form of colour correction, he had not fully appreciated the difference that this would have in stimulating the visual receptors.

Joly had also realised that the direct application of the primary filter colours, as chosen by Maxwell to project an artificial representation of the prismatic spectrum by synthesis upon a screen, would not provide an accurate colour picture. He wrote: "The C red, for example, is not the wave-length which most strongly stimulates the red sensation; a wave-length which appears orange to the eye possessed of both red and green vision, will far more effectively excite the red sensation."

Additional problems with colour correction arose as a result of the spectral sensitivity of the emulsions of the time. Their 'blindness' to certain colours, and unequal response to those colours to which they were sensitive, led to considerable inaccuracies in density and contrast in the negative. Since the subject colours were modified by the dye colours of the analysing or taking screen, the problems became more complicated.

Having noted Ives' observations and those independently arrived at by Abney, Joly based his research on the colour vision curves produced by König, and found dyes which transmitted a broad spectral band about an axis centred on each of the three colours he required. He first defined, by spectroscopic tests, a green dye which carried an even proportion of red and violet at all luminance levels. Similar tests for red and blue dyes followed. His patent indicates the use of chrysoidine orange for the red lines, a mixture of ethyl green and chrysoidine orange for the green, and water-blue for the blue lines of the taking screen.

In a letter, Joly mentions: "There is — with correctly chosen colours on the taking screen — no want of truth observed or to be expected, except what arises owing to the complex nature of the green sensation. The want of fidelity here is but small."

Actual measurements produced in 1898 gave the red transmissions from 550 nm to 670 nm with a peak between 580 nm and 600 nm; green transmission ranged from 470 nm to 570 nm peaking between 515 nm and 530 nm, and blue transmission extended from 430 nm to 520 nm with the maximum between 460 nm and 480 nm.

Separations made with such dyes could be obtained with short exposures, but gave poor results when synthesised. Joly introduced a separate viewing screen with a narrower cut in the dye transmissions to create the appropriate visual stimuli within the receptors of the eye. A yellow tinted filter in front of the lens, to absorb unwanted blue and ultra-violet wavelengths, fulfilled the final requirement necessary to enable the eye to appreciate a full range of colours.

It was perhaps more through the thoroughness of his research and depth of understanding of the physical concepts underpinning the work of Maxwell, Helmholtz and König rather than his overall appreciation of the subjective application of colour theory which led Joly to his conclusions. There is no doubt that without his work on colour correction, his initial results would have been tantalising but unsatisfactory, and would have been welcomed with little enthusiasm. However, as *The Times* saw it, "A large share of interest was displayed at the recent soirée of the Royal Society in the exhibition by Dr. Joly, of Dublin, of some photographic transparencies upon glass plates, representing various objects in their natural colours. That every range of colour and texture could be dealt with according to the new method by which these were obtained was evident upon examination of the subjects portrayed."

It is particularly apt that this paper should be delivered in the centenary year of Joly's patenting his colour process, a process from which so many others stemmed and which still finds practical application in colour photography today.

Language

Primary Confusion

When I was a student I was taught what I will call 'Traditional Art School Colour Theory':

Primary colours: Yellow, Red and Blue. *Secondary colours*, mixed from the primaries: Orange, Violet and Green. Primaries and secondaries, arranged in spectral sequence, form the *colour circle*. The colour circle can be used as a guide to colour mixing and colour composition.

I found this useful and passed it on. However, when I got serious about colour, I encountered problems with this model. I don't teach it any more. One demonstration can serve to illustrate the kind of discovery I made which turned my colour world upside down.

A disc can be painted different colours in segments and then spun very fast; the different colours blend into a single colour. The colour of a particular spinning disc might be described as a greyish pink. It comes as no surprise, when the disc slows down and stops, to see that the segments are red, white and black (Fig. 1a). A second spinning disc appears the same greyish pink as the first, but when this one stops it is seen to be half blue and half yellow (Fig. 1b) (Note: to duplicate this demonstration it will be necessary to experiment with several different reds, blues and yellows.) When I was younger I thought that a mixture of blue and yellow would be green. In one sense it often is, but clearly not always.

For mastery of colour we need control and understanding. Understanding needs clarity of thought, and clarity of thought is helped by clarity of language. From my early investigations (Green-Armytage, 1980, 1983) it became clear that many of the problems I had encountered were due to language, in my case the English language.

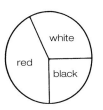 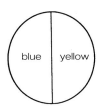

(Fig. 1a and Fig. 1b)

Language for the Senses

Our understanding of the world around us depends on the information we receive through our senses. The language we use in relation to our understanding is an expression of our experience.

Double Duty Words

One feature of everyday English which can contribute to confusion is the use of one word to mean two different but related things. For example consider the sentence "The dog smells". This could be understood in one or both of two ways, one of which would correspond to the sentence "I smell the dog", and the other to the sentence "The dog smells me". Our sense of smell depends on molecules which are given off by things and which we sniff in through our noses. The word "smells" is what I will call a *double duty word*, it can refer both to the giving off and the sniffing in of molecules.

Language Short Cuts

Confusion can also arise from our use, in English, of what I will call 'language short cuts'. What single word might you use to complete the sentences:

1. The rose ... sweet
2. The rose ... red

1. The rose *smells* sweet. This is a short sentence to refer to what is in fact quite a complex process, a cycle of information and understanding which can be shown in a diagram (Fig. 2).

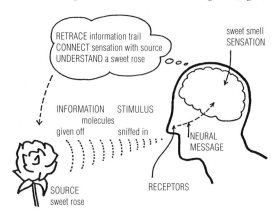

Fig. 2. Cycle of Information and Understanding related to smell.

We can be quite conscious of this process in the case of smell because sniffing can be such a deliberate act, but the process tends to get compressed in normal conversation. I would not say: "I am experiencing a sweet smell *sensation* as a result of a *neural message* transmitted to my brain from my nose. The *receptors* in my nose are responding to the *stimulus* of molecules which I am sniffing in and which are being given off by that rose. The rose is the *source* of the molecules and the molecules carry *information* about the physical nature of the source, the rose. As I *retrace* the information trail and *connect* the sensation with the source I *understand* that the rose has certain physical characteristics which I can label 'sweet'.

The everyday expression "The rose smells sweet" is a short cut way of referring to this process. Notice that both "smells" and "sweet" are double duty words. "Smells" refers both to the giving off and the sniffing in of the molecules and "sweet" refers both to the physical nature of the rose which causes it to give off the molecules, and to the sensation, the sweet smell.

2. The rose *is* red. This is correct, normal, everyday English. It could be another language short cut like "The rose smells sweet". But there is a crucial difference. Now there is no word for the transfer of information between me and the rose. Such a word might be used. We might say "The rose *looks* red". The word "looks" could play the same role in establishing the cycle of information and understanding as was played by the word "smells". The cycle itself is essentially the same with a source, information, stimulus, receptors, neural message to the brain, a sensation, retracing, connection of the sensation with the source and understanding (Fig. 3).

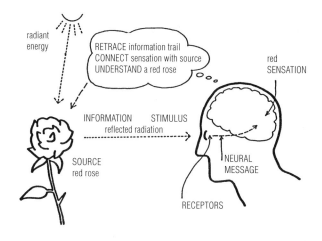

Fig. 3. Cycle of Information and Understanding related to Colour.

The source is the rose which has certain physical characteristics. Because of its physical nature, when it is illuminated, the rose interacts with the radiation in a particular way. Part of the radiation is absorbed and part is reflected. The reflected radiant energy contains information about the rose and is the stimulus to which the receptors in our eyes respond. A neural message is generated which reaches the brain and we experience a particular sensation.

Primary Confusion

As with "smells" the word "looks" could be a double duty word, referring both to the reflection of radiant energy and to its reception in the eye. Certainly the word "red" is a double duty word. It refers both to the physical nature of the source, the rose itself, and to the sensation. Double duty words need not be a problem if one is conscious that two meanings are possible and if one can know from the context which meaning is intended. Red referring to the source and red referring to the sensation might be kept separate by the word "looks", but with the word "is" they get collapsed together as though the two kinds of red, instead of being just connected, were actually the same thing. It is this identification of source with sensation in the case of colour that I am calling *primary confusion*.

Language is one reason for the confusion, but language may simply be a reflection of another reason which goes deeper. We experience smells within ourselves, if not in our brains, at least in our noses. We are conscious of the distinction between the sensation of smell and the corresponding aspect of the object responsible - the dog, the rose or whatever. It is easy to appreciate that there may be a more complex process involved and that the sentence "the rose smells sweet" is a language short cut. Colours, on the other hand, we experience out there, not in our

brains or in our eyes, but on the surfaces of the objects themselves. So when I say "the rose is red" it is a natural expression of my experience. It would not occur to many people to consider that there is a complex process involved or that the sentence might be a language short cut.

Greater clarity of language could help resolve this primary confusion. It can certainly be resolved by greater clarity of thought. If we think about it we must appreciate that the aspect of the rose's physical nature which we might label "red" is not the same thing as the sensation, which we also label "red", and which we experience when we look at the rose. They are two different things. Keeping that distinction clear is essential for understanding, and understanding makes control and mastery of colour that much easier.

Taking Colour Apart

I am far from being the first to draw attention to the distinction. Newton himself (1966 [1704] Book 1, pt. 2, pp. 90-91) made it very clear when he wrote that: "Colours in the Object [the source] are nothing but a disposition to reflect this or that sort of rays more copiously than the rest; in the rays [the stimulus] they are nothing but their dispositions to propogate this or that Motion into the Sensorium [i.e. the brain], and in the Sensorium they are Sensations of those motions under the forms of Colours."

More recently David Wright (1967) proposed a 'Philosophy of Colour' which recognises the processes which lead to a sensation in the brain but also includes the projection of that sensation back into the world outside and its association with the object. For Wright, colour as a concept embraces the whole information/understanding cycle.

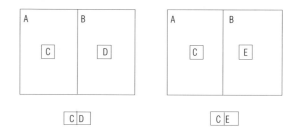

Conceptual Fission

Barry Maund (1981), however, argues that with colour there is "a case for conceptual fission". The concept needs to be broken apart. Maund describes the process whereby an "old concept", which has been found to have shortcomings, may get divided into two new concepts. In the case of colour the old concept has two aspects, a physical aspect and a sensuous aspect. The latter, though associated with the object, is in fact a feature of our sensation. If conceptual fission took place we could form two new concepts from the old one: (a) colour as a physical property of an object, and (b) colour as the sensation we experience when we look at an object.

The old twofold concept of colour may serve well enough in most situations, but for those who are serious about understanding colour it is in the way. If I do not recognise that colour words can be double duty words, and If I regard the "red" physical aspect of the rose as *the same thing* as the "red" sensation I experience when I look at the rose then I am suffering from primary confusion.

Primary confusion is best illustrated by the phenomenon identified by Chevreul (1967 [1839]) as 'simultaneous contrast'. Josef Albers (1975) has provided many dramatic examples; Fig. 4 is derived from one in his book *Interaction of Color* (plate VII-4).

The colours of the two large rectangles A and B are very different. On the left the two small squares C and D are cut from the same piece of uniformly printed paper. On the right the papers from which C and E are cut have been printed with different inks. In which situation are the small squares the same colour?

Fig. 4. Designs for demonstrating two possible ways of establishing that two colours are the "same".

On the left they are physically the same so they fit new concept (a); in that sense they are the same colour. But because of the simultaneous contrast phenomenon they do not *look* the same. We get a different sensation. So for new concept (b) they are not the same colour.

The situation is reversed on the right. By careful mixing of the inks for printing square E it can be made to appear the same as square C in this context. Now the two squares are the same colour according to new concept (b) but are no longer the same according to new concept (a).

It would seem that both Chevreul and Albers suffered from primary confusion. Chevreul (1967, p. 57) wrote: "If we look simultaneously upon two stripes ... of different colours placed side by side ... the eye perceives certain modifications .... Now as these modifications make the stripes appear different from what they really are, I give to them the name of *simultaneous contrast of colours* ...." And Albers (1975, p. 1): "In visual perception a color is almost never seen as it really is - - as it physically is. This fact makes color the most relative medium in art."

If we consider colour only as a physical property of objects (new concept (a)), there would be great difficulty in the notion of 'seeing a colour as it really is'. Under what circumstances could we ever see a 'real colour'? On the other hand, if we consider colour only as what we see, as the sensation we experience when we look at an object (new concept (b)), we always see colour 'as it really is' because that is all that colour is, what we see.

New Names for Old?

What now should we do with the word "colour" and words like "yellow", "red" and "blue"? One option would be to reserve them exclusively for one or other of the new concepts (a) and (b) and to define the narrower meanings with great care. My own preference had been for new concept (b) and to confine colour words to sensations. So there would be no 'colour' inside a tube of paint. A mixture of gamboge and vermilion should not be described as a "colour mixture" but as a mixture of pigments, and "yellow" paint should not be thought of as Yellow but as a substance which gives rise to a sensation of yellow. In the abstract for this paper, written some months ago, I indicated that such an approach would be recommended. However I am now inclined at least to reconsider. Hering (1964 [1920], p. 41) pointed out in a related context that "the clearest definition of a word is of little use if it is already known to the reader in a different sense; he (sic) automatically continues to associate the word with the old ideas".

A solution is offerred by Gunnar Tonnquist (1989, p. 162). He has summarised what I call the cycle of information and understanding in a simple model (Fig. 5) and used a qualifying word in conjunction with the word colour for the different stages.

```
                        PHYSIOLOGY
                        Eye and
                        neural system
                        NEURAL RESPONSE

PHYSICS                                   PSYCHOLOGY
Illuminant                                Visual cortex
Stimulus object                           Signal evaluation
COLOUR STIMULUS                           COLOUR PERCEPT
                        PSYCHOPHYSICS
                        Colorimetry
                        COLOUR VALENCE
```

Fig. 5. Gunnar Tonnquist's model for Colour

On the left the *Colour Stimulus* refers to the physics of the situation and corresponds to new concept (a). (It should be noted that Tonnquist includes both object and light here since both contribute to the stimulus.) On the right, for new concept (b), is the *Colour Percept*. Tonnquist shows two ways to connect the Stimulus with the Percept. The *Neural Response* refers to the workings of the eye and nervous system. *Colour Valence* refers to the science of colorimetry (Tonnquist, 1989, p. 163):

"The term 'colour valence' (= the capacity of a stimulus to evoke a colour percept) is translated from the German 'Farbvalenz' (Richter 1954). The usual English term is 'Psychophysical colour', as a parallel to 'perceived colour'. Both are unfortunate, implying 'colour' to be dual in character and to exist outside the observer.

Two stimuli with the same colour valence will - under equal observing conditions - look alike. Also, if the observing conditions are different (e.g. different surrounds), equal stimuli with the same colour valence may look different. Colorimetry can only be used for stimuli, not for percepts."

It might be clumsy in everyday English to say "I am enjoying the red colour percept which I associate with this rose", but such use of language, at least in thought, should help keep primary confusion at bay.

Primary Colours

Primary confusion is especially evident in definitions of the so-called *primary colours* as "colours from which all other colours can be mixed" or as "colours which cannot be mixed from other colours". The first is a definition of *primary colour stimuli* and might be revised as "colour stimuli which can be combined to provide a comprehensive range of colour percepts". The second is a definition of *primary colour percepts* and might be revised as "colour percepts resulting from particular colour stimuli which cannot be matched in combinations of any other stimuli".

Tonnquist's model can be used to illustrate another kind of primary confusion, that is the confusion between different sets of primary colours. In fact Tonnquist's model could be seen as an argument for further conceptual fission. Perhaps the old concept of colour is not twofold but fourfold and we need not two but four new concepts to replace it. In addition to (a) colour as a physical property of an object and (b) colour as the sensation we experience when we look at an object we might also want (c) colour as the neural response to a stimulus and (d) colour as the capacity of a stimulus to evoke a colour percept. It certainly is the case that in each situation there is a place for some notion of primary colours which means that there is scope for confusion and misunderstanding between people working in the different areas.

Colour Stimulus

Painters, printers, dyers, lighting designers and technologists concerned with monitor displays for computers and television are all working with various colour stimuli to achieve a certain range of colour percepts. According to circumstances, usually economic, they will choose the smallest number of different paints, inks, dyes, filters or phosphors to achieve the largest range of colour percepts.

Printers who need to reproduce coloured photographs have long been satisfied that what works best for them is four inks that look yellow, magenta (a pinkish, purplish red), cyan (a slightly greenish blue) and black, on paper that looks white. What makes this set primary is nothing more than the fact that these inks deliver the "mostest for the leastest". Similarly, for reproducing photographic images on a television monitor the best results are achieved with three phosphors which look red (a yellowish red), green (also yellowish) and blue (tending slightly towards violet).

Perhaps there should be further subdivision in this part of Tonnquist's model to take account of the difference between pigment primaries and light primaries. There is scope for confusion here, and more confusion arises from the fact that colour percepts which result from pigment mixture are not always a reliable guide to the colour percepts likely to result from light mixtures. We saw this with the spinning disc demonstration at the beginning; spinning disc mixtures behave more like light mixtures.

Colour Valence

The primaries used in colorimetry are related to the red, green and blue for lights and the glowing phosphors of the television screen. They are primary lights, but they are lights that could not be made. The mathematics makes it possible to work with theoretical lights, the advantage being that measurements do not result in negative values.

Neural Response

In the neural response two stages have been identified, each of which could have its own set of 'primary colours'. In the eye the three types of cone receptor cells each has different degrees of sensitivity to the different wavelengths of radiant energy. Different colour percepts are associated with the different wavelengths so the 'primary colours' could be those wavelengths to which each cone type is most sensitive. Further along the neural pathway between the eye and brain there are three kinds of neural signal. One carries information about redness or greenness, another about yellowness or blueness and the third about lightness and darkness.

Colour Percepts

Artists, architects and designers need not be over concerned with colorimetry or the neural response. They may need to know how to generate and manipulate colour stimuli, but what ultimately matters is what things look like, the colour percepts.

The clearest articulation of the distinction between colour stimulus and colour percept was made by Ewald Hering (1964 [1920]). It became clear to him that there are six fundamental colour ideas (primary colour percepts) to which we can relate all the colours we see. The six primary colour percepts are White, Black, Yellow, Red, Blue and Green. Having established absolute White and absolute Black at either end of a scale of pure greys which vary from end to end in their degrees of resemblance to White and Black he defined the other four (p. 42): "... there are four outstanding loci in the series of hues that make up the closed circle: first the locus of the yellow that shows no remaining trace of redness, and yet reveals no trace of green; second the locus of the blue for which the same is true. These two hues may be called *primary yellow* and *primary blue* [*Urgelb* and *Urblau*]. Likewise we can name, third, the red, and, fourth, the green that are neither bluish nor yellowish *primary red* and *primary green* [*Urrot* and *Urgrün*]"

Hering's *Natural Colour System* has been developed in Sweden (Hård and Sivik, 1981) and adopted as the country's national

standard (Swedish Standards Institution, 1978). Referred to by its initials, NCS, this is the only comprehensive system for ordering colour percepts. Among the many advantages it offers is the possibility of illustrating what colour percepts can or cannot be delivered by a given set of primary colour stimuli.

The position of any colour percept can be plotted on the NCS circle. Its position is an indication of its relative resemblance to one or two of the primary colour percepts - Yellow, Red, Blue and Green, and of its relative resemblance to a pure grey (in the centre of the circle) and the most vivid colour percept imagineable (on the circumference of the circle). The appearance of each primary printing ink can be plotted on this diagram (Green-Armytage, 1989) as can the appearance of the various mixtures. (Fig. 6). Similarly, for television, computers etc., the appearance of the primary phosphors can be plotted (Nilsson, 1993) together with their mixtures (Fig. 7).

The range of colour percepts that can be delivered by the process inks is revealed to have some deficences. To make up a deficiency in one area a new ink could be substituted for one of the old ones, but then it could be shown how a gain in one area would result in a loss elsewhere. The range achievable on a television or computer screen can also be shown, and gaps are revealed here as well.

We may be so overawed by the claims that a computer can deliver 16 million colours (surely every conceivable colour must be included!) that we may not notice the deficences, especially in the areas of blueness and greenness. This is a clear case of primary confusion. The 16 million 'colours' are simply the 16 million electronic possibilities for a pixel where there are 256 degrees of excitation possible for each of the three phosphors.

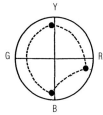

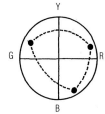

Fig. 6. Printing inks and their mixtures plotted in NCS space

Fig. 7. CRT phosphors and their mixtures plotted in NCS space

Traditional Artists' Primary Colours

To finish where we began with Traditional Art School Colour Theory: Are the primary colours Yellow, Red and Blue to be understood as colour stimuli or colour percepts? They seem to be understood and used as both - as "colours from which all other colours can be mixed" and as conceptual reference points.

Among the most influential and widely used of all books on colour theory for artists are *The Art of Color* and the condensed version *The Elements of Color* by Johannes Itten (1961 and 1970). Itten's account should be read carefully (*Art* p. 34, *Elements* p. 29):"... let us develop the 12-hue color circle from the primaries - yellow, red and blue. As we know, a person with normal vision can identify a red that is neither bluish, nor yellowish; a yellow that is neither greenish, nor reddish; and a blue that is neither greenish, nor reddish."

These definitions are reminiscent of Hering's except that Green is not included as a primary. However Green is used in the definitions of the primaries Yellow and Blue. Itten did not (could not?) describe primary Blue as neither reddish nor *yellowish* or primary Yellow as neither reddish nor *bluish*.

Itten goes on (*Art* p. 34, *Elements* p. 29) to describe the secondary colours as "... three mixed colours, each composed of two primaries". Later in the books (*Art* p. 136, *Elements* p. 88) he describes green as "... the intermediate between yellow and blue. According as green contains more yellow or more

blue, the character of its expression changes." Did he mean that there could be more or less *yellow* or *blue* paint in the mixture which resulted in the green colour percept? Or did he mean that in the green colour percept there might be more or less resemblance to the primary colour percepts Yellow and Blue?

It is not clear from the books whether Itten associated his primary Yellow, Red and Blue with any particular pigments. There is certainly no claim that with three such paints it would be possible *to mix all other colours*. But what is clear from experiment is that three paints which might fit Itten's definitions would not work so well for producing a comprehensive range of colour percepts as would three paints which look the same or similar to the process inks of the printers (Fig. 8).

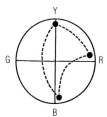

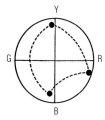

Fig. 8. Comparison of colour percepts achievable with artists' primaries (left) and paints that resemble printers' primary inks.

If one accepts the revised definition and thinks of them as "three colour stimuli which can be combined to provide a comprehensive range of colour percepts" the artists' primaries Yellow, Red and Blue are not very satisfactory as primary colour stimuli. And without Green they are not satisfactory as primary colour percepts. For artists who want to understand what is going on it is unfortunate that with the traditional Yellow, Red and Blue primaries, primary confusion, in every sense, is total.

Acknowledgements

I would like to thank Alun Price and Barry Maund, who read the first draft of this paper. I hope that I have overcome the weaknesses in the argument and inaccuracies of detail to which they drew my attention.

Postscript

Following the presentation of this paper I was very fortunate to receive feedback from Osvaldo da Pos.

He cautioned me about trespassing into the realms of Physics as when I referred to two squares cut from the same piece of uniformly printed paper as "physically the same". For a physicist such a statement might reflect some other kind of primary confusion. If I am being particular in one area and drawing attention to the inadequacies of everyday language for a clear understanding of colour I should at least acknowledge the lack of precision of my own language here. There are many kinds of Physics. Mine is clearly the 'Naïve Physics' of everyday language.

He also objected to my implication that the perceptual processes related to the senses of smell and sight are essentially the same, and that conclusions drawn from one can be applied to the other. As he pointed out, one fundamental difference is that in the case of smell, unlike sight, there is no instantaneous connection between the sensation and the source. It would be possible to walk into a room, experience a sweet smell sensation and never know the source. (I am sure it is a common experience to "wonder where that smell is coming from.") In the case of colour this could only happen in very exceptional circumstances - dreams, hallucina-

tions etc. If I walk into a room and experience a sensation of redness it is only as I recognise redness in the light or focus on a particular object and connect the redness with that object.

Alun Price had made the same objection about relating sight to smell when he read the earlier draft of this paper. I made substantial cuts as a result but still kept the reference to smell because it provided such clear examples of 'double duty words' and 'language short cuts'. I introduced the topic of smell to illustrate such uses of language and should have made that clear from the start. No doubt I should also do something about the passage where I suggest (page 193) that the cycle of information and understanding related to colour is "essentially the same" as the cycle related to smell. Perhaps it would be more acceptable if I were to say, instead, that it is "in some respects similar" to the cycle related to smell.

More seriously Osvaldo da Pos objected to my referring to the source as a "rose". While trying to be careful with words when dealing with particular aspects of an object I was not so careful when dealing with the whole object. Perhaps this is larger scale primary confusion. If nothing is 'red' until it is perceived to be so, then nothing is a "rose" until it is perceived to be so.

Alternatively one could say that 'rose' itself might also be a double duty word. Perhaps 'rose' refers both to the source and to the sensation, to the object in all its 'physical' aspects (physical in the naïve sense), as well as to the perception, the understanding which results from the several sensations (shape, size, colour, texture, smell, touch etc.) associated with the object. In everyday language both the physical object and the perception associated with the object are a 'rose'.

200 *Clearly it would be possible to get drawn further and further into debate about the subtleties of language and the exact meaning or meanings of words. But however fascinating such a debate might be for some people, it is not likely to hold the interest of art students for long. They prefer to be left alone with their paints. That has been a constant dilemma: how to make clear the distinction between colour stimulus and colour percept and shift a lifetime's habit of thinking without losing my audience, a task made more difficult in the face of long established and supposedly authoritative books which perpetuate what I have called primary confusion. It is a delicate operation to hold one's audience without alienating a wider audience that has expertise in related fields.*

References

ALBERS, J. (1975) Interaction of Color. (Revised ed.). New Haven: Yale University Press.

CHEVREUL, M.E. (1967) The Principles of Harmony and Contrast of Colours and their Applications to the Arts. (Original French edition, 1839). New York: Reinhold Publishing Corp.

GREEN-ARMYTAGE, P. (1980) Violets aren't Blue - Colour Sensations and Colour Names. In: J. Condous, J. Howlett and J. Skull (Eds:.), Arts in Cultural Diversity. (pp. 166 - 175) Sydney: Holt, Rinehart and Winston.

GREEN-ARMYTAGE, P. (1983) Brightness, Whiteness and Lightness. In: A. Hård and L. Sivik (Eds.), Colour Report F 26. The Forsius Symposium on Colour Order Systems. Stockholm: Scandinavian Colour Institute.

GREEN-ARMYTAGE, P. (1989) Printers and Designers should be Friends. Invited paper. 10th Biennial convention of the Lithographic Institute of Australia. Fremantle.

HÅRD, A., and SIVIK, L. (1981) Natural Colour System: A Swedish Standard for Colour Notation. In: Color Research and Application. 6. (3), pp. 129 - 138.

HERING, E. (1964) Outlines of a Theory of the Light Sense. (Original German edition, 1920). Cambridge, Massachusetts: Harvard University Press.

ITTEN, J. (1961) The Art of Color. New York: Van Nostrand Reinhold Co.

ITTEN, J. (1970) The Elements of Color. New York: Van Nostrand Reinhold Co.

MAUND, B. (1981) Colour - A Case for Conceptual Fission. In: Australasian Journal of Philosophy. 59. pp: 308 - 322.

NEWTON, I. (1966) Opticks. (Facsimile of original 1704 London edition.). Brussels: Impression Anastaltique, Culture et Civilisation.

NILSSON, A. (1993) NCS Color Selector. Systems extension for Macintosh computers. Stockholm: Scandinavian Colour Institute.

SWEDISH STANDARDS INSTITUTION. (1978) Colour Atlas - Swedish Standard SS 01 91 02, Stockholm.

TONNQUIST, G. (1989) Colour Order Systems and Colour Atlases. In: Grupo Argentino del Color (Eds.), Color 89. Proceedings of the 6th Session of the Association Internationale de la Couleur. Vol. 2. Buenos Aires.

WRIGHT, W.D. (1967) Towards a Philosophy of Colour. In: The Rays are not Coloured (pp. 17 - 31). London: Adam Hilger.

The Role of Language in the Teaching of Colour

Good afternoon ladies and gentlemen! How are you feeling to-day? 'Perhaps you're feeling .... Blue.'

'Maybe you are feeling a bit homesick and you've got *the blues*'? Perhaps the northern climate of Finland is not for you and you're feeling *blue with cold*. Or, maybe you watched a porno-graphic film - *a blue movie* - at your hotel last night. But if you are French, your blue feelings may reveal your overpowering desire for something or someone - *envie bleue*. If, however, you are German, your blueness could be a sign that you are not be-ing honest with us - *das Blaue vom Himmel lügen*.

'But which blue do you feel'? Perhaps you aren't feeling blue at all. Perhaps you feel ... Green. But then we need to know where you are from, and which language you speak, before we can interpret your green feelings. If you are from an English speak-ing country then perhaps you ate too much of the sumptuous Scandinavian breakfast at your hotel this morning and conse-quently you feel *green about the gills*. Or maybe you are new to the International Conference circuit and your greenness arises from feelings of being *inexperienced, naive, gullible*. In France, however, a novice or *greenhorn* is blue - *un bleu!* Any French amongst the audience who are feeling green may be hav-ing a rough time - *en avoir vu des vertes et des pas mûres*. Or perhaps, while others stayed up late last night watching blue movies, you were exchanging rude stories with your Gallic chums - *en raconter des vertes* - because you are just a dirty old man - *un vieillard encore vert*.

But if you are German it could be that you are feeling green be-cause you are a lonely suburban housewife - *eine grüne Witwe*. Maybe you should get together with the vieillard encore vert and have some fun! Or is the Teutonic green feeling because you aren't getting on with the other delegates - die heiden sind sich

gar nicht grün. Our Italian colleagues may be feeling green because they have already spent all their pocket money on Hel-sinki's night-life - *ridursi al verde*. Beware of the Spaniard who feels green - he may be about to put you down - *poner verde a alguien*. And I must be wary of any Portuguese delegate who is feeling green. He may be about to ask me leading questions - *jogar verde para colher maduro*.

The Dutch, apparently, feel green when their heads start to swim - *het werd hem groen en geel voor de ogen* while a green Dane may be fast asleep - *sove på sit grønne øre*. Make friends with the Norwegian who feels green for he is a prosperous man who is doing well for himself - komme på den *grønne gren*. But be-ware of any Norwegians feeling green and yellow for they may be demonstrating their annoyance - *han ergret seg gul og grønn*. If any delegates from Hungary are in a greenish mood it could be because attending this conference represents the attainment of their goal - *zöld agra vergodik*. Or because they think I am talk-ing a load of nonsense - *zöldeket beszél*. As for our Finnish hosts, if they look green they are keeping their secrets from us by sweeping them under the carpet - *panna vihreän veran alle*.

This is all very interesting - it may be the subject of my next re-search paper - but it is not the aspect of language and colour which I wish to address in this presentation. My introductory observations have been what we call in English a red herring.

John Gage is an authority on the history of colour. In his fasci-nating and comprehensive book *Colour and Culture* published last year, he wrote: "...although the human eye is capable of dis-criminating some millions of colour-nuances, most colour-lan-guages in all cultures and throughout recorded history, include a vocabulary of from eight to eleven 'basic' terms". (Gage, but see also Berlin and Kay).

Gage acknowledges that this is neither his discovery nor even a recent one. "The problem was also a familiar one in Antiquity... in the second century AD Aulus Gellius introduced the question of colour vocabularies in his *Attic Nights* where Favorinus pointed out that that eye sees far more facies (nuances) of colour than language can distinguish." (Gage) Other philosophers have also considered this question: C L Hardin, the author of *Colour for Philosophers: Unweaving the Rainbow* draws our attention to "...the enormous disparity between the number of possible colour discriminations and the numher of color terms in normal use" (Hardin).

Returning to John Gage: "...colour space has never been more than partially and crudely mapped by colour-language. There has been a far more remarkable tendency towards the 'basic' term than towards the development of more and more subtle distinctions."…" As colour terminology is so vague, this presents real problems for the modern reader of historical texts" (Gage). And if we accept Gage's view that colour terminology is so vague, then we should ask whether this also presents real problems for those who teach colour in Universities and Colleges of Art and Design.

Let us for a moment consider the importance of language in learning across the whole spectrum (excuse the pun) of undergraduate education. *Literacy by Degrees* - a book published in the UK jointly by the Society for Research into Higher Education and the Open University - brings together a number of papers which address this subject and which assert that "There is a close connection between the nature and quality of our students' language and the nature and quality of their learning ... language is a necessary (though not sufficient) condition for both public and individual learning to take place" (Taylor).

In their paper, *Literacy in the University*, Brigid Ballard and John Clancy conclude from their research that: "The second dimension of linguistic competence involves control of the disciplinary 'dialect': those meanings, items and forms of language peculiar to the discipline." (Ballard and Clancy).

Those of us who have fine-tuned our colour knowledge and powers of chromatic discrimination over many years may too easily forget the situation of the layperson and the student which was succinctly expressed by Rush Rees in his work *Can there be a Private Language?*: I cannot learn the colour unless I see it; but I cannot learn it without language either. I know it because I know the language... I can remember the sensation I had, just as I can remember the colour I saw. I feel the same sensation, and that is the same colour. But identity - the sameness - comes from the language" (Rees).

His view reinforces the conclusion which P Nightingale favours in her bibliographical essay *Language and Learning*: "...having the language (in the broadest sense of the term) does seem to make it easier to learn, which brings us once again to the subject teacher's role in offering instruction in the language of the subject" (Nightingale).

This interdependence of language and learning is not confined to the educational arena. Umberto Eco observes in his essay *How Culture Conditions the Colours We See*: "Just as language is determined by the way in which society sets up systems of values, things, and ideas, so our chromatic perception is determined by language." "We are dealing with verbal language in so far as it conveys notions about visual experience, and we must, then, understand how verbal language makes the non-verbal experience recognisable, speakable and effable." And further: "The names of colours taken in themselves, have no precise chromatic content: they must be viewed within the general context of many interacting semiotic systems" (Eco).

We possess the perceptory potential to discriminate a vast number of colours - estimates vary but accuracy to about half a Munsell step can be achieved by trained observers (Hardin). The *Methuen Handbook of Colour* suggests that approximately 8,000 colour names are current in the United Kingdom alone. But the authors qualify this statistic with the advice that: " ...constantly changing fashion demands an ever-increasing variety of colour names - often in such fantastic combinations that a name becomes vague or meaningless" (Kornerup and Wanscher).

And just how adequate is this minimal vocabulary to articulate our complex sensations of and responses to colour. As Stephen Melville put it in his essay intriguingly entitled *Color Has Not Yet Been Named*: "We know how to describe color in strictly physical terms. We also know something about how to analyse it semiotically, and indeed color can easily appear a prime candidate for semiological investiture, displaying the full force of 'cultural construction'. But color can also seem bottomlessly resistant to nomination, attaching itself absolutely to its own specificity and the surfaces on which it has or finds its visibility, even as it also appears subject to endless alteration arising through its juxtaposition with other colors. Subjective and objective, physically fixed and culturally constructed, absolutely proper and endlessly displaced, color can appear as an unthinkable scandal" (Melville).

The views quoted here suggest that there is clearly an inextricable link between language and colour, a relationship and interdependency which poses important questions for those who teach colour to Art and Design students. In the absence of a universally accepted lexicon of colour nomenclature and terminology, how do Art and Design educators select words and phrases to articulate information, opinions, ideas and questions about colour for a meaningful dialogue with their students? And given the importance of language in the processes of learning, what difficulties are experienced by students as they strive to acquire an informed understanding and awareness of colour in a variety of Art and Design contexts?

I interviewed lecturers and their students in Fine Art, Graphic Design, Three-Dimensional Design, Textile Arts, Environmental Design and Art History. I questioned my colleagues at the University of Plymouth about the sources of their vocabulary, but I also asked them questions about colour to test whether the vocabulary which they actually used matched what they claimed to use.

For the first questions I deliberately chose a colour which provided not merely a visual sensation but one which also had definite associations of one form or another. This was to accommodate the very important distinction between sensation and perception where the former (sensation) is defined as "directly associated with stimulation of the organism while the latter (perception) is the combination of different sensations and the utilisation of past experience in recognising the objects and facts from which the present stimulation arises" - a distinction defined by the Optical Society of America (Optical Society of America).

My first question asked respondents to 'describe the colour of the University's logo in whatever way you consider appropriate'. Perhaps not surprisingly no-one responded 'Pantone 167' - the precise description. Answers ranged from names such as 'Terracota', 'Salmon' and 'American Tan' and comparative phrases such as 'face-mask pink' and 'not quite shit brown' to value judgements including 'non-colour', 'badly-mixed brown', 'dead, no vibrancy' and 'bland and unexciting' and those which anticipated my second question by describing how the colour might be mixed, for example 'a tint of burnt sienna', 'orangey brown', 'enriched fawn', 'sort of subdued red-brown' and 'a tint of Indian Red mixed with a tiny amount of blue and of white'.

When asked for a description of how to mix or match the colour, most responses drew heavily upon the eleven basic colour terms identified by Berlin and Kay freely interspersed with more specific pigment names such as Vermillion, Cobalt, Sienna and Alizarin. Modifiers including 'warm', 'neutral', 'natural', 'deep', 'pastel', 'dirty' and 'dull' were used abundantly, while some respondents drew frequently on associations using words and phrases such as 'like a make-up, cosmetic colour', 'sandy', 'chalkish' and 'brick-like' and made specific comparisons with 'quarry tiles' and 'ceramic plant pot'.

The students' replies to my first question - 'describe the colour in whatever way you consider appropriate' - were heavily oriented towards subjective responses rather than more objective descriptions of the visual sensation, and they were universally negative - 'Nondescript', 'non-inspiring', 'inoffensive, too subtle', 'drab, muddy', 'not really any colour', 'safe', 'tacky, irrelevant, inspires no idea of a University', 'old-fashioned', and '1970's colour' (two students made this latter observation). In describing how to mix or match the colour, students' responses were similar to those of their tutors but with fewer references to pigment names and a greater reliance on comparisons and associations of a more imaginative but perhaps less accurate nature such as 'a mixture between chocolate spread and peanut butter', 'uncleaned copper', 'clay out of ground mixed with sand', and 'flesh colour (almost)'.

The students were then asked to describe the differences between two colours in three pairs of swatches. I chose the swatches to provide pairings where one of the three basic properties of hue, tone, and saturation was significantly different while the other two were very similar. Which words would students use to compare these colours? Would they, for example, refer to 'hue', or 'colour'? Would they talk of the colour's 'tone', 'value', 'brightness', or 'lightness and darkness'? And what word would each use to describe the 'purity' of the colour - 'saturation', 'intensity', 'chroma', 'brightness'? Would their answers indicate a common shared vocabulary or a mixture of terminology?

Their responses were very interesting. Most of the students showed little interest in the formal properties of the colours. They were as - if not more - concerned to identify their subjective responses to the colours, to the colours' emotional effects and associations. None of the respondents used names more specific than the basic 'green' and 'blue' to compare the first two swatches. With the exception of a few references to 'pure', 'bright', 'tone' and 'warm cool', the colours were evaluated in terms of opposing qualities such as (blue first) 'passive/aggressive', 'peaceful/sickly', 'wet/dry', 'clean/dirty', 'attractive/unpleasant', 'recedes/stands out', 'emblematic/independent' and 'calming/vivid'. (Clearly the designer of our University logo should have chosen a blue!) Both colours were perceived as 'striking', 'nice and bright, not muddy', 'unnatural, can't associate them with anything', 'obvious colours', 'young colours', 'TV colours', and 'acidic'.

The red/pink pairing elicited frequent but not universal references to the obvious tonal difference between the swatch colours - these were most commonly described (accurately) by references to 'light' and 'dark' or 'tone' and (inaccurately) by 'shade' - the latter term being used for both shade and tint. Some students identified differences between 'old and young' and 'ancient and modern' - pink was considered to be a 'twentieth century colour'. Several referred to feminine qualities and associations which the colours had for them, while others described them as 'process' and 'lipstick' colours. Many had difficulty articulating the differences between the red and the pink and concentrated on describing the similarities.

Finally, a more subtle contrast where the principle difference lay in the 'saturation' of each blue. Words chosen by the students to articulate this included 'sharper/muted', 'brighter, more striking/duller, more subdued', 'stands out/sits back', 'new/old', 'natural/faded' and 'purer/pastelly'. One student described the contrast as 'denim/cotton', and another made an obscure observation that both colours were 'political'.

I then showed each student a list of terms frequently used in textbooks and other writings on colour to establish which were familiar to the majority of the students and which were not (appendix 2). Only one student understood the term 'chroma' while 'value' was only marginally better understood - this would suggest that the Munsell system has clearly not had a significant or lasting effect on the vocabulary of colour. The other terms with which students showed least familiarity (and therefore presumably they are unfamiliar with the concepts) were additive, subtractive and optical mixtures.

My next step was to find out which sources the lecturers believe they use for their choice of vocabulary when teaching colour, and whether they used these sources 'usually', 'often', 'sometimes' or 'rarely'. The majority were of the opinion that they rarely or only sometimes drew upon established colour theories for names and terminology. Those who conceded to 'often' or 'usually' drawing upon colour theories mentioned Itten most frequently then Albers as their principle source. Chevreul was the other most cited source. Understandably, the Art Historians indicated that they would refer to established colour theories only when the theory in question had been acknowledged as an important influence on an artist's thinking.

There was an almost universal rejection of any colour systems such as Munsell, Pantone or the Natural Colour System as a source of names and terminology with most respondents stating that they 'rarely' or 'never' used these sources.

The names given to pigments by manufacturers appears to provide a more fertile source of names, but even here there is no evidence of the beginnings of a common vocabulary as each lecturer favours the names derived from the medium through which they teach - painters use the names given to oil and acrylic paints; printmakers use the names of printing inks and the tri-chromatic colours; textile artists the names or code numbers of dyes. One Graphic Designer used names from Pantone and Gouache paints, while a Fine Artist working with computers also used Pantone because he said it is employed in Photoshop software.

Several respondents conceded that they mostly relied upon commonly used names and terms rather than drawing upon more specialised and specific vocabularies, and this led conveniently to my next set of questions. Given that many colour terms are composites of a basic colour name and some form of 'modifier', what kinds of modifier were most frequently used in their teaching'?

Modifiers which are based upon visual qualities, for example 'dark' green, 'pale' blue, 'bright' red, and the suffixes -ish and -

ey as in 'yellowish' or 'orangey', were almost universally claimed to be used 'often' or 'usually'. This was consistent with their descriptions of the logo. Conversely, modifiers derived from associations such as 'grass' ~reen, 'chocolate' brown, or 'copper' red were, in most cases, believed to be 'rarely' or even 'never' employed. This was at odds with their descriptions of the logo where many had resorted to making such comparisons in their descriptions of the colour. However, when asked how frequently they would use modifiers based upon emotions, feelings and other subjective responses such as a 'sombre' grey, a 'restless' red, or a 'quiet' purple, there was a full range of responses ranging from 'usually' to 'never if I can help it'!

Few of my colleagues indicated that they take any substantial measures to establish a common vocabulary of names and terms for discussing colour with their students. Those that gave an affirmative response do so only to a basic level - "keep it straight forward, simple, not too complex" was a typical reply. One felt it was necessary to keep the common vocabulary at a base level so as not to disempower students (he is a colleague who provides special support for dyslexic students which may account for his concern in this matter); another stated bluntly that it was not a problem - students are not interested in the formal aspects of colour, contemporary Fine Art practice has moved into new arenas of inquiry where colour theory has little or no significance. This latter view was consistent with some of the responses from the Fine Art students whom I interviewed, whereas Design students recognised their need to have an understanding of colour. Finally, I asked my colleagues and their students to indicate the extent to which they felt that language and vocabulary presents difficulties in teaching and learning about colour.

A significant proportion clearly do not find this issue a problem, but in most cases this view was expressed by those who attach little or no importance to the formal and theoretical aspects of colour in contemporary Art practice. Others acknowledged a communication problem but most attributed this to the students' lack of previous learning about colour. There was a consensus of opinion that the basics of colour should be taught prior to a student entering undergraduate study even though experience shows that colour education at these levels is erratic to say the least. Only a small number identified the absence of an adequate vocabulary as an important factor although many colleagues resort to using swatches or other available coloured surfaces to communicate to students. "Language can become a bit convoluted" claimed one colleague.

There was no clear consensus of views given in the responses to the three final questions which I put to the students, but it would be reasonable to draw some tentative observations from the results although these would clearly have to be tested against a much larger and more comprehensive sample before setting out any authoritative conclusions.

From my relatively small sample of students the following situation emerged:
- most students acknowledge at least some difficulty in commu nicating their thoughts about colour in verbal terms;
- students understand most of the names and terms used by their tutors when they talk about colour, but
- most students would find it useful if their tutors would employ a common vocabulary to teach and discuss colour.

In this paper I have attempted to address the potential for inadequate and imprecise communication which can arise when Art and Design lecturers need to articulate information and ideas about a complex visual phenomenon - colour - for which the available lexicon is both severely limited and for which there exists a diverse and unrelated body of nomenclature and terminologies. I have outlined how educational research has demonstrated the importance of language in the learning process even at undergraduate level, and I have referred to some of the work of linguistic theorists and philosophers who have explored the relationship between colour and language.

I have produced some evidence to suggest that the teaching of colour relies on the use of a hybrid vocabulary which mixes quite specific and scientific terms with a generalised layperson's vocabulary and the jargon or *dialect* of the Art and Design communities. This does not, however, constitute a standard lexicon which is used selectively and with differing emphasis by each individual. By and large there is an uncritical and unquestioning use of this inadequate vocabulary which therefore fails to serve as a common shared vehicle for communicating about colour.

Viewed in the contemporary context of teaching increasingly larger classes of students, and the associated shift towards more student-centred learning, both of which place greater importance on verbal communication, reading, group-teaching, and other language-dependent activities, it is surely essential that any Art and Design programme where colour plays a significant role must incorporate at the very least a debate with the students about the ways in which language is and can be deployed to support learning about colour.

Finally, the scale of the problem of attempting to establish a common or universal lexicon for colour may be summed up by the following anecdote. In researching for this paper, I came across a questionnaire compiled by the Colour Reference Library at the Royal College of Art in London. The purpose of the exercise was "to discover what measure of agreement can he found for colour terms in everyday use...So many different words are used to describe colour that there is often doubt and confusion over what is actually meant .... we would like to adopt the terms most acceptable to our user's in Art, Science, and Technology".

When I wrote to the Royal College asking for information about the outcome of their survey I did not know that it had been launched as long ago as 1985. The Colour Librarian replied apologetically to state that "as far as I can establish, this survey did not produce any information".

Appendix 1

the blues: depression of spirits, melancholy.

blue: colour of the skin as a result of cold, fear, etc.

blue: obscene, indecent, profane.

envie bleue (French): overpowering desire.

das blaue vom Himmel lügen (German): to tell a pack of lies.

go green about the gills: miserable- or sickly-looking.

green: inexperienced, naive, gullible.

un bleu (French): a new recruit, a novice.

en avoir vu des vertes et des pas mûres (French): to go through a lot of hardship, to have a rough time.

en raconter des vertes (French): to tell spicy, risque, 'blue' stories.

un vieillard encore vert (French): a 'dirty old man'; an old man who is still hale and hearty.

grüne Witwe (German): a lonely suburban housewife.

die beiden sind sich gar nicht grün (German): there's no love lost between them.

ridursi al verde (Italian): to loose all one's money, to go broke.

poner verde a alguien (Spanish): to give somebody a dressing down, to abuse somebody violently, to run somebody down.

jogar verde para colher maduro (Portuguese): to fish, to ask leading questions.

het werd hem groen en geel voor de ogen (Dutch): his head began to swim.

sove på sit grønne øre (Danish): be fast asleep.

komme på den grønne gren (Norwegian): do well for oneself, to prosper, to get on in the world.

han egret seg gul og gønn (Norwegian): it irritated him beyond annoyance.

zöld agra vergodik (Hungarian): to get on, to reach one's goal.

zöldeket beszél (Hungarian): to talk garbage, talk nonsense.

panna vihreän veran alle (Finnish): to sweep under the rug.

a red herring: something intended to divert attention from a more serious question or matter; a misleading clue, a distraction.

Appendix 2

Hue	Tint	Subtractive mixtures
Tone	Shade	Optical mixtures
Value	Complementary contrast	Opaque
Brightness	Primary Colours	Transparent
Saturation	Secondary colours	Translucent
Chroma	Tertiary Colours	
Intensity	Additive mixtures	

References

BALLARD, B. and CLANCHY, J. (1988) Literacy in the University: An 'Anthropological' Approach. In: Literacy by Degrees. Taylor, G. et al. Milton Keynes. SRHE and Open University Press.

BERLIN, B and KAY, P. (1969) Basic Colour Terms. Their Universality and Evolution. Berkeley and Los Angeles: University of California Press.

ECO, U. (1985) How Culture Conditions the Colours We See. In: Blonsky, M. (Ed.) (1985) On Signs. Oxford: Blackwell.

GAGE, J. (1993) The Spectrum's Shades of Meaning. Edited version of a 1993 Darwin Lecture at Darwin College, Cambridge. The Times Higher, 6 August, 1993

GAGE, J. (1993) Colour and Culture. London: Thames and Hudson.

HARDIN, C L. (1988) Colour for Philosophers. Unweaving the Rainbow. Indianapolis: Hackett.

KORNERUP, A. and WANSCHER, J.H. (1978) Methuen Handbook of Colour. London. Methuen .

MELVILLE, S. (1994) Color Has Not Yet Been Named: Objectivity in Deconstruction in Deconstruction and the Visual Arts. ed. by Peter Brunette and David Wills. New York: Cambridge University Press.

NIGHTINGALE, P. (1988) Language and Learning: A Bibliographical Essay. In: Literacy by Degrees. Taylor, G. et al. Milton Keynes. SRHE and Open University Press.

OPTICAL SOCIETY OF AMERICA, COMMITTEE ON COLORIMETRY. (1953) The Science of Color. New York. Crowell.

REES, R. (1954) Can there be a Private Language?

TAYLOR, G. (1988) The Literacy of Knowing: Content and Form in Students' English. In: Literacy by Degrees. Taylor, G. et al. Milton Keynes. SRHE and Open University Press.

References used for word and phrase defnitions

Cassell's Dutch-English Dictionary. Seventh Edition (1967). London. Cassell.

Collins German Dictionary. Second Edition (1991). Glasgow. HarperCollins.

Collins Portuguese Dictionarv (1991). Glasgow. HarperCollins.

Collins Sansoni Italian Dictionary (1988). Third Edition. Florence. Sansoni.

Collins Spanish Dictionary (1992). Third Edition. Glasgow. HarperCollins.

Harrap's French-English Shorter Dictionary (1991). London. Harrap.

Harrap's New Standard French and English Dictionary (1972). London. Harrap.

HERAIL, R.J. and LOVATT, E.A. (1984) Dictionary of Modern Colloquial French. London. Routledge and Kegan Paul.

KIRKEBY, W.A. (1986) Norsk Engelsk Ordbok. Oslo. Kunnskapforlaget.

MARKS, J. (1970) Harrap's French-English Dictionary of Slang and Colloquialisms. London. Harrap.

New Shorter Oxford English Dictionary (1993). Oxford. Clarendon Press.

Standard Danish Dictionary (1984). Eastbourne. Holt, Rinehart & Winston.

WUOLLE, A. (1986) The Standard Finnish Dictionary. Eastbourne. Holt, Rinehart & Winston.

I also wish to acknowledge the help I received with the non-English phrases and colloquialisms generously given by Laszlo Acs (Hungarian), Alba Chapman (Italian), Christine Cornish (French), Martine Esser (German) and Mercedes Williams (Spanish)

The Rainbow, Colours and Science Mythology

The rainbow as an extraordinary and attractive natural phenomenon has fascinated human beings throughout the ages. However, the cognitive representation the human mind has created concerning it, has been variable to a high degree in different periods.

Usually the interpretation of the rainbow by an ordinary Estonian is as follows: "A rainbow is seven colours in the sky. It is a phenomenon which makes its appearance when it is raining at the same time as the sun is shining." The answers can undoubtedly vary to some extent, sometimes there can be a longer explanation about refraction and reflection of the sunbeams in the raindrops, but in outline they are similar. To the people of today the rainbow seems to be without exception a source of positive emotions and an experience gladdening the heart, a symbol of beauty and singularity.

It is quite apparent that the ordinary image of the rainbow is fused with the image of the spectrum.

Etymology

The etymology of the Estonian word *vikerkaar* - 'rainbow' is rather ambiguous. The word *viker* has several derivation possibilities, it could have originated from the following meanings: from 'multicoloured', 'scythe' or 'thunder', as its name is in Livonian - a cognate language to Estonian - *pit'kiz kōr* 'thunder bow'. In other Balto-Finnic languages the rainbow is usually connected with rain: Finnish, Ingrian and Karelian *sateenkaari*, Izhorian vihmakārDo.

The connection with rain seems to dominate in Germanic languages as well: German *Regenbogen*, Swedish *regnbåge*, Old Norse *regnbogi*, Danish *regnbue*. Widespread is the connection

with heaven - German dialectal *Himmelring,* French *arc-en-ciel.* In Latin there are several different expressions denoting rainbow: *arcus pluvius* 'rainbow', *arcus caelestis* 'bow of the heaven or gods', *arcus colorātus* 'coloured bow'. One can also refer to the Greek word ιριζ. In Greek mythology Iris was the daughter of Thaumas and Electra, the sister of harpies and a messenger of Olympian gods. Since Hesiodos she has been represented both as a goddess of rainbow and its impersonation. At the same time the rainbow could be the belt of Iris and a footpath between heaven and earth. The original meaning of the word iris is 'path, band'.

Interesting also is the Latvian word for rainbow - *varaviksne*, meaning literally 'copperelm'.

So, the Estonian word *vikerkaar* is rather curious compared with other languages. It is not quite clear if the meaning of the word *viker* 'multicoloured' is secondary, derived from rainbow or vice versa, but nevertheless it is a unique word referring probably to the colours of the rainbow.

Mythology

One of the most interesting mythological presentations of the rainbow is the Eddic *Bifröst* (or *Bilröst, Bilfröst*). In the Younger Edda it is described as a tricoloured bridge to Asgard, very skillfully built by the gods. The colours are not mentioned, but the bridge is very strong and destroyable only by the sons of Muspel, the giants of fire as it happened in Völuspá. *Bifröst* was kept guard by Heimdall, one of the Aesir, 'who casts bright rays'. In the Younger Edda there is also a remark, that the Bifröst appears red as there is a burning fire on it to show the way to Asgard (Gylfaginning XIII, XV).

The most well known rainbow representation in the European cultural area is the version in the Bible, where the rainbow is the sign of the covenant between Jehovah and Noah: "I do set my bow in the cloud; and it shall be for a token of a covenant between me and the earth" (Genesis 9.13). The Old Testament treatment of the rainbow is ambiguous, denoting both Gods wrath and mercy. In the Old Testament there is likewise found an image of Jehovah's bow with which he sends arrows to the earth to punish the misdoers. It can be explained by the earlier Hebrew mythological motifs, where the rainbow was connected with the bow and the arrows with lightning.

In the New Testament the rainbow appears in a new relation. It is a symbol of the covenant between God and people, which has expanded to Christ as an establisher of the new covenant. "And he that sat was to look upon like a jasper and a sardine stone: and there was a rainbow round about the throne, in sight like unto an emerald" (Relevation 4.3). Still, in the Bible there is found no reference to the colours of the rainbow or to their number. Apparently with these apocalyptical motifs the rather popular role of the rainbow in the late Gothic painting can be explained. In Romanesque art it is possible to associate the rainbow with a mandorla or halo surrounding the body of God or a saint. In Gothic art Christ is depicted sitting on the rainbow in scenes of the Last Judgement as *Maiestas Domini*, it is the Lord's throne.

Older representations of the rainbow in different mythologies can be divided into animate and inanimate ones. From the latter the already mentioned image of bridge and path of gods, which binds heaven, the ulterior or the gods' world and this, the human world, is rather common everywhere (e.g. Greece, Japan, Indonesia, India, Mesopotamia). The heroes of Polynesian and Hawaiian myths take the souls of the dead by it to paradise, in Indonesia it is the bridge of soul boats. In the myths of Finno-Ugric and other Nordic nations many features supposedly attributed to the rainbow have been melted with the image of the Milky Way, supported largely by their similar outward appearance. Last but not least, the folk legends grounded on Christianity depict the rainbow as a bridge along which the dead will rise to Heaven on doomsday, with an angel sitting on it beckoning them with a trumpet. Under the feet of the wicked dead the bridge will break down. So the rainbow as a bridge has nearly always been connected with the other world, the realm of gods and the dead.

The image of the rainbow as a bow, with which the (thunder)god sends down arrows and rain, is rather widespread as well. Besides already mentioned images in the Old Testament there are data about it from the Arabs and several African tribes. The rainbow was the bow of Indra. Among the Balto-Finnic nations a similar image is referred to by the Estonian dialectal (Saaremaa) word for rainbow *ammukaar*, and Finnish and Karelian idiomatic *ukon kaari* (Ukko as a mythical impersonation of a god of thunder).

Further, the rainbow was considered to be somebody's belt or robe. It occurs among other cultures in the Slavonic and German folk-beliefs. In Albania the rainbow was a belt of the goddess of beauty and a later Catholic Saint Prenne (or Prende), whose name is derived from the word *perëndi* meaning 'heaven'. Swallows who were harnessed to her carriage drew it over the vault of heaven. The concept of the rainbow as a belt of a mother of the heavens is known likewise by the Livonians.

In the late German folk-beliefs the connection of the rainbow with hidden treasures were popular. The ends of the rainbow showed its location or could drop gold coins themselves.

From the animated imaginations one of the most essential ones was a serpent as a simile of the rainbow - *the rainbow snake* or *the rainbow serpent*. The most typical area of occurrence of that mythical figure is throughout the Australian continent, but similar legends are known likewise in equatorial Africa and in Brazil. It is an important figure in initiation and rainmaking rites, carrying often a dangerous and destructive character (Eliade 1989).

Rather close to the latter is the image of the water-drinking rainbow, found in myths of almost every part of the world. According to it, the rainbow draws the water up to the sky, from where it falls down to the earth again. The water could be drawn from everywhere, from rivers, lakes and wells. It is always accompanied by the danger of grabbing together with the water, fish and all kinds of other stuff, including human beings. At Siebenbürger in Germany, for example, the rainbow has drawn up an inquisitive shepherd boy with the whole flock of sheep and in Livonia a fisherman with his boat (Hwb. d. Abergl.; Loorits 1926)

As to rainbow beliefs in Estonia, they are broadly speaking not very original and similar to the above-mentioned themes. The imagination is general of the water-drinking rainbow which can draw up people too, when they are under the bow (H II 10,55 (4) < VJg). Still, there are not so many records in the archives about drawing up fish and people as in Livonia. The belief is common to the other Balto-Finnic nations.

Secondly, it is commonly prohibited to point one's finger at the rainbow, as at the result of this, the finger will fall away, mortify or rot. It is analogically not allowed with the other heavenly phenomena and quite known also by other nations. The image of the rainbow as a belt is not so common in Estonia as it is in Livonia, but still known, especially as a belt of God (e.g. EKS 4

1,220 (6) < VNg). In addition there is the above-mentioned connection with the bow in the Estonian islands and analogical similes with the Finnish, Livonian, Lapp, Mordvinian and other Finno-Ugric nations.

Rainbow Colours

On the grounds of the preceding analysis, it is interesting to mention that almost all rainbow beliefs are inspired by its shape - the large arc - and not by its colours (except to some extent the Younger Edda's one where the colours are not mentioned). The seven colours, which are fixed in the consciousness of modern man, one can't find anywhere. There are even rhymes for children to acquire the names of these seven colours more easily, in English: *Richard of York gave battle in vain* = red, orange, yellow, green, blue, indigo, violet (McLaren 1985). The Estonian analogue is more sporadic: *Peremees ootab kitselt raha sulane tema liha* 'Master waits money from goat, man its meat'.

However there are several references to the colours of the rainbow as a mean of weather forecast. Most common are the colours red and green, e.g. *Kui vikerkaar punane, ei tule vihma, kui roheline siis sajab* (RKM II 245,106 (41) < Vagivere) 'When the rainbow is red, it will not rain, when green, it will rain'. Or: *Mida selgem vikerkaare punane karv on, seda enam tuult* (H IV 8,647 (38) < Pal) - 'The clearer the red colour of the rainbow, the more wind'. However, one can find an opposite or different meaning to nearly every colour - so, seemingly such forecasting was not very fixed.

A couple of Estonian riddles refer to the colours of the rainbow, as generally the connection between an object and its colour is much more common to riddles. The most characteristic ones are:

(i) *Punane puuder, sinine siider, ripub rikka mehe räästa all*
(< Jõe) or in Finnish *Sininen siirto, punainen puurto,*
keskellä kamarin kattoa (Korhola 1961). This riddle is hardly
translatable, but broadly speaking, the rainbow is described
here through two colours, red and blue.

(ii) *Üle ilma pihelgas* (Eisen 1913:1110) 'The rowan-tree over
the world'.

(iii) *Seitse linti üle ilma seotud?* (Eisen 1920:215, E 46993
(5) < Saarde) 'Seven ribbons bound over the world'.

The first type is widely spread in Finland and Ingria, likewise in
other Balto-Finnic languages and probably originates from Finnish. Still, it is possible to find parallels in other languages, where
the simile of the rainbow contains a limited number of colours,
two or even one. The russian riddle *Krasnoje koromõsloje*
tsherez reku povislo refers to the colour red (Mitrofanova
1968:330) or Irish: *Whom do I see (coming) toward me*
through the sea but the sunny gewgaw, the red-coated man
with a red thread in his shirt. (Hull-Taylor "A collection of
Irish Riddles": 201). Further it is possible to find connections
with some clichés of the old Estonian alliterative folk songs:

Pilve tõuseb soost sinine,
soost sinine, maast punane,
Ei saja sinine pilve,
sajab sauekarvaline.
Mis seal pilvete seessa?

Vikerkaar pilvete seessa.
Mis seal vikerkaare vahella?
Hani vikerkaaride vahella.
(VK VI:1, 10 A "Kulla põlemine")

'A blue cloud is rising from the bog,
from the bog blue, from the earth red,
It's not raining from the blue cloud,
it's raining from the claycoloured.
What's there in the clouds?
There is a rainbow in the clouds.
What's there between the rainbow?
There's a goose between the rainbow.'

Or further:

Pilvel on puhas purje,
purjel on hani punane,
hanil on saba sinine,
(ER1A I:1, 165, 2 "Pilves veepisarad")

'A pure sail is on a cloud,
a red goose is on the sail,
the goose has a blue tail'

This type of folk song has contaminated several other types allowing hypothetical treatment of the similes, with a maiden sitting on the edge of the cloud, or the goose replaced by a
woman, as rainbow metaphors. While in Estonian folk songs the
cliché *hani punane, saba sinine* ('red goose, blue tail') de-
note a rainbow, then in Finnish and Karelian songs the analogical widespread cliché is *veno punainen* 'red boat':

Pilvess' on vesipisaret,
Pisariss' on loajat lammit,
Lammiss' on veno punaset
(SKVR I:1,216; Koski 1983:72)

'In the cloud there are drops of water,
In the drops there are wide pools,
In the pools there are red boats'

A hypothesis based on the grounds of the preceding could be the proposition, that for the Estonian, Finnish and other neighbouring nations there were only two significant colours connected with the rainbow - red and blue. Still, such a conclusion could be precipitate, as the use of red and blue is rather frequent in other clichés of alliterative folk-songs. As a rule the combination is used to emphasize (colour) differences between beings or things and to refer to extraordinary phenomena.

Interesting connections emerge likewise with the riddle *Üle ilma pihelgas* ('The rowan-tree over the world'), the typical Finnish version from it being *Pitkä vitsa pihlajainen yli meren ulottuu.* The finnish folklorist Uno Harva has referred to an Estonian Swedish variant (the Estonian Swedes lived in the western part and on several islands of Estonia from 13th century to 1944, their selfname was *aibofolket*): *Iwe wärde raunträ* in connection with the Finnish deity Rauni. According to Agricola Rauni was the wife of the thundergod Ukko, known also by Swedish Lapps under the name of *Ravdna* and the rowan-tree (*raudna* in Swedish Lappish) was dedicated to her. Harva supposed that the rowan-tree could be a code-name, a euphemism for the rainbow and rauni meant originally both rowan and rainbow. Later from it there developed the personification of the rainbow as the wife of the thunder god (Harva 1948).

Without considering the essential role the rowan-tree has had in folk-beliefs one may refer to its protective properties against thunder (e.g. Hwb. d. Abergl. sub *rot*). Analogical properties were attributed to other things with red details. So, one can suppose the holiness of the rowan-tree was to some extent derived from its red berries. One can also refer to the Old Norse word *rauda* 'red' (Islandic *raudr,* Lithuanian *raûdas,* Sanskrit *rudhir*). The Estonian word *raud* 'iron' is derived from it, as rust is also red. Likewise, the name of the deity *Rauni* could be derived from the Old Norse *rauda.* One can again recall the connection of red and rainbow in the Balto-Finnic folk songs and suppose that the rainbow and rowan-tree were linked by the red colour.

The third riddle - *Seitse linti üle ilma seotud?* 'Seven ribbons bound over the world' refers quite clearly to a later origin, as the number seven wasn't earlier linked with rainbow in any way.

Science

The well-known modern conception of the cause of rainbows - the refraction and reflection of sunbeams in the raindrops - was first apparently grounded by René Descartes (1596-1650) in 1637. The common understanding of the seven colours of the rainbow descends still from another source - it comes from Sir Isaac Newton's famous prism experiments. In his Optics, published in 1704, Newton described seven prismatic colours. From that claim is derived the common 'scientific truth' mixing completely the concepts of rainbow and spectrum, caused partly by Newton himself, as he subsequently said that the rainbow consists of seven homogeneous gleams.

The reason for exactly seven primary colours of the spectrum is quite a sophisticated theme (McLaren 1985; Parkhurst, Feller 1982; Schweizer 1982). The first one seems to be the desire to find analogy with the musical scale. The idea didn't belong to Newton, as synaesthetical concepts were expressed already by Aristotle in his *De sensu et sensibili* and in *De anima.* The idea of seven principal colours originates likewise from Aristotle (*De sensu:* IV, 442). From that paragraph, however, it is not quite clear, whether the number of colours is inspired by some kind of Pythagorean symbolism of numbers or not. Aristotle derived all other colours from the two, black and white, which belonged to his linear colour concepts. It was not based on the hues but on the brightness of colours.

The concept of seven principal colours was very persistent throughout the Middle Ages and found support especially from all kinds of mystical and alchemical theories. It found full observance in Renaissance colour theories, e.g. Girolamo Cardano (De gemmis et coloribus 1563), Cennino Cennini (Il libro dell'arte ca 1400) and especially in the magnificent system of Gian Paolo Lomazzo (Trattato dell'arte della pittura 1584; Idea del tempio della pittura 1590), who was inspired by many other authorities, especially by Cornelius Agrippa (Gavel 1979; Kemp 1990). He linked together under the seven-based-system the planets, humours, temperaments, famous Renaissance artists, animals, plants, metals, etc. The 18th century natural philosophical doctrine of harmonious relationships, grounded on Johannes Kepler's *Harmonices mundi* (1619), is in some degree also based on the system of seven.

Aristotle's concept of the rainbow is presented in another book of his, the *Meteorologica*. In its third part there is a discussion about the colours of the rainbow and the proposition: "The rainbow has three colours, and these three and no others" (*Meteorologica* III, 2. 371-372; 4. 374-375). These three primaries are not manufactured by painters, and they are named by Aristotle as αλουργης 'violet, purple', translated also as 'blue', πρασινος 'green' and ερυθρος 'red'. Sometimes there can be seen the fourth colour - ξανθοζ 'yellow, orange-yellow'- but it is not a primary one. The question of these names is of course complicated by the often polysemantic character of the Greek colour terms.

Homer described the rainbow only with one colour - purple (Iliad 17.547) - an interesting parallel recalling the rainbow riddles of Balto-Finnic folklore. Xenophanes mentioned three: 'purple', 'yellow' and 'crimson'. The Aristotelian three-coloured rainbow doctrine was so impressive, that it dominated throughout the Middle Ages. The one and main reason for that was doubtlessly the possibility to connect it with the Trinity. This concept was supported by several authors such as Albertus Magnus and Thomas Aquinas; Jacob Böhme (1575-1624) and Emanuel Swedenborg (1688-1772) gave the explanation for the three colours inclining more to the symbolic and mystic point of view.

Still, from the 6th or 7th century there began the parallel development of the four-colour rainbow theory. Its main conceptual basis was the connection of the colours with the four elements (earth, air, water, fire), humours, seasons etc. The idea of linking the colours and elements was already followed by the Greek philosophers (Empedocles as the first known, but mentioned also by Plato and Aristotle). The rainbow colours were probably associated with the elements by Arabs and the main authority was here Ibn al-Haitam or Alhazen (965-1038): *De aspectibus or Perspectiva.* In European tradition the same trend was followed by the Dominican Theodoric of Freiberg in his treatise on the rainbow from ca 1310. From the Renaissance authors there is known Leon Battista Alberti's reference to the four colours of the rainbow (De pictura 1435) which are linked with the four elements (Gavel 1979).

So it seems obvious that the honour of "discovering" the seven-colour rainbow belongs to Newton. It's a typical example of secondary mythology still very common in the cognitive representation in the human consciousness. Such firm doctrine is represented, even in Brockhaus Enzyklopädie (Band 24 1992; sub Regenbogen: *Ein bunter Haupt-Regenbogen hat von innen nach aussen die Farbfolge Violett, Indigo, Blau, Grün, Gelb, Orange, Rot (sieben sprichwörtliche Regenbogenfarben)).*

A good compendium and a remote Estonian echo of the history of discovering the seven-colour rainbow could be the following description from the1890, reflecting the knowledge one could get from a village school of that time in Estonia: "The sun is running so fast around itself that it overshadows the seven colours it has, but when there is a rain cloud near the sun, it draws these seven colours in its water vapour into sight. The sun is as a wheel of a spinning wheel that has 7 spokes, each spoke of different colour, but the fast running of the wheel doesn't allow us to see the colours". (E 54367 (21) < Tori: *Janseni seletus koolis vikerkaarest. Päev oma väga kiire jooksuga enese*

ümber varjab omas vee aurus 7 värvilist karva aga kui vihma pilv päeva vastu se tõmbab omas vee auurus 7 värvilist karva nähtavale. Päike on kui vokki rattas kel 7 kodarast iga kodaras isi värvi aga ruttuline ratta jooks ei lase värvisi näha)

or: "The rainbow is an odd thing created by God. Nobody believes that it appears when the sun is shining on the cloud, so that the raindrops falling down change themselves to seven-coloured ones in the sun". (H II 65,628 (11) < Jüri: *Vikerkaar arvatakse üks iseäralik Jumalast loodud asi olema. Seda ei usu keegi et ta siis nähtavale tuleb kui päike vihma pilve peale paistab, et maha sadavad vihma piisad ennast päikese paistel seitsme karvaliseks muudavad).*

216 ## References

ARISTE, Paul (1979) Vadja mõistatusi. Tallinn.

CHRISTIANSEN, Reidar Th. (1965) Myth, metaphor, and simile. In: Myth, Thomas A. Sebeok, ed., 64-80. Bloomington, London.

EDDA Snorra Sturlusonar (1848). Copenhagen.

EISEN, M. J. (1913) Eesti mõistatused. Tartu.

EISEN, M. J. (1919) Eesti mütoloogia. Tartu.

EISEN, M. J. (1920) Mõista, mõista, mis see on. Tartu.

EISEN, M. J. (1927) Eesti vana usk. Tartu.

EILIADE, M., ed. (1989) The Encyclopedia of Religion. Vol 12. New York.

ERFFA, H. M. V., ed. (1989) Ikonologie der Genesis. Band I. München.

ERIA: Tedre, Ü., ed (1969, 1970, 1971, 1974) Eesti rahvalaulud. Antoloogia. I - IV. Tallinn.

GAVEL, Jonas (1979) Colour. A study of its position in the art theory of the quattro- and cinquecento. Stockholm.

HARVA, Uno (1948) Suomalaisten muinaisusko. Porvoo, Helsinki.

HWB. d. Abergl.: Hoffmann-Krayer, E. (1935) Handwörterbuch des Deutsches Aberglaubes. Band VII, sub Regenbogen. Berlin, Leipzig.

IRWIN, Eleanor (1974) Colour terms in Greek poetry. Toronto.

KEMP, M. (1990) The science of art. Optical themes in western art from Brunelleschi to Seurat. New Haven, London.

KIRCHBAUM, E. (1971) Lexikon der christlichen ikonographie. Band III.

KORHOLA, Leena (1961) Suomalaisista sateenkaariarvoituksista. In: Kalevalanseuran vuosikirja 41. Porvoo, Helsinki.

KOSKI, Mauno (1983) Värien nimitykset suomessa ja lähisukukielissä. Savonlinna.

LOORITS, O. (1949, 1951) Grundzüge des estnischen Volksglaubens. I, II. Lund.

LOORITS, O. (1926) Liivi rahva usund. I. Tartu.

MACADAM, David L. (1970) Sources of color science. Cambridge, London.

MCLAREN, K. (1985) Newton's Indigo. In: Color Research and Application, Vol 10, 4, 225-229.

NEWTON, Isaac (1704, reprint 1952). Optics. New York.

PARKHURST, Charles; Feller, Robert L. (1982) Who invented the color wheel? In: Color Research and Application, Vol 7, 3, pp. 217-230.

RÄSÄNEN, Martti (1948) Sateenkaaren nimityksistä ja uskomuksista. In: Kalevalanseuran vuosikirja 27/28, pp. 158-175.

SCHNELLBACH, Ingrid (1959) Das Wogulische Rätsel. In: Ural-Altaische Bibliothek, VIII. Wiesbaden.

SCHWEITZER, Paul D. (1982) John Constable, rainbow science, and English color theory. In: The Art Bulletin, Vol 64, 3, pp. 424-445.

SKVR I: HURT, Jakob. (1904) Setukeste laulud. I. Helsinki.

MITROFANOVA, V. V., ed. (1968) Zagadki. Leningrad.

VK III: Vana Kannel III (1938) Kuusalu vanad rahvalaulud. Toim. H. Tampere. Tartu.

VK VI: Vana Kannel VI:1, VI:2. (1989) Haljala regilaulud. Tallinn.

HAUSSIG, H. W., hrsg. (1973) Wörterbuch der Mythologie. Band II. Stuttgart.

In this article manuscript folklore collections from the folklore archives of the Estonian Literary Museum have been used.

Wittgenstein, Colour Concepts, Teaching

Ludwig Wittgenstein (1889-1951) was a lousy teacher, disasterous educator and he hated the academic nomenclature. When his students wanted positions in universities he advised: "don't go there to die". However, he had a huge impact on his students and those who got hooked, never escaped the intellectual research. Many of his publications rely totally on the notes of his students. Examples of such are *The Blue Book* and *The Brown Book,* named after the colours of their covers. Of course there is a double contradiction here, there would not be a Wittgenstein without Cambridge and Oxford.

Without a consistent theory, without a valid structure of thinking, and without a law-like system he become one of the most influential philosophers in our century. He operated mainly with questions. He avoided definitions for his major concepts. What is his "language game"?

Where did Wittgenstein's interest in colour come from?Was it his passion for black-and-white films? Or did the heavy propaganda of the first and second world wars support his search for the meaning of colour?

Cycle of Landscape Colours

The Norwegian philosopher *K.E. Tranoy*[1] has published two interesting photographs, which, from an artistic point of view, are valid in documenting his desire for a colour experience. The photographs depict the magnificent location of the hut Wittgenstein built for himself in the beautiful Norwegian fjord and mountain area. *Skjolden* is one of the remotest, wildest, and most spectacular spots in western Norway, in Wittgenstein's days quite inaccessible.

Skjolden lies at the bottom of one of the innermost arms of the

longest of all the fjords, *Sognefjord,* which cuts its way some 170 kilometers inland to the foot of the highest and wildest mountains in Norway. The colour expressions of the landscape are easy to imagine as totally impressive, when the sun gets up in the morning from east and travels to the west over the mountain peaks for the evening and hit the yard and windows of Wittgenstein's house. Cold and warm, light and shadow, blue and orange dominate the scene in constant daily cycle. Here Wittgenstein prepared his *Tractatus* before the first world war, and *Philosophical Investigations* before the second world war, his two major works, two totally opposite concepts by the same author.

Tractatus Logico-Philosophicus

From Skjolden Wittgenstein travelled back home to take part in the first world war, and completed his Tractatus -manuscript[2] on the battle fields. He had to struggle until 1926 to get the book published. *Tractatus Logico-Philosophicus* became a great success in the logical empirism circles, especially the school of analytical philosophy in Wienna hailed his ideas as groundbreaking. Tractatus remained the only book by Wittgenstein to be published during his lifetime.

Tractatus introduced the picture theory of language. The cryptic short sentences are pose questions outside language. What can one not speak about? Inside the border of language are all the real and possible "Sachverhalte", situations of things. What is outside the borders cannot be described by language, but it can show its existence; we can "see" it by understanding that we cannot say it.

The last paragraph of Tractatus has become the symbol of the theory: "*Wovon man nicht sprechen kann darüber muss man schweigen*"[3]. The slogan became famous especially inside the abstract expressionist art movement. The existence of the world outside language was just what the abstract expressionist artists searched for and tried to paint on their canvases. How to formulate something which is only a hint, a quest, a feeling of a feeling, existing only in instinct and even there without outlook? I want to refer here to the main theoretician, the artist *Barnett Newman*[4:] "Aesthetics is for me the same as ornithology is for birds". It is hard to find a theory for events which themselvelves appear in quite a formless existence.

Space, time and colour are forms of things[5] for Wittgenstein. For an artist they are the basic tools and substance for the handwork. Grammar was for Wittgenstein a "Russellian" theory of logical types. The conventions of grammar need the interpretations of language, but they do not give rules. No facts can be the paradigma of grammar. "We do not formulate the grammar of words 'red' or 'grey' so that they would suit together with the reality"[6].

Philosophical Investigations

After Tractatus Wittgenstein left philosophy. He acted as a school teacher, made dictionaries, practiced architecture by planning the rectilinear functionalistic house for his sister in 1926 and studied sculpture, with a very traditional classisistic overtone. Slowly he returned to philosophy, where the main theory was formulated in 1946 to the manuscript Philosophical Investigations, published 1953.

The concepts of language, expression and meaning began to be much less stable. They became living in time and place and people. The sense of past time characterises the imagination. Behind understanding there acts always remembering and experi-

ences. Language, game, rule and expression are social institutions, which are not ruled by individual sovereignity, but the social dependency of human beings. The meaning of a word is not an individual image, but the use of the word. The unity of language is based on the lifeform, not individual opinions. "The eye tells me the blueness, but not the role of blue"[7] On what do the possibilities of the meanings of our words depend?

He sees the language games as communication systems which change all the time when the words and their usages change. How does understanding and explaining happen? How do words and realities depict? To see something as something is naming. The use of language depends on the strength of argument and the strenght of expression. And now you can have similar blindness for meaning as in colour blindness or tone deafness.

Turning from the logic of strict truth value to a more self directing logic opened his colour conception. Now he is using terms such as *family resemblance* and *language game*, which give wider vistas for expressions.

Colour in the Total Production

To research Wittgenstein's colour sentences I read closely his total production translated into Finnish, 13 books. The Finnish literature is valid, because in Finland there is a keen interest in Wittgenstein. One of the three editors of Wittgenstein's papers after his death is his Finnish colleague, *Georg Henrik von Wright*. His depth of research is revealed also in the Tranoy photographs: he appears on the site of the now demolished Wittgenstein house in *Skjolden*. My question with every page of the Wittgenstein books was: "How much and in what circumstances does Wittgenstein speak of colour?" In the following table[8] the numbers indicate how many pages or numbered paragraphs the book contains, how many of those speak of colour, and how many of them deal with colour.

Colour as a Subject in the Production of Wittgenstein
(books in the order of their writing)

		pages	paragraphs total	paragraphs on colour	%
1.	Notebooks 1914-1916	188		1 p *	0,5
2.	Tractatus Logico-Philosophicus	83	526	9	1,7
3.	Philosophical Remarks	320	1101	111	10
4.	Writings 1929-1938	156		17 p	10,1
5.	The Blue and Brown Books	267		33,1 p	12,4
6.	Remarks on the Foundations of Mathematics	354	719	12	3,4
				30	4,2
7.	Zettel	150	717	53	7,4
8.	Remarks on the Philosophy of Psychology, part I	247	1137	92	8,1
9.	Remarks on the Philosophy of Psychology, part II	316	1816	82	4,5
10.	Philosofical Investigations, part I	250	693	55	7,9
	part II	85		5,23 p	6,1
					7
11.	On Certainty	107	676	26	3,8
12.	Remarks on Colour	82	350	350	100
	Total	2605 p		253 p	9,7 %

* = page

The table is astonishing. Wittgenstein comments colour in every one of his books. In 2605 pages there are 253 pages about colour. Ten per cent on one theme is muchin the production of any philosopher. Wittgenstein showed unusually strong interest towards the theme of colour.

Inside such a small group of concepts as colours there exists a huge asymmetry. You cannot find many identical properties. Colours do not act symmetrically. The ways of appearing, which have been developed for white, are not proper in researching red; brown and green act differently. You cannot draw conclusions of the interaction between black and red by observing blue and yellow. This is one of Wittgenstein's conclusions.

What is Wittgenstein's main starting point? Colour is for him a reason to talk about physics, chemistry, optics, information theory, theory of observation, logic of colour concepts, phenomenology, logic, usages of language, theories of meaning, consciousness. Colour is both a handy source of practical everyday facts and a sphere of theoretical structuring.

He combines rational empiristic facts to speculative, even metaphysical discussion. In his own words, what he least wants to establish is a physical theory of colours. But of course he constantly comments on just that theme. He wants "to discuss the logic of colour concepts"[9]. And the logic of literal expressions. "...we are not able to describe how something white and clear weould look, and this means: we don't know, what description, portrayal, these words demand from us"[10]. "When dealing with logi, 'one cannot imagine that' means: one doesn't know what one should imagine here"[11].

What is seeing? How to compare objects and experiences? What are the relations of physical objects and consciousness? What kind of descriptions are there for words, actions and phenomena? How do the public colour games function? Which kind of ways of acting are there in colour discourse? What are colour sensations and what are their relations to reality? How do we talk about colours? Are there private colour concepts?

The questions above are but a small portion of Wittgenstein's themes. He is saying: "Visual world is the world of colour impressions, but we can talk about those impressions only by pointing at the physical colours." For him observing and seeing are different actions, they do not have the same identity. And practice gives the meaning to words. "The indefinitiveness of the visual space is the clearest for us, when we do not see anything, in the complete darkness"[12]. When reading this sentence from the cybernetic information theory point of view, it resembles the utterance: the most information exists in entropy, in chaos.

We create for ourselves the images of facts. The comparisons of observations are as the sense organs of picture elements, by which the image touches the reality. The complex issue of matter and colour awakens his interest. What are the properties of the matters of coloured objects, for example milk, glass, paper, varnish, water; and what are the properties of colours?

These comments arise much from reading *Goethe* and *Runge,* partly *Newton.* Wittgenstein had often Goethe's *Zur Farbenlehre* on his table. "I have again read parts of the Farbenlehre by Goethe, which both draws me in and pushes me out. For certain it is philosophically interesting.[13]" "Goethe's theory of the constitution of the colours of the spectrum has not proved to be an unsatidfactory theory, rather it really isn't a theory at all. Nothing can be predicted with it.[14]"

The "weak remarks" on Goethe carry the character of the dear enemy, where the negation has to overflow in vast quantities. But he also agrees: "No lightness can come out of darkness - just as more and more shadows do not produce light"[15]. If Goethe had been with Wittgenstein through his life, colour became the issue for the last one-and-a-half years. When Philosophical Investigations became ready in 1946 Wittgenstein devoted the rest of his life to three themes: 1) certainty, 2) epistemology and the philosophy of psychological concepts, and 3) colour.

General Philosophical Colour Interest

For artists it is nice to imagine the discussions between the philosophers in Cambridge and Oxford at the beginning of the 1950's as Wittgenstein, and thus his favorite theme colour had an important role in it. Georg Henrik von Wright has recollected those events with warmth: "the best drawings of Wittgenstein as a person are impressionistic notions of discussions and episodes"[16].

Remarks on Colour was written in 1950-1951, and published for the first time in 1977. The theme is the last one Wittgenstein dealt with and kind of a testament. Already in *Philosophical Remarks* (first German edition 1964) Wittgenstein had introduced the image of the colour cone. For him the cone was a general description of the grammatical rules and it tells us what we can and cannot do. So again, we are not dealing with a physical colour theory. "That a dot cannot be simultaneously red and green, does not have to be a logical impossibility"[17].

The most interesting thought in *Philosophical Remarks* deals with the multifaceted possibilities of building colour spheres, especially the fourth dimension. "If someone believes he can imagine four-dimensional space, then why not also four-dimensional colours - colours which in addition to the degree of saturation, hue and intensity of light, are susceptible of being determined in yet a fourth way.[18]" This very important new aspect for all colour spheres stays without an answer from Wittgenstein.

Remarks on Colour contain now hundreds of different starting points for thinking about colour. *Jonathan Westphal* has collected a few philosophical aspects in his book *Colour, Some Philosophical Problems from Wittgenstein* under the term puzzle propositions[19]. He lists the following from Wittgenstein's book *Remarks on Colour:*

"Something can be transparent green or any other colour, but not transparent white."
"Grey cannot be luminous."

"There cannot be a pure brown or brown light."
"There is no blackish yellow."
"There can be a bluish green but not a reddish green."

Strenght of the Argument

The strength of Wittgenstein's argument lies in his philosophical and psychological remarks. In his days the developments of light theories and optics were not as advanced as today, and many of his real life colour observations are built on shaky theoretical ground. But what a sphere of issues!

The early, first Wittgenstein had four titles: the world, language, the unspeakable, philosophy. His interest concentrated on the most simple, absolute primitive building blocks of the world and their relation to each other. Their state of affairs told how the world was structured. The language was an ideal language and thus an image of the world. The late, second Wittgenstein wants to avoid generalisations. Everyday language must be described by everyday language. To explain the character of language one must understand it as a game, a language game, or as an instrument or machine, which deep down is a life form. This way of life builds up a cultural togetherness, family resemblance. It is the usage of the expression, the meaning family, which fibrates the net, where there is not only one meaning, but many families of meanings.

Sameness of meaning, sameness of expression, or in colour theory, sameness of colour, was the topic Wittgenstein does not want to follow. How to distinguish nearly similar colours? What is sameness? "We are never able to say that someone considers as blue the same object, which we name as blue. What seeing is, I know only out of my own seeing."[20] "I point a blue blouse. How does showing a colour differ from showing a form? The difference lies in the environment of the act in use of language."[21]

He takes an example from the colour red. We should think of the autumn and all the red in nature. How to determine the sameness? "But why would I not say, that it has only one meaning, but it will be used through the circumstances?"[22]

We know throught the paintings of Bosch or drawings of Esher, what so called impossible three dimensional spaces and objects would look like, if they would exist. This is not enough to prove that they would be possible in the object reality, or in other words, that complete descriptions of them are logically consistent. We repeat experiences for ourselves, also colour experiences, and these experiences form a word, and in colour, our concept of the colour. And now "We do not need an explanation, but practice".

Notes

1. K.E. Tranoy: Wittgenstein in Cambridge 1949-51. Some Personal Recollections, p. 14.

2. Lugwig Wittgenstein (1926) Tractatus Logico-Philosophicus.

3. Tractatus, p. 7.

4. Barnett Newman in an interview in the Emil de Antonio film: Painters Paintings.

5. Tractatus 2.0251.

6. Wittgenstein's Lectures, Cambridge 1930-32 (1980). Edited Desmond Lee. Basil Blackwell, Oxford, p. 86.

7. Wittgenstein: Remarks on the Foundation of Mathematics, p. 179.

8. Antero Kare (1994) Wittgensteinin väriä koskevat huomiot vuoteen 1944. University of Helsinki.

9. Wittgenstein: Remarks on Colour, p. 5.

10. Ibid. p. 5.

11. Ibid. p. 6.

12. Witgenstein's Philosophical Remarks, p. 292.

13. Nyman, Heikki: Translators preface in the book Huomautuksia väreistä (Wittgenstein; Remarks on Colour), p. 129.

14. Wittgenstein: Remarks on Colour, p. 11.

15. Ibid. p. 12.

16. von Wright, Georg Henrik: Wittgenstein. Basil Blackwell, Oxford. 1982. p. 2.

17. Wittgenstein: Notebooks 1914-1916. p. 96.

18. Wittgenstein: Philosophical Remarks, p. 96.

19. Westphal, Jonathan (1987) Colour: Some Philosophical Problems from Wittgenstein. Basil Blackwell, Oxford, p. 1.

20. Wittgenstein: The Blue and Brown Books, p. 111.

21. Ibid, pp. 139-140.

22. Ibid, p. 223.

References

BLOCK, Irving, ed. (1981) Perspectives on the Philosophy of Wittgenstein. Basil Blackwell, Oxford.

HINTIKKA, Merrill B. & HINTIKKA, Jaakko (1987) Investigating Wittgenstein. Basil Black well, Oxford.

KARE, Antero (1994) Wittgensteinin väriä koskevat huomiot vuoteen 1944. Helsingin yliopisto.

NYMAN, Heikki (1982) Translator's Preface in the book Huomautuksia väreistä (Wittgenstein: Remarks on Colour), Werner Söderström Osakeyhtiö, Juva.

TRANOY, K.E. (1976) Wittgenstein in Cambridge 1949-51. Some Personal Recollec tions. In: Acta Philisophica Fennica Vol.28, Nos.1-3. North-Holland Publishing Company, Amsterdam.

WEDBERG, Anders (1978) Ludwig Wittgenstein, Filosofiska undersökningar, Bonniers, Stockholm (c 1953 Basil Blackwell, Oxford).

WESTPHAL, Jonathan (1987) Colour: Some Philosophical Problems from Wittgenstein. Basil Blackwell, Oxford.

WITTGENSTEIN, Ludwig (1956) Bemerkungen über die Grundlagen der Mathematik. Suhrkamp Verlag.

WITTGENSTEIN, Ludwig (1958) Blue and Brown Books. Basil Blackwell: Oxford.

WITTGENSTEIN, Ludwig (1978) Bemerkungen über die Farben - Remarks on Colour. University of California Press, Berkeley and Los Angeles. Editor G.E.M. Anscombe.

WITTGENSTEIN, Ludwig. (1953) Philosophical Investigations.Basil Blackwell, Oxford.

WITTGENSTEIN, Ludwig (1975) Philosophical Remarks. Basil Blackwell, Oxford. (first German edition 1964).

WITTGENSTEIN, Ludwig (1971) Tractatus Logico-Philosophicus. Werner Söderström Oy. Porvoo. Finland.

WITTGENSTEIN, Ludwig (1984) Tractatus Logico-Philosophicus. Suhrkamp, Frankfurt/M (original 1926).

VON WRIGHT, Georg Henrik (1982) Wittgenstein. Basil Blackwell, Oxford.

The Authors

Albert-Vanel, Michel
Professor, Painter
Ecole Nationale Supérieure des Arts Décoratifs
Le Plessis-Robinson, France

Albrecht, Hans Joachim
Professor, Painter, Sculptor
Fachhochschule Niederrhein in Krefeld
Krefeld, Germany

Bagley, Marian-Ortolf
Professor
University of Minnesota
Department of Design, Housing and Apparel
St. Paul, Minnesota, USA

Blomstedt, Juhana
Professor, Painter
Helsinki, Finland

Burton, David
PhD, Associate Professor
Virginia Commonwealth University
Richmond, Virginia, USA

Buss, David
Associate Dean, Painter, Photographer
University of Plymouth
Faculty of Arts and Education
Plymouth, UK

Caan, Shashi
Architect and Instructor
New York, New York, USA

Coonan, Stephen
Lecturer
Dublin Institute of Technology
Dublin, Ireland

Dohr, Joy H.
PhD, Professor
University of Wisconsin
Madison, Wisconsin, USA

Green-Armytage, Paul
Designer, Educator
Curtin Universty of Technology
School of Design
Perth, Australia

Janssens, Jan
Architect, Techn. Dr., Researcher
Lund Institute of Technology
Lund, Sweden

Kare, Antero
Critic, Artist, Lecturer
Helsinki, Finland

Lewis, Garth
Senior Lecturer
The London Institute
Central Saint Martins College of Art and Design
School of Fashion and Textile Design
London, UK

Linton, Harold
Professor, Assistant Dean, Artist and Author
Lawrence Technological University
College of Architecture & Design
Southfield, Michigan, USA

Marx, Ellen
Sculptor, Painter, Colour Researcher, Author
Jumeauville, France

Maycock, Bryan
Associate Professor, Foundation Division Chair
Nova Scotia College of Art and Design
Halifax, Nova Scotia, Canada

Minah, Galen
Professor
University of Washington
College of Architecture and Urban Planning
Seattle, Washington, USA

Portillo, Margaret B.
Assistant Professor
University of Kentucky
Kentucky, USA

da Pos, Osvaldo
Professor
University of Padua
Department of General Psychology
Padua, Italy

Sarapik, Virve
Lecturer
Tallinn Art University
Tallinn, Estonia

Thompson, Wade S.
Professor
Southwest Missouri State Univer
Department of Art and Design
Springfield, Missouri, USA

Tomcik, Andrew M.
Professor
York University
Faculty of Fine Arts, Depart
North York, Ontario, Cana

Warfel, William B.
Professor Emeritus
Yale School of Drama
New Haven, Connecticu

Willard, Christopher
Instructor
City University of Ne
Hunter College
New York, New Yor

Zwimpfer, Moritz
Professor, Designer, Author
Schule für Gestaltung Basel
Basel, Switzerland

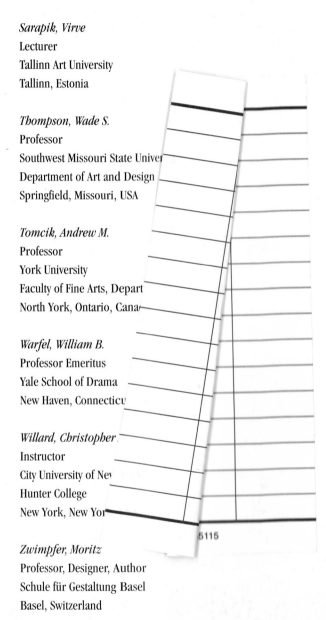

5115